1943
Days of Peril, Year of Victory

VICTOR BROOKS

Guilford, Connecticut

An imprint of The Rowman & Littlefield Publishing Group, Inc.
4501 Forbes Boulevard, Suite 200, Lanham, Maryland 20706
www.rowman.com

Distributed by NATIONAL BOOK NETWORK

British Library Cataloguing in Publication Information Available

Library of Congress Cataloging-in-Publication Data

Names: Brooks, Victor, author.
Title: 1943 : days of peril, year of victory / Victor Brooks.
Description: Guilford, Connecticut : Lyons Press, [2021] | Includes
   bibliographical references and index. | Summary: "Military historian
   Victor Brooks argues that the year 1943 marked a significant shift in
   the World War II balance of power from the Axis to Allied forces"—
   Provided by publisher.
Identifiers: LCCN 2020052621 (print) | LCCN 2020052622 (ebook) | ISBN
   9781493045082 (cloth) | ISBN 9781493045099 (epub)
Subjects: LCSH: World War, 1939-1945. | United States—Armed
   Forces—History—World War, 1939-1945.
Classification: LCC D755.5 .B76 2021 (print) | LCC D755.5 (ebook) | DDC
   940.54/1273—dc23
LC record available at https://lccn.loc.gov/2020052621
LC ebook record available at https://lccn.loc.gov/2020052622

♾™ The paper used in this publication meets the minimum requirements of American
National Standard for Information Sciences—Permanence of Paper for Printed Library
Materials, ANSI/NISO Z39.48-1992.

Contents

PREFACE

FOUR YEARS AGO, I WROTE AN ACCOUNT OF THE AMERICAN NATION AT war during the year 1944 as a follow-up to previous, well-received books on the Normandy campaign and the battle for the Marianas Islands. I continue to believe that the events of 1944 essentially doomed the Axis powers to ultimate surrender or total destruction. Yet, as I was finishing that project, I became increasingly fascinated by the series of events during the previous year, 1943, a period in which America and its allies clearly seized the initiative away from the Axis and set up the conditions under which the battles of 1944 had a far better than even chance to end as Allied victories. Before I began this current book, I had a general understanding of the events of 1943, but less perception about the sense of peril that confronted American military and civilian leaders and the general public as the nation faced the occupation of American territory with the Japanese occupation of Attu and Kiska; the depressing films of captured American soldiers being paraded by the Roman Colosseum after the defeat at Kasserine Pass; and the appalling loss of merchant ships as the German U-boats closed within sight of bathers on American beaches.

These "days of peril" also held a fascination for me because of a very *Back to the Future*–like series of events that significantly affected my birth four years later, as my father, nearing engagement to a woman in Pennsylvania, became the sole survivor of an Army Air Force plane crash and was shipped to an Air Force hospital in upstate New York, where he met my mother, who was also nearing engagement to her high school sweetheart, who had just been sent to fight in the Pacific Theater. As happened more than once in 1943, propinquity held the upper hand, and a new relationship was initiated that would provide four new baby boomer children from two people who never would have known each other existed prior to 1943.

If 1943 did not produce the decisive quality that prompted postwar films and television programs such as *Combat*, *The Battle of the Bulge*, and *The Longest Day*, the year was hardly ignored by Hollywood, as *McHale's*

Navy, Broadside, Baa Baa Black Sheep, The Rat Patrol, PT 109, The Great Escape, and *Von Ryan's Express* are merely the tip of the iceberg of television and cinema coverage of that year.

In the very real world of war, by 1943, most of the cast of characters who would crush the Axis in 1944 and 1945 were all very much in place and already sending the enemy much closer to their final redoubts. Dwight Eisenhower, George Patton, Henry "Hap" Arnold, Douglas MacArthur, Chester Nimitz, and Omar Bradley are major actors in the drama, although often serving against a different backdrop than they would in 1944, with Tunisia, Sicily, Tarawa, and New Guinea standing in for the 1944 counterparts: Normandy, Rome, the Philippines, and the Marianas. Yet, not only were the Americans in 1943 fighting over different place names than the following year, they were in combat with fewer forms of backup American bomber aircrews flying missions over occupied Europe in 1943 had to watch their escort fighters head home before they reached their targets, as "little friends'" gas tanks slipped into the danger zone. A year later, new drop tanks allowed them to accompany their charges all the way to Berlin. The American invaders of Tarawa would challenge the Nipponese defenders with less air cover, fewer battleships, and fewer flamethrowers than the men who would storm Guam and Saipan a year later.

PROLOGUE

December 1942

MONDAY, DECEMBER 7, 1942, DAWNED ON A UNITED STATES THAT HAD probably undergone more significant changes during the past twelve months than at any time since the Civil War, eight decades earlier. Exactly 365 days before, 130 million Americans had woken on an early winter Sunday morning in a nation at peace and went to bed that night as a nation under attack by a formidable and aggressive Japanese Empire. The year that followed was a sensory kaleidoscope of air raid sirens, children searching creekbeds and empty lots for discarded metal and rubber products, women donning bandanas and slacks and standing along assembly lines, and uniformed men insisting without conviction to their loved ones that they would return safely after trouncing the forces of Hitler and Hirohito.

The key phrases in early December 1941 were "Preparedness Rallies" and "Neutrality Patrols." A year later it seemed that the key word in the entire English language was *Victory*, from "V-mails" to "Victory Gardens." A single excuse covered every annoyance from poor service in restaurants to overcrowded, delayed trains to shoddy cardboard children's toys: "Don't you know that there is a war on?", as if anyone older than a toddler could possibly think otherwise. The Lone Ranger and Tonto now faced Nazi-employed cattle rustlers. Dick Tracy confronted Axis agents, and children noticed that their parents' green packaged Lucky Strike cigarettes were now white as "Lucky greens have gone to war."

The events on the war front during the past twelve months had created a national emotional rollercoaster. In April of 1942, twenty thousand American servicemen and fifty thousand troops of the still technically American-controlled Philippine Commonwealth surrendered to the Imperial forces while soon after, beachgoers from Florida to New England gasped in horror as American and Allied ships burned and sank from U-boat torpedo attacks seemingly just beyond the surf breaker waves. Japanese submarines fired cannon shells into West Coast oil refineries. Nazi agents set fire to the majestic *Normandie*, docked in New York harbor, and Imperial troops occupied American soil at the edge of Alaska. However, a wide variety of voices ranging from President Roosevelt to newspaper and magazine columnists to high school history teachers reminded that the Republic had endured dark times before the current crisis, including the virtual disintegration of the patriot army at Christmas 1776, the British burning of Washington in 1814, all the way to the stock market crash and ensuing Depression that had only been partially resolved during the past few months.

In fact, the second half of the year since Pearl Harbor had provided Americans with far more positive news that promised to become even more encouraging in the coming months. Only a month after the American surrender of the last fortified post of Corregidor in the Philippines, a badly outnumbered American fleet had destroyed four first-line Japanese aircraft carriers in the vicinity of Midway Island at a loss of only a single American "flat-top." Then, a few months later a division of American Marines, with eventual aid from a significant Army contingent, had sent the Japanese reeling backwards in a Guadalcanal battle that was still raging late in 1942.

A half a world away, forty thousand American assault troops landed on the beaches of the Algerian city of Oran and in concert with British and Commonwealth units induced Vichy French defenders to switch sides, forcing the German forces in North Africa into a gradually closing vise between Algeria and Egypt.

A year after Pearl Harbor, the commander-in-chief of a military force that seemed to be growing by geometric progression and preparing offensives around the globe was a sixty-year-old patrician who was easily one of the most recognizable faces and voices on the planet. Franklin Delano Roosevelt, now paired with Josef Stalin and Winston Churchill, had become the arch nemesis of Hideki Tojo, Benito Mussolini, and Adolf Hitler, all of whom were now united in an unspoken "temporary" defensive posture from which none of them would emerge alive.

In the final days of 1942, Benito Mussolini had the dubious distinction among this trio of becoming the first Fascist dictator to be facing expulsion. Only three years earlier *Il Duce* had been at the peak of his power after authorizing his generals to attempt to recreate the Roman empire of the Caesars by invading seemingly hopelessly outmatched lesser nations. Easily disposing of adversaries, such as an Ethiopian army that was still hurling spears at Italian armored cars invading their land, the Duce's fame reached a crescendo when Italy declared war on a French nation that was disintegrating under the blows of a German *Blitzkrieg*, and like a vulture swooped down on an imploding French republic to extend the boundaries of the new "Roman Empire." However, when faced with British and Commonwealth forces that would actively fight back with guns and tanks instead of spears, the forces of the Roman Empire were forced into an unseemly retreat only partially halted when the *Führer* committed crack Wehrmacht divisions to the desert war in North Africa. Led by an increasingly legendary Gen. Erwin Rommel, the tide temporarily turned once again with an embarrassing British surrender of nearly thirty thousand men at the port city of Tobruk, Libya, but even the optimistic, pugnacious Desert Fox admitted to German headquarters that the days of the Axis control of North Africa were increasingly numbered once the British and Americans were able to straddle the opposite ends of the vast desert battlefield.

While Italian and German forces were becoming more and more squeezed in a shrinking North African battlefield by a British army under Field Marshal Bernard Montgomery gradually advancing from Egypt in the east and an American, French, and British juggernaut under Gen. Dwight Eisenhower rumbling eastward from Morocco, much of Adolf Hitler's attention was increasingly drawn northward toward what was shaping up as one of the most titanic battles in history.

In autumn 1942, a massive German and German allied army swooped down on the Soviet megacity named after the unquestioned dictator of the Soviet Union, Stalingrad, a super-factory, population center, and propaganda prize all rolled into a single ugly metropolis squatting on the River Volga while residents accustomed themselves to a new name after generations of residing in "Volgograd." The idea of surrendering a city named after one of the least forgiving leaders in history was simply ludicrous, and party officials simply transferred weapons from dead men to untrained living men in an endless conveyor belt of fatalities.

However, while the Wehrmacht fought street to street and house to house against the defenders, General von Paulus had assigned the broader outer defense of the huge area of operation to role players under the flags of German allies from Italy to Romania. These non– "Nordic supermen" were now being hunted from all sides by Soviet armies that seemed to appear from nowhere, and though swastikas flew over many important Stalingrad buildings, the supply routes to feed and equip the new conquerors were being snapped shut one by one in the fading days of 1942. Hitler and his generals were adroit at moving division symbols on huge maps in a war room in Germany, but of the quarter million "victors" of Stalingrad, only five thousand would be destined to return alive to a defeated Germany.

At about the same time Hitler and his generals were moving pieces on their chessboard of war, Hideki Tojo and his colleagues were leaning over even larger maps of the Pacific Theater which, for the first time, displayed some ominous symbols. While America, Britain, and other Allies clearly placed their joint European adversaries, Hitler and Mussolini, as Enemy Number One, the jury was still a bit unclear regarding their Nipponese foe. One segment of American opinion clearly felt that Hirohito was the poster villain for the public to scorn. Since Hirohito was supposed to be a god in Japan, it seemed that this relatively young monarch was the center of an evil anti-West, anti-American cabal—that turned Japan into a nation of deadly predators. However, relatively few military officers even seemed to actually interact with Hirohito in that nation's strange political system, while Hideki Tojo was far more frequently photographed and filmed, including poses with the European Fascist dictators.

In Washington, Franklin Delano Roosevelt was just completing his first year as a war leader, and by December 1942, he and the nation he led were in the process of comprehending both the extent of American losses during the past twelve months and the prospects of initiating some form of retribution against the Axis powers. Roosevelt, unlike most of his Allied and Axis counterparts, was intelligent enough to largely avoid meddling in war plan activities and allowed the three American service chiefs—George Marshall, Ernest King, and Henry "Hap" Arnold—to develop a cogent strategy to defeat the Axis while avoiding Civil War– or World War I–like bloodbaths. In turn, the American people overwhelmingly supported the war effort and even Republicans, who opposed the administration's domestic policies, supported the president in his role as commander-in-chief.

By December of 1942, Franklin Roosevelt was just beginning to consider the viability of a possible unprecedented attempt to win a fourth consecutive term in the White House in the next presidential election twenty-three months in the future. It was no secret that a "win the war in '44" outcome would be a far more amenable background to a presidential campaign than a deferral to "home alive in '45," or even worse, "the Golden Gate in '48." The president realized that a World War I that was not expected to see a decisive conclusion before 1919 ended before that year was reached. Yet in early December of 1942, the president and his party were grappling with the sting of an unexpected Republican surge in the just completed national elections.

As one national news magazine noted in the aftermath of that contest, "Last week the voters of the United States staged a major political upset and stumped the experts good and plenty." A Republican Party that had seemed to have burrowed itself into a hole of perpetual minority status scored stunning gains throughout the nation. In New York, California, Michigan, and Connecticut, voters turned out Democratic governors, and nine new Republican senators and forty-four GOP representatives were elected to Congress—the most significant swing in political power since the Depression year of 1932. Republicans were clear winners in twenty-three of the forty-eight states, Democrats held sway in nineteen states, and the other six states seemed to be largely a political standoff. Roosevelt's party still held almost unanimous control in a "Solid South" that permitted virtually no African Americans to vote and fumed at even the modest civil rights initiatives of the Roosevelt Administration. However, just beyond the borders of the original Confederacy, in Maryland, West Virginia, Kentucky, and Oklahoma, Republicans enjoyed significant gains, and Vice President Henry Wallace admitted that it was a "miracle" that the Republicans had not enjoyed even more spectacular gains. Every single candidate who had received the "personal" selection to run by the president lost, which prompted Republican senator Arthur Vandenberg to suggest forming a joint Republican/Conservative/Democratic coalition to "get rid of New Dealers for the duration of the war."

Young Republican victors, such as Thomas Dewey of New York and Harold Stassen of Minnesota, hinted that the young people of America were the future of the Republican Party, yet, ironically, Stassen, who was still too young to run for president, then went on active duty as a naval officer, perhaps to add a valuable extra dimension to a prospective postwar presidential candidacy. Earl Warren, the new, young governor of California, found himself on a fast track to higher potential office, which would put him on the short list for the Republican presidential nomination in 1948 and 1952. He would become chief justice of the Supreme Court after the election of Dwight Eisenhower. Clare Boothe Luce, the photogenic, youthful spouse of media baron Henry Luce, was elected to Congress from Connecticut as she campaigned for a "hard" war to guarantee total victory against the Axis. Winifred Shantz, the thirty-three-year-old assistant district attorney of Buffalo, echoed this GOP call for an even more expanded emphasis on relatively quick victory while advocating veterans' benefits far more generous than those given to the veterans of World War I.

One of the major paradoxes of this outpouring of anti-administration sentiment just before the end of 1942 was that the American people seemed to be clamoring for an even more intensive war against the Axis, while lambasting the negative effects of the war on their personal lifestyles. For example, a late autumn poll of high school students by *Forbes* magazine revealed that an overwhelming 90 percent of the nation's teens strongly believed in a concept of unconditional surrender by the Axis powers but equivocated over whether the draft law should allow eighteen-year-olds to enter combat situations. The mixed message sounded by the nation's youth on the eve of 1943 was strongly echoed by the adult voting public.

Support for a war prosecuted to a final unconditional surrender of the Axis powers was still very high, even as casualty lists began to soar, yet civilians moaned about the incompetence of rationing bureaus and officious government drones. The print news media carried numerous articles on regional and even national shortages of traditional American food and beverages. As the Christmas shopping season began moving into high gear, it seemed that the nation was running out of everything. In a single week, nine hundred restaurants were forced to close due to a shortage of food, fuel, and labor. A *Life* magazine report sampled substitute fare in several restaurants and decided horsemeat was "dark, coarse, sweet and palatable," while buffalo meat was "tasty but gamey." Restaurants began displaying signs, "Sorry, no meat today—maybe tomorrow," and then were forced to add milk, butter, cheese, and eggs to the list crossed from the menus. A few days later the coffee supply seemed to evaporate as the U-boat fleets began to pick off ships laden with precious beans as they wended their way north from Brazil. One plucky restaurant owner boldly admitted that "plenty of coffee" was available in his establishment and then astounded customers with the fine print that noted that although the first cup was only a nickel, refills soared to $100 each. A Baltimore photographer snapped a nationally distributed photo of a long line snaking toward what seemed to be the entrance to a church and then clarified the scene when a second photo showed that the huge crowd was actually in line at an adjacent grocery store that had just received a fresh supply of coffee. Ration boards then provided the civilian public with a further holiday shock that allotted forty-five pounds of coffee a year to all service personnel and dropped the civilian ration to only twenty-one pounds.

One of the few items that seemed to be in adequate supply in December 1942 was a huge new bestseller, *So Your Husband's Gone to War*, which the publisher Doubleday was selling off the shelves at two dollars a copy. Advertising writer Ethel Gorman of Bonwit Teller department stores offered a survival guide to the thousands of women who were married to a spouse who qualified for draft deferment in the first year of the war and was now being scooped up as the net for military personnel widened.

The American people may have been shocked at the prospect of less steak and coffee and more horsemeat and chicory, but if nothing else, this holiday season was set against a strategic background far brighter than only six months earlier. Between early April and early May, the then only actively engaged elements of the American combat force were essentially wiped off the chessboard of war in two agonizing surrenders. First, in early April, Maj. Gen. Ernest King authorized the largest surrender of American personnel in history when the Filipino-American garrison on Bataan Peninsula capitulated to Gen. Masaharu Homma unconditionally. A combination of roughly twenty thousand American troops and sixty thousand Commonwealth of the Philippines service personnel stacked their arms and were herded northward toward prison camps in a carnival of enemy blood lust in which as many as twenty thousand of the captives may have died through neglect or outright murder in what became known as the Bataan Death March. While only one full combat regiment and about fifteen thousand support troops, grounded fliers, and beached sailors were actually members of the American military establishment, the sixty-thousand-member Filipino contingent were still technically American personnel as the July 4, 1946, Act of Philippine Independence was still four years in the future. Thus, Edward King would surrender a larger force than either Gen. John Pemberton at Vicksburg in 1863 or Gen. Robert E. Lee at Appomattox in 1865. Four weeks later, Gen. Jonathan Wainwright surrendered the American garrison on Corregidor Island off the tip of Bataan and effectively turned the Philippines into a forced member of the Greater East Asia Co. Prosperity Sphere, the front title for the forcibly conquered Japanese puppet states.

Few American or Axis leaders realized it at the time, but General Wainwright's capitulation would be the last official American surrender of a significant force in World War II. Within forty-eight hours after the eleven thousand surrendering American military personnel on Corregidor were marched into captivity, a Japanese fleet attempting to secure Port Moresby in New Guinea was deflected by an outnumbered American fleet in the Coral Sea. Adm. Frank Jack Fletcher's task force centered around aircraft carriers *Lexington* and *Yorktown* came within aerial attack distance of a Nipponese carrier force under Adm. Takeo Takagi. In a battle in which the deck crews of the two fleets never came within sight of one another, American pilots sank the carrier *Shoho*, while their Nipponese counterparts sank the *Lexington* and for the first time in World War II, the Imperial commander ordered a cancellation of an operation as the Port Moresby invasion was "temporarily" postponed.

The Imperial navy had actually gained a tactical victory at Coral Sea. Of their meager fleet of three aircraft carriers then operating in the Pacific, the American fleet had lost one carrier sunk and another, the *Yorktown*, was badly damaged, while the Japanese lost only one relatively small carrier out of nearly a dozen that plowed through the ocean from the North Pacific to the South Pacific. Adm. Isoroku Yamamoto, the hero-worshipped architect of the Pearl Harbor attack, now determined to settle matters once and for all with a highly complex offensive that dispatched ten carriers and virtually the entire Imperial fleet on a massive offensive that stretched from Alaska to Australia in a complex sequence of feints, deceptions, and attacks designed to sweep the Pacific Ocean of the remnants of the American Navy.

The Battle of Midway, fought during the first week of June 1942, would quickly achieve prominence as one of the most decisive naval encounters in history, the Trafalgar of the twentieth century, and the clear choice as the turning point of the Pacific war. Adm. Chester Nimitz, a Texan who grew up in a community where the local creek was the largest body of water, coolly parlayed a fortuitous breaking of the Imperial naval code, excellent fleet commanders, and youthful pilots and flight crews who would suffer astronomical casualties that in one case resulted in the survival of only one member of an entire torpedo squadron to turn a looming defeat or stalemate into a one-sided victory in only ten minutes. While Japanese fighters were decimating the slow-moving American torpedo planes flying at high altitudes, a small contingent of divebombers swooped down on a momentarily vulnerable Japanese carrier fleet and turned three almost irreplaceable flat-tops into raging infernos in ten minutes.

The United States had now won its first major victory in World War II, even if it was primarily a defensive triumph, and now two less than hospitable places would dominate the American newspaper headlines through December 1942.

American civilians reading daily newspapers and weekly magazines, listening to nightly newscasts on the radio, and viewing the "news of the week" in neighborhood theaters had become increasingly accustomed by December of 1942 to the familiar names in otherwise exotic parts of the world. Guadalcanal, in the South Pacific, was an exotic location with a rather pedestrian name. Few Americans had ever been anywhere near this part of the world, and the rather innocuous name initially may have prompted visions of scantily clad South Seas denizens engaged in gathering pineapples and coconuts in a heat-induced torpor and then engaging in frequent dips in the sea between ritual dances and songs. The other focal point, Morocco/Algeria in North Africa, was possibly a bit less fantasized but still high on the exotic scale to an American population that virtually never traveled beyond its own borders, and if they did, it was for a quick glimpse of Canada or Mexico.

North Africa before World War II began hinted at desert sheiks, exotic dancers, steamy nightclubs with ceiling fans, hookah pipes, and the consummation of shady deals among a melting pot of natives and foreign adventurers. It seemed questionable who actually governed the region's nations at any one moment in time, which was perfectly acceptable, since they provided nothing that Americans particularly needed or cared about. Now, a year after Pearl Harbor, exotic lands suddenly mattered if for no other reason than preventing the Axis enemies from controlling them or their future use as jumping-off points to begin the long march to Tokyo, Berlin, or Rome.

The third probable battleground for the upcoming year, 1943, was culturally less alien but still thousands of miles from the conference rooms of the Pentagon. As part of the complicated Japanese offensive of June 1942, Imperial forces had bombed Dutch Harbor, Alaska, and occupied the thinly populated Aleutian Islands of Attu and Kiska. At their most optimistic moments, Imperial commanders saw the bleak islands as the jumping-off point for a "victory offensive" in which Japanese forces would sweep through Alaska, push southward into Washington and Oregon, and finally invade California as a first step in forcing the United States to come to the bargaining table to recognize the new order in the Asian/ Pacific world.

Now, six months later, North Africa, the Solomon Islands, and the Aleutian Islands were all emerging as major battlegrounds between the Americans and their Allies and the Axis powers that were interested in securing the huge territorial gains they had made in the opening phase of the war.

By December 1942, the long Arctic winter had turned the Aleutian front into a literal and figurative cold war. American bombers from XI Bomber Command made regular runs against Attu and Kiska. Nearly five thousand American soldiers occupied the island of Adak, and Gen. Simon Bolivar Buckner's Alaska Defense Command rose to eighty-seven thousand troops in December 1942, with 1943 clearly viewed as the decisive year in the battle for the Northland.

As American leaders celebrated the six-month anniversary of the victory of Midway in early December, that small sand speck in the Pacific was both an outdoor museum and an active defense site. According to one war correspondent who had visited the island on assignment for a news magazine, "The two mile long island still is seen as a strategic location of immeasurable importance," but noted that "Since June, the Japs have not troubled Midway but the Marines are ready for them." While bored garrison members munched on Spam, apples, and oranges and drank endless cups of coffee, "This island seemed to take on the aura of a strange combination of battlefield museum and municipal trash dump." Spit and polish gave way to a more relaxed atmosphere as an operations officer slouched in a chair that had been a seat on an abandoned transport plane and put his feet up as other members of the garrison showered in an outdoor stall that had once been the fuel tank for a now wrecked plane. The news reporter sensed that the war had moved well beyond Midway. "Even though planes are kept in readiness day and night for an enemy return, most formal rules are forgotten as a garrison of men in shorts, tee shirts and baseball caps play volleyball, horseshoes and baseball," waiting for an unlikely Japanese invasion.

The mellow mood on Midway was not shared by many of the servicemen on Guadalcanal. As the shattered remnants of a victorious but decimated 1st Marine Division were evacuated from this particular antechamber to hell, the Army GIs slowly pushed the still ferocious Japanese forces into an ever-shrinking perimeter while the Japanese high command debated whether the surviving troops should be evacuated. Yet even as the enemy hold on the island weakened, malaria began felling the soldiers and Marines faster than bullets. During October, just over nineteen hundred men were hospitalized for that illness; in November, the toll soared to over thirty-two hundred. As late as November 2, Imperial forces had been able to stage a counter landing of the 230th Regiment near the Nalimbu River, a landing that forced the Americans to abandon their own planned offensive in order to address the new threat.

On November 11, the increasingly famous Marine Raiders led by Col. Evans Carlson entered the jungle and did not emerge until a month later, as they pushed the 230th Imperial Regiment back toward the ocean. Carlson, who had seen active service with Chinese Communist forces battling the Japanese in China, had organized a special unit of fifteen hundred volunteers who were willing to adopt the concept of "gung ho" (work together) of Mao's Special Forces. Living on a meager ration and heavily trained in judo fighting, Carlson's Raiders turned the jungle from a Japanese refuge to a killing ground, and when they emerged a month later, a significant enemy force had been mauled at a loss of only seventeen Raiders. Now, December 1942 became the month of deliverance for the Marines, as on December 9, Gen. Alexander Patch of the Army "Americal" Division was handed command on Guadalcanal from Marine general Alexander Vandergrift, making the closing act of Guadalcanal an Army affair as 1943 dawned.

American and Japanese forces had spent most of the second half of 1942 contesting an island of two thousand square miles. At much the same time, American forces and their allies were dueling with German and Italian forces on a battlefield far more vast in scope that encompassed over a million square miles of endless desert, snow-capped mountains, and mysterious cities filled with enigmatic residents who often turned from enemy to ally and back again, depending on which side seemed to be winning at that particular moment in time.

By most standards of American military theory, Operation Torch and its Mediterranean sequels were never supposed to happen. Even as work crews cleared the wreckage around Pearl Harbor, senior members of the American Army high command were already convinced that Nazi Germany was a far greater long-term threat than Imperial Japan and that the Pacific Theater would essentially devolve into a holding action, while the cream of a hugely expanded American ground Army stormed ashore on French beaches as early as 1942. Actually, fifty American Rangers did storm ashore at Dieppe, France, in 1942, along with several thousand British and Canadian commandos tasked with testing the strength of Hitler's hugely publicized Atlantic Wall. Unfortunately, a few hours later, the majority of the assault force was either dead on the beach or being processed into German prisoner-of-war camps, and two years would pass before that particular strategy would be given a second chance.

Yet the Dieppe disaster had a silver lining. By the autumn of 1942, Hitler's forces were so overextended in their attempt to take and hold Stalingrad, lunge at the supply cornucopia that was Cairo, and defeat an Anglo-American landing in France that was more than just a raid, that there simply were not enough forces to adequately defend every gateway to Third Reich territory. Anglo-American planners studied their maps with great diligence, and on July 30, 1942, Franklin Delano Roosevelt approved the plan his commanders had cobbled together: Operation Torch. Much like a Monopoly player who puts houses and hotels on Baltic and Mediterranean Avenues when Boardwalk and Park Place are divided between other opponents, a successful landing in French Morocco would get the American forces into the European Theater "game," with minimal risk of being thrown back into the sea.

An invasion of French Morocco was hardly a high-risk assault compared to a mass paratroop assault into Berlin before Allied ground troops ever set foot on the continent of Europe, but if the eight Vichy French divisions stationed in Morocco put up something less than a last stand fight, American forces would finally be at least on the same side of the Atlantic Ocean as the Third Reich. Just under thirty-five thousand troops would be crowded onto transportation in both the United States and Britain, with much of the force centered around the Iowa and Minnesota members of 34th Division who had hardly experienced much desert activity in their hometowns.

The commander of this still relatively modest expeditionary force was just beginning to make the almost fantastic transformation from middle-aged major sitting in a windowless War Department office with few future prospects to the overall command of the largest Army that the United States would ever raise. Although he was never reduced to selling Christmas trees on a street corner like his predecessor, Ulysses S.

Grant, Dwight David Eisenhower grew up in a small Kansas community enduring physical punishment and verbal abuse from a father who was descending the social scale from bankrupt store owner to less than successful dairy employee.

Like Grant, Eisenhower was a non-entity at West Point, grateful simply for the free education. He was a middling student preparing to become a middling officer in a sort of alternate universe to his Pacific war counterpart, Douglas MacArthur. While MacArthur spent the 1930s pontificating and commanding, Eisenhower spent that decade as a major who implemented other people's decisions. Yet Eisenhower was energetic, diplomatic, easy to deal with, and would make a perfect fit for an American Army that would spend most of the war dealing with a more glamorous Navy that Franklin Delano Roosevelt considered his favorite service; an equally glamorous and increasingly autonomous Army Air Force that had first pick of the best inductees and expected to divorce itself from its senior service as soon as the war ended; and a British ally that had spent the previous war giving the fledgling American Expeditionary Force everything from its helmets to its own airplanes. Now, the Americans under Eisenhower would have their own war planes, their own helmets, their own largely superior rifles, and their own significant uncertainty as to whether the French garrison of Morocco would join them as brethren in arms or fight to the death for what they still considered French territory.

On November 8, 1942, a campaign that would take American forces from the desert sands of North Africa all the way to the vineyards of Italy during 1943 was set in motion when Maj. Gen. Orlando Ward's 3rd Battalion of the 6th Armored Infantry Regiment landed on the beaches of Oran, while a second assault force centered around the 1st Infantry Division and 1st Armored Division stormed ashore along the fishing village of Arzew, sixteen miles to the east. Within hours, seven more assault forces hit a wide swath of beaches along the Algerian and Moroccan coastline, and for much of the next five days, the amity of World War I between French and American soldiers was shattered by grim battles in which outnumbered defenders killed over five hundred American troops at a cost of roughly *twice* as many casualties as their own largely outgunned defenders. However, like President John Adams's "undeclared" war on the French Directory in the 1790s, the sting of conflict would soon largely fade as Hitler quickly managed to destroy Franco-German amicability by occupying the southern half of France, which had existed as a relatively autonomous state since the debacle of 1940.

CHAPTER 1

Buna to Bismarck Sea

ON DECEMBER 24, 1941, GEN. DOUGLAS MACARTHUR STOOD ON THE balcony of the penthouse suite of the Manila Hotel and pondered a scene not witnessed by an American since Jefferson Davis stood on the balcony of the Confederate White House on April 2, 1865, and watched his army evacuate the capital in the first stage of a weeklong retreat that would end in surrender a week later at Appomattox Court House. The suite of rooms behind MacArthur still projected the feasting of the holiday season and the general could still glance at a glass-front case displaying numerous medals of most likely the most famous American warrior since John J. Pershing a generation earlier. Along with the glass case, the most noticeable item in the room was a bronze vase given to the general by the emperor of Japan, which commemorated MacArthur's role as an official observer of the Japanese triumph over Russia four decades earlier. Now the son of that emperor had given his divine blessing to a massive attack on Nippon's Great War allies, Britain and America, and the first extended, large-scale clash between Japanese and American forces was occurring not far from MacArthur's balcony as American and Philippine units backpedaled from the enemy landings at Lingayen Gulf and swung ever closer to their last redoubt, Bataan Peninsula just across the bay from Manila. On paper, MacArthur's retreat order seemed a bit perplexing, as he commanded nearly eighty thousand Philippine and American soldiers, and his antagonist, Gen. Masaharu Homma, was attacking them with only a little more than forty thousand invasion troops who were under orders to bring the Philippine Commonwealth into the Greater East Asia Co. Prosperity Sphere along with numerous other "fortunate" Asian nations.

MacArthur may not have lacked for warm bodies in uniforms, but unfortunately for the Filipino-American allies, most of these men had been untrained civilians only a few weeks earlier, and the mass of troops was even less trained than the Union and Confederate armies at Bull Run. Moreover, in July 1861, at least *both* armies were virtual newcomers to battle. Now MacArthur could only substantially depend on one regiment of American regulars, two regiments of "Philippine Scouts" who were moderately well trained, and a badly understrength American Marine regiment that was currently deployed on the island of Corregidor in Manila Harbor. This provided the general with about twenty thousand men who might be considered trained soldiers but even the barely tolerable two to one odds they faced were lengthened by two more massive Imperial advantages. First, on the day before Pearl Harbor, the American Far East Air Force in the Philippines could put in the air about one hundred more-or-less modern fighter planes and thirty-five front-line B-17 Flying Fortress bombers. However, after fog delayed a Japanese, Pearl Harbor–like dawn attack on American airmen in the Philippines, the attackers returned when almost the entire defense force was grounded and promptly obliterated more than half the American air strength in only a few minutes. Now, in late December, the bombers had been pulled back to Australia, and perhaps twenty American fighter planes could still take off to confront four hundred enemy aircraft. MacArthur hoped the retreat into the largely jungle-covered Bataan Peninsula would potentially negate enemy air superiority.

The siege of Bataan was the first American ground battle of World War II, and the gritty defense of the peninsula would provide Hollywood with a treasure trove of Alamo-like "last stands" against an overwhelming, merciless foe, from *Bataan* with Robert Taylor to *Back to Bataan*, starring John Wayne and filmed after MacArthur returned. Douglas MacArthur settled down inside the massive tunnel complex built to defend Corregidor Island with his wife and a preschool-age son, and while he showed admirable courage in refusing to retreat back into the bombproof tunnels when he ventured outside during bombings, the general only made one brief visit to the actual Bataan battlefield. He began to acquire the nickname "Dugout Doug" from the American troops being whittled down by enemy ambushes, malaria, and a meager diet of one-quarter rations centered around moldy World War I hardtack and an occasional stray iguana or monkey.

Despite Gen. Douglas MacArthur's enormous ego, he was still emerging as one of the most talented commanders in the Pacific Theater. MacArthur, right, poses with Maj. Gen. Jonathan Wainwright.
LIBRARY OF CONGRESS

As nurses and doctors in open-air hospitals near the tip of Bataan heard the enemy guns get a bit closer with each food-scarce day, Franklin Roosevelt and Gen. George Marshall realized that while there was no way that the garrison could be relieved with much of the Pacific Fleet sitting on the bottom of Pearl Harbor, there was little sense in providing the enemy with the propaganda coup of capturing the most senior American commander in the Pacific Theater. While MacArthur insisted that he would not be taken alive, rumors that the enemy might exhibit the captured general in a cage throughout the Empire helped to expedite the presidential order that the American commander was expected to leave the Philippines and transfer his headquarters to theoretically organize a rapid return to the Philippines with substantial reinforcements.

MacArthur, along with his wife and young son, underwent excruciating bouts of seasickness after boarding Lt. John Bulkeley's PT-41 in a meandering odyssey from Corregidor down to the Mindanao city of Cagayan, where the small party was expected to board B-17 bombers for the flight to Australia. Seasickness was quickly exchanged for airsickness on a fifteen-hundred-mile flight in the cramped bombers, never designed to carry passengers. When MacArthur reached Darwin on St. Patrick's Day morning, the general received a new shock that the Army that he was told he would command in an early attempt to relieve Bataan simply did not exist and, in fact, a Japanese invasion of Australia was expected shortly. The general had commanded over seventy-five thousand men on Bataan. Now, with most of the Australian army fighting abroad, MacArthur discovered that the Allied garrison in Australia was closer to twenty-five thousand men. Despite the initial shock, the general held a press conference that proved to be a turning point, as he told the press, "I have come to Australia to organize an offensive against Japan ... I came through, and I shall return." Bataan and then Corregidor would soon surrender, and the proud tradition of the Japanese honor code would become a mockery in the Bataan Death March and subsequent prison camp mistreatment of American prisoners that may very well have cost the life of every captured solder if their escaped commander did not return. For the next two and a half years, Douglas MacArthur's eyes were always on the emaciated American soldiers and the mistreated Filipino civilians who were unwilling protagonists in the Imperial fraud of Asia for Asians. However, the defeat in the jungle of Bataan could only be eventually redeemed by an initial American victory in the equally challenging jungles of New Guinea, and the first step on the trip back to Bataan began at a small village in another jungle.

While the surrender of the American garrison on Bataan in April and the capitulation of an even larger British army at Singapore a few weeks earlier effectively cleared the board for a massive Nipponese territorial expansion, the Imperial staff could not declare total victory in the Great East Asian War until Australia was either captured or neutralized.

In the wake of the 1940 German defeat of France and the British evacuation at Dunkirk, the Australian government had sent most of its army units to the United Kingdom to aid the mother country in an expected Nazi invasion of the British Isles. While Axis allies Japan and Germany were both too far apart geographically and too suspicious of one another's motives to provide more than token assistance, the transfer of much of Australia's armed forces to the war against Hitler provided the Imperial high command with a possibility of conquering or at least neutralizing Australia by capturing a jump-off point at Port Moresby, New Guinea, and then possibly besieging or invading Australia. Soon after Gen. Douglas MacArthur settled into his new headquarters in a comfortable office of a Melbourne insurance company, the battle to push back the Nipponese tide began in earnest.

Just as few Americans in 1860 had ever heard of Gettysburg, Pittsburg Landing, Tennessee (Shiloh Church), or Appomattox Court House, few Americans in 1940 could identify Port Moresby, Buna, or Guadalcanal; yet, as 1943 began, these locations were the sites of headlines.

Part of Admiral Yamamoto's complex Midway campaign plan was to distract Allied forces on Midway by launching an operation across Papua, New Guinea, to capture the dockyards at Port Moresby, a relatively short hop across the water to northern Australia. A Japanese assault force hacked its way through dense jungle from the village of Buna on the Solomon Sea coast of Papua, New Guinea, struggled over the Owen Stanley mountains, and arrived close enough to Port Moresby to see the lights of the airfield and harbor of this town opposite the northern Australian coast.

However, Douglas MacArthur also quickly appreciated the strategic value of a port town that could become a jumping-off point for a Japanese invasion of Australia, and reinforcements were funneled into the area at a rapid pace. These included the Australian 14th Infantry Brigade, the largely African-American 96th Engineer Battalion, an American antiaircraft battalion, and other assorted units that turned the sleepy town into a major military base that could most likely repulse the enemy assault forces.

Yet Douglas MacArthur was at heart a riverboat gambler who emphasized offensive operations, and after the disastrous siege of Bataan, the general was willing to take substantial risks in order to carry the war to the enemy. Thus, Port Moresby would not be the site of a heroic Australian-American last stand but merely a jumping-off point in chasing the enemy back across the Kokoda Trail all the way back to the eastern shore of Papua, New Guinea. The ultimate target was the tiny port town of Buna on the far side of the Owen Stanley mountains, which would become the first baby step back to the general's ultimate target, liberation of the Philippines.

The remaining weeks of 1942 became a push and shove shooting match on the Kokoda Trail, as MacArthur flew over the battle scene in his specially modified B-17 Flying Fortress, the *Bataan*. MacArthur's ground commander, Maj. Gen. Robert Eichelberger, had been a classmate of George Patton at West Point, and like both MacArthur and Patton, he was moody, dramatic, sometimes engaging, sometimes a martinet to everyone around him. Eichelberger did not welcome his new assignment, as he had emerged as a possible major figure in the upcoming invasion of North Africa, which he considered a much better path to significant promotion. In many respects, the clear winner in this command shuffle was Maj. Gen. Robert Richardson, who was initially chosen for the thankless job of serving under MacArthur but was shunted over to command all Army forces in the Central Pacific, under the far more agreeable Adm. Chester Nimitz, to form an Army-Navy team that worked together with very little friction for the remainder of the war.

Eichelberger's assault force for what would eventually become the Battle of Buna was the 32nd Infantry Division, composed primarily of

National Guard enlistees from Wisconsin and Michigan and the 41st Division, another National Guard unit centered around personnel from Oregon and Washington. As the Americans and allied Australian units set off on their long march across the Kokoda Trail, MacArthur, never a person to miss an opportunity for a dramatic gesture, wished Eichelberger good luck and then insisted, "Take Buna, Bob, or don't come back alive!"

On New Year's Day, 1943, Robert Eichelberger and most, but not all, of his men were still alive and had managed to push the enemy out of the town of Buna. However, the Japanese forces had retreated to a twentieth-century version of the Alamo, Buna Mission, which was a fortified trading post and headquarters for British/American merchants and government officials in this part of Papua, New Guinea. A *Life* magazine war correspondent noted that, "Buna Mission is a pleasant settlement with native huts, warehouses, and a general store around the district headquarters of the Papuan government." Yet, now on the first day of 1943, the Japanese garrison was playing the role of the Texan defenders of the Alamo, except that, unlike Davy Crockett, Jim Bowie, and company, these Japanese troops were armed with automatic weapons and machine guns, and much of the main building was constructed of corrugated iron.

The Imperial commander had also studded the numerous jungle trees with sharpshooters, and as the Americans attempted to move in for a final assault, the sniping became so persistent that wounded men returning from the front line to the aid station walked "Chicago gangster style" with bodyguards front and rear, constantly on the watch for snipers. One American private noted with some astonishment, "I was walking down the trail when I saw some fellas talking; they grinned, I grinned, one pulled a gun, I pulled mine, and I killed him. It was just like in the movies."

As American casualties mounted, a single chaplain often rotated among Catholic, Protestant, and Jewish funeral services, while wary armed bodyguards eyed the treetops and bushes for potential enemy snipers. Sgt. Herman Bottcher, a German immigrant to the United States, led an assault force that finally opened a passable corridor between already captured Buna village and the still contested Buna Mission and was given a spot promotion to captain for his bravery. General Eichelberger, with MacArthur's win or die exhortation still ringing in his ears, was frequently

The bloody battle of Buna Mission emerged as the first significant American victory in New Guinea.
LIBRARY OF CONGRESS

photographed with a tommy gun, and as he stepped over a long line of enemy bodies was quoted as exclaiming, "What! Another 100 Japs killed; isn't it beautiful!"

The Battle of Buna was the first American offensive victory over the Japanese as the battle for Guadalcanal was still being conducted, and the publicity surrounding the campaign for Buna was enormous. Newspapers and magazines featured lengthy articles on the battle. *Life* magazine followed a thirteen-page photo essay on the battle featuring photographs by George Strock, with a follow-up piece the next week that focused on the enormous booty taken at Buna. Photos displayed grinning but obviously exhausted men of the Sunset (41st) and Red Arrow (32nd) divisions holding samurai swords and paper fans with rising suns, while one shot featured an American barber cutting the hair of a soldier using a rising sun flag as the "wrapper" covering his "customers."

Correspondents related stories of hand-to-hand bayonet duels and extremely close quarters combat that taught them that "jungle fighting differs radically from any other kind: one American soldier pitted against one enemy soldier. Americans must become independent, self sufficient fighters experienced with a rifle, grenade and bayonet, capable always of personally killing his enemy and saving himself."

Twelve hundred miles to the east, many of these same lessons were being put to practice as the battle for Guadalcanal entered its final stage in January of 1943. On New Year's Day, the US Army forces that had relieved the battle-weary First Marine Division began to push the Imperial defenders from their strongpoints in the jungle back onto the relatively open grasslands that fronted the looming heights of Mount Austen. The redeployed Nipponese soldiers were now issued the last rations in the Japanese larder, two crackers and one piece of candy each. Even Imperial soldiers who were taught to make do with minimal supplies could not continue to fight much longer on such meager fare, and back in Tokyo, Japanese army and navy officials argued about what to do with the perhaps ten thousand survivors that remained of the thirty-thousand-man invasion force that had battled for Henderson Field back in the summer and early autumn.

The situation had become so dire that an initial Japanese plan to reinforce Guadalcanal with the 41st Division was canceled, and the unit rerouted to a New Guinea campaign where the situation was a bit less dire. Army and navy officials had used a New Year's audience with Emperor Hirohito to present a new "victory plan" that actually was tantamount to a heretofore unthinkable evacuation of the island. Apparently, the emperor received the evacuation plan with barely concealed shock, as he was at that moment preparing an "Imperial Rescript thanking his military forces for defeating the Americans on Guadalcanal." While the American victory at Midway could be partially masked by simply abandoning the assault on that island in order to launch attacks on more "suitable" war targets, the evacuation of an island that had been technically absorbed into the Japanese Empire the previous summer was simply unfathomable in the Imperial palace.

Vague and hollow promises from military and naval leaders that the garrison on Guadalcanal was simply being redeployed for more promising and strategically important "new projects" were accepted by Hirohito with barely concealed concern, but a united palace-military front needed to be maintained, lest Japanese subjects begin to wonder why it now appeared that American forces might be moving closer to Tokyo when Japanese forces were preparing to deploy against California.

On January 9, 1943, the Combined Fleet and 8th Imperial Army set in motion Operation KE that would center around an evacuation of all able-bodied surviving personnel on Guadalcanal, beginning during the final week of January. All soldiers still capable of walking would retreat to the western end of the island in a series of phased withdrawals with each unit, in turn, covering the fallback of the next retreating force. Every available combat aircraft would provide air cover for the evacuation, while submarines would be assigned to slip in at the last moment and evacuate any personnel who had not been able to get away on a destroyer or landing craft. Those sick or badly wounded not able to take part in the evacuation would be assigned to keep the enemy in the dark by firing their weapons to dissuade an American advance, then commit suicide by holding a hand grenade over their chests. Surviving sick and wounded too weak to perform even these last services to the emperor would simply be injected with poison to ensure that not one live prisoner be taken by the enemy.

Admiral Yamamoto now set in motion the distasteful KE operation that seemed little more than a Japanese version of the British disembarkment from the beaches of Dunkirk three years earlier. The admiral hoped that the concentration of a still formidable Imperial fleet that included two carriers, two battleships, four heavy cruisers, and twenty-one destroyers would somehow entice an equally battered American fleet into a foolhardy overconfidence that might end in a repetition of the Imperial triumph at Java Sea and Savo Island.

Gen. Alexander Patch now commanded a newly activated mixed service unit centered around the Americal Division, the 25th Division, the independent 147th Infantry Regiment, and the 2nd Marine Division. This formidable array could field over fifty thousand front-line troops now facing perhaps fifteen thousand Imperial defenders with an

American artillery advantage of 170 pieces of field artillery to confront enemy battery that had shrunk to perhaps three dozen field pieces.

The defenders were now hemmed into a shrinking perimeter about six miles wide that extended from the Matanikau River and its adjacent town to the Kokum Bona River and its nearby settlement. One of the most visible leaders in the final battle for Guadalcanal was Maj. Gen. J. Lawton Collins, a relatively young, energetic Louisianan who had emerged as a popular professor at both West Point and the Army War College, and then gained command of the 25th "Tropic Lightning" division in his early forties. Collins was now embarked on a whirlwind career at age forty-five that would place him on magazine covers and in newspaper

The army commanders in the Pacific Theater were talented, aggressive soldiers who often operated in the shadow of the more glamorous Marines. Pictured here are Maj. Gen. Alexander M. Patch Jr., left, Gen. Millard F. Harmon, and Maj. Gen. Nathan F. Twining.
LIBRARY OF CONGRESS

headlines, and a rare transfer to the European Theater where he commanded VII Corps in Normandy and eventually rose to Army Chief of Staff and commander of NATO ground forces during the 1950s.

Collins's Tropic Lightning soldiers and the leathernecks of the 2nd Marine Division now teamed up to push the still dangerous Japanese defenders from the heights of Mount Austen that loomed over the island. The Imperial forces had carefully designed a series of forty-five interconnected pillboxes known collectively as the Cifu Strong Point, and the soldiers of the Americal division had been probing the enemy complex since Christmas. Now the final battle for Guadalcanal began as a powerful array of American artillery batteries opened fire under a new attack scheme called Time on Target, which placed a hurricane of explosives on a sequential timed barrage. Then the Army artillery dropped white phosphorous rounds that became markers for Navy Dauntless divebombers that used depth charges in a new and unique way.

This combined Army, Marines, and Navy operation provided numerous instances in which the integration of forces contributed significant dividends. For example, the reconnaissance troop of the 25th Division borrowed light trucks from the Marines and knocked out eight enemy machine-gun nests in a terrain that textbooks insisted was a poor place to deploy armored vehicles. As the swarming Japanese defenders backpedaled toward their final defensive position at Kokum Bona on the northwest coast of the island, the intermingling of Army and Marine units became more of an asset than a liability as Collins even took the unheard of step of combining soldiers and leathernecks into a provisional Combined Army and Marine Division (CAM), which added a new dimension to the campaign.

A final battle for Guadalcanal in open terrain such as Tarawa later in the year would have produced a near annihilation of the Japanese garrison on Guadalcanal. However, Guadalcanal's much larger land mass and dense jungle growth delayed American operations just enough that roughly ten thousand Imperial defenders were able to retreat to Cape Esperance before their pursuers could organize a final assault.

On the night of February 8-9, 1943, leaving twenty thousand of their comrades dead somewhere on Guadalcanal, ten thousand Imperial troops were ferried out to destroyers and clambered aboard so they could die for the emperor on an occasion that offered more benefit to the throne. For the first time in World War II, the Japanese Empire had actually lost a ground battle, and the experience was so novel that the idea of a banzai charge to the last man had not really occurred to commanders who had only experienced victory. The search for a rationalization of this disaster quickly produced a new "spin" on a Pacific war that was, for the first time, not going entirely according to plan. The battle for Guadalcanal was quickly linked to the battle for New Guinea with the explanation that New Guinea was so vital to the Empire that victory there would easily right the embarrassing outcome on Guadalcanal. As this new reality took hold, the reinforcement of Imperial units on that battlefront took on an increasingly critical importance.

As Imperial navy destroyers were evacuating the emaciated survivors of the Battle of Guadalcanal, senior Nipponese commanders converged on the massive air base complex and port of Rabaul at the northeast tip of New Britain and discussed a new strategy for the New Guinea campaign in light of the loss of Buna and the evacuation of Guadalcanal. Gen. Hitoshi Imamura, commander of an army group composed of the 17th and 18th Armies, was seeking some action that could contain MacArthur's possible breakout from Buna to advance westward along the coast of New Guinea while possibly even closing the strategically important Huon Gulf to Imperial shipping. The linchpin of an unraveling Japanese control of much of the central coastline of New Guinea was the port at Lae, and American and Australian troops were edging closer to the town every day.

General Horii felt that the situation was becoming so critical that he proposed an enormously risky roll of the dice. He would beat the enemy at its own game of amphibious invasion by employing the 51st Division, carried from Rabaul by eight transports escorted by eight destroyers that would steam west through the Bismarck Sea and land at Lae in time to tip the balance of forces back in favor of the Japanese army.

Unfortunately for Lieutenant General Hatazō Adachi, the 51st Division commander, American cryptographers had intercepted much of the Imperial plan, and Gen. George Kenney's invaluable fleet of bombers

The agony of the Marines' experience on Guadalcanal ended in triumph as the Imperial navy evacuated the starving survivors of the Imperial attack force. Japanese dead lie on the beach as US Marines establish their position.
LIBRARY OF CONGRESS

had already transmitted reports that an enemy fleet was already steaming out from Rabaul. Kenney was flexible enough to realize that American Army Air Force commander General "Hap" Arnold's cherished vision of high-level percussion bombing on targets in Europe would not necessarily transfer well over the seemingly endless waters of the Pacific Ocean. Kenney and his energetic alter ego, Ennis Whitehead, felt that they had almost perfected an entirely new technique called "skip bombing" designed to hit moving targets at sea. Like skipping flat stones across a pond, American medium bombers would skim along the water at two hundred to three hundred feet and use four- or five-second delay fuses to skip across the sea and hit an enemy ship on its vulnerable side either slightly above or below the waterline. Then the bombers and their fighter escorts would let loose with every machine gun available and minimize antiaircraft fire by distracting Japanese gun crews.

On the morning of March 2, 1943, the Japanese fleet, designated Operation 81, passed Cape Gloucester on the far end of New Britain from Rabaul and prepared to make the relatively short passage between the Bismarck Sea to the north and the Solomon Huon Gulf to the south. This narrow channel called Vitia Strait soon became a death trap as American medium bombers suddenly swooped from the sky and roaring at virtual mast level loosed bombs and opened fire with dozens of machine guns. As each attack force veered off, American P-38 Lightning fighters and Australian twin-engine Beaufighters shot up Imperial soldiers as they scrambled to make a hasty exit overboard. One by one, all eight transporters began to slide to the bottom of the sea as the next wave of bombers then concentrated on the now badly overcrowded rescue destroyers, which quickly saw their numbers cut in half. Moments later, PT boats based in Buna appeared to finish off the damaged ships.

Two days later, Gen. Douglas MacArthur issued a press communication describing the outcome of what was quickly labeled the "Battle of the Bismarck Sea," which proved unusual in the sense that one side had fielded only planes, and the other deployed only ships. MacArthur's statement included an overly generous tally of twelve enemy transporters and ten warships sunk, which would have been quite a feat, considering that only sixteen ships were afloat at the start of the battle. He also noted that fifteen thousand Imperial soldiers were wiped out almost to the last man.

The actual tally of enemy ships was well below these inflated figures, especially when the attack force was credited for killing over twice as many enemy soldiers than debarked on the vessels. However, the task force did lose three thousand Imperial soldiers, all eight transports sunk, and four of the eight destroyers sent to the bottom of the sea, while General Adachi himself had to be fished from the sea to take command of a badly decimated force.

The series of battles from Buna to Bismarck Sea, including the primarily Army-directed final battle on Guadalcanal, received far less wartime and postwar publicity than the Marine-dominated first stages of the seesaw struggle for Henderson Field and the nearly disastrous battle of Savo Island in the opening phase of the Solomons campaign. However, New Guinea would have been a far more important addition to the Japanese Empire than Guadalcanal, and the failure to win that contest kept a very vulnerable Australia at arm's length from Japanese seizure. March of 1943 would see the Solomon Islands and New Guinea share top billing as Allied forces set their sights on capturing the massive enemy-held harbor and multiple airfields of Rabaul. Imperial generals and admirals longed for a reversal in fortunes on New Guinea that might eventually plant the rising sun flag on the shores of Australia. Neither side would get what they dreamed of in 1943, but half a world away, Axis and Allied commanders were dueling for the gateway to southern Europe over an equally enormous battlefield as unforgiving, exotic, and dangerous as the "green hell" of the New Guinea and Solomon Island jungles.

CHAPTER 2

Debacle at Kasserine Pass

WHILE AMERICAN SOLDIERS AND MARINES SLOGGED THEIR WAY through the green hell of New Guinea and Guadalcanal jungles in early 1943, their counterparts in the other major theater of war at that time, North Africa, were experiencing for the first time the shock of Blitzkrieg launched from a German army that had swept across northwest Europe three years earlier. Most American service personnel assigned to this region had experienced "desert" culture and warfare primarily through silver screen depictions, from Rudolph Valentino's *Sheik* to more contemporary films such as Gary Cooper's *Beau Geste*. Even though the film sets were strictly limited to Hollywood backlots, producers and directors of desert movies attempted to portray with some authenticity the shimmering heat and exotic settings. Yet now, in the winter of 1943, a large force of American service personnel were ensconced in a real North African desert with days on end when the sun never appeared, as cold rain and even occasional snow showers destroyed the myth of never-ending heat. Unlike Guadalcanal and New Guinea, which had virtually no climate equivalent in the continental United States, the battles around the Western and Eastern Dorsal Mountains of Algeria and Tunisia would be fought by men who were seeking warmth, not shade, in what they viewed as a cruel irony when they first learned that they would be engaged in a campaign in North Africa.

The main reason tens of thousands of American military personnel were now experiencing the less-than-comfortable life of a denizen of the desert was that Prime Minister Winston Churchill had effectively engineered an end run around President Franklin Roosevelt's senior generals and convinced the American commander-in-chief that the American military plan to launch a cross-Channel invasion in 1943 was sheer suicide. The British prime minister was as ardent a supporter of total victory over the Germans as his American counterpart, but he was convinced that a cross-Channel invasion without total command of the air and sea was tantamount to self-destruction. Churchill convinced a reluctant President Roosevelt to commit massive American ground forces to a Mediterranean campaign already being conducted by a large portion of his British army. The plan was to trap a sizable Axis army between Gen. Bernard Montgomery's Eighth Army advancing westward from Libya and an American expeditionary force pushing eastward from Morocco. If all went according to plan, the advancing Allied forces would trap the enemy forces against the sea in Tunisia; launch an invasion of Sicily and southern Italy; and then essentially hit Hitler's vulnerable flank in Austria in concert with eventual Russian offensives from the east.

Gen. George Marshall, the senior officer of the US Army, resolutely opposed Churchill's plan as a possibly disastrous loss of focus on the real prize, the invasion of northwest Europe. Eventually, a compromise was secured. Operation Roundup, the invasion of France in 1943, morphed into Overlord, with a 1944 deadline, while a separate American expeditionary force tackled the enemy in North Africa with further campaigns to be decided as events progressed.

On January 9, 1943, Franklin Roosevelt, who had recently viewed the film *Casablanca* in the White House theater, boarded a special train waiting on a secret spur line beneath the United States Printing Office and launched a roundabout odyssey that would terminate in the very Casablanca that he had just seen on the silver screen. A twenty-seven-hour train ride to Miami led to a Pan Am flight to Trinidad, where he then caught a flight to Brazil, then Gambia, and eventually a final hop to Morocco. The commander-in-chief was welcomed to Casablanca by rising star Gen. George Patton who, in a symbol of the way in which the tide of the war was changing, requisitioned the hotel that up to a few weeks earlier had been occupied by the members of the German Armistice Commission which effectively dictated policy to a defeated colonial French government.

The Casablanca Conference solidified the image of the Anglo-American allies as the probable victors against Mussolini's now besieged Fascist empire. Winston Churchill is seated third from left; to his left is FDR.
LIBRARY OF CONGRESS

Josef Stalin was an invited no-show at the supposed Big Three Conference as the battle for Stalingrad absorbed all of his energies, and there were no colorful adventurers like Humphrey Bogart's "Rick" in the box office smash hit film, but Winston Churchill was highly visible, and President Roosevelt was also pleasantly surprised to see the youngest son of his closest personal adviser near at hand. Corporal Hopkins, the son of the president's boon companion, Harry Hopkins, was a photographer/reporter for the Army who was dispatched to Casablanca on a five-day odyssey from Tunis and exchanged a tent for a plush room near the center of action. As Hopkins photographed Churchill puffing on an enormous fifteen-inch cigar and Roosevelt fitting a new cigarette into his trademark holder, plans for the final defeat of the Axis in North Africa were bandied back and forth.

The first major confrontation between the German Wehrmacht and a largely novice American Army was about to occur against a vast, harsh North African backdrop that in real life differed significantly from the "desert" soundstages of Hollywood films. The vast panoramic desert that stretched across North Africa may have been relatively arid but did feature at least some foliage and trees, functioning farms, and fruit orchards, and the cold dampness of the Carolinas and Georgia in wintertime.

The penetrating cold and vast spaces of this battleground produced occasions when killing one another temporarily dropped from prime importance as the climate and topography mastered both armies. One bemused American bomber pilot related to a new reporter that upon his return from a mission against a German airfield in Bizerte, as the Americans flew eastward, the attack force met a large formation of Ju-88 German bombers on their way to attack an Allied convoy. The pilot noted that the two armadas passed within close proximity to one another, and instead of opening fire, "just ignored each other . . . what a war! . . . we meet each other on the way to bomb one another."

As reports of the utter ferocity of the Pacific war and the numerous atrocities committed by the Nipponese enemy that had little value for life reached the North African camps, there was at least some comfort in the realization that the German and Italian forces did allow surrender and treated prisoners tolerably well, so that as hard as conditions were in North Africa, they were far worse in New Guinea and the Solomon Islands.

However, real bullets were still being used by both sides, and even if native brigands might be more bloodthirsty in their actions than Axis soldiers, even in a "clean war" those bullets resulted in an ever-lengthening casualty list. By the winter of 1943, the Axis position in North Africa was clearly becoming more precarious, but the tide had not yet turned completely in favor of the Allies. The far harsher winter months that held Stalingrad in their icy grip in early 1943 had helped to almost totally blunt the Axis offensive in the previous autumn, and now the survivors of the quarter-million-man German and Reich allied armies were slowing starving to death on a daily ration of one piece of bread, one ounce of horsemeat, and one cigarette a day, so that by the time that the planned Allied spring offensive rolled into action, two hundred fifty thousand enemy soldiers would be dead or prisoners who could offer no possible aid to their comrades in the Mediterranean. Yet, as all German cinemas, theaters, and restaurants were closed for three days of mourning and radio stations played only somber dirges, two talented German generals were cobbling together a complicated offensive designed to stop the Allied advance in North Africa in its tracks and return the initiative to a Wehrmacht that hoped to compensate for the Stalingrad disaster by giving a smart defeat to the newly arriving American forces.

As the Soviet ring around the besieged German garrison in Stalingrad closed ever tighter, Wehrmacht intelligence officers became increasingly aware that Allied defenses in Tunisia were poorly arranged and generally weak, while the whole southern flank was held by woefully inexperienced American units that Erwin Rommel dismissed as "Britain's Italians" in a comparison hardly flattering to his fellow Fascist allies. If Bernard Montgomery continued his leisurely pace through Libya, there might well be an opportunity to smash into the carelessly deployed Americans strung out along the Tunisian-Algerian border, then pivot and smash into Montgomery's British forces before that general could cobble together the conditions he required for a full-scale battle.

What would become the Battle of Kasserine Pass was neither a slapped-together desperation move that would plague the Germans in the closing months of the war, nor the perfectly timed and executed romp through France and Belgium in the Blitz of 1940. The two complementary operations, Spring Wind and Morning Breeze, were designed to weaken American morale, drive a wedge between the two main Allied armies, and buy extra time to more fully consider the future direction of the Axis operations in the Mediterranean Theater.

In the winter of 1942-1943, the single most important point in North Africa was the port city of Tunis, Tunisia, as that city's docks and harbor provided the Axis powers with a port of entry for reinforcements if the tide of war shifted in their favor, and an embarkation point if the German and Italian armies were pushed to the tip of Africa and decided to mount a Dunkirk-like evacuation back to Sicily, only ninety miles to the north. As the German defenses in Stalingrad crumbled, the two senior commanders in Sicily, Field Marshal Erwin Rommel and Gen. Hans-Jürgen von Arnim, began to cobble together a counterpunch that would throw the Allied advances off balance and open up fresh options to salvage something from a rapidly deteriorating African adventure.

While Erwin Rommel was a household name across Europe and America as the "Desert Fox" and even achieved grudging recognition in the British Parliament in a Winston Churchill speech, the major defeat at El Alamein in the autumn had reduced the German contingent of the Afrika Corps to about thirty thousand men, compared to fifty thousand Italian troops who were seen by Rommel as, at best, a very mixed bag. Arnim's 5th Panzer Army had seen less action and still numbered about seventy-five thousand troops bolstered by twenty-five thousand Italian servicemen. Contrary to both Allied and German barbs against them, the Italian soldiers were individually brave but suffered under the worst leadership of any major forces in World War II. Officers tended to ignore the needs of their men and focused on either their own careers or their personal safety, and many were nothing more than political hacks of a now fraying Fascist party.

In turn, there was also a division between the two senior German commanders. Rommel was the son of a lower middle class elementary school teacher and had risen to prominence at least partially due to the more egalitarian National Socialist army expansion, while Arnim, who carried the key prefix "von," belonged to a military class that was mature at the time of Frederick the Great. The Desert Fox's gradual move to an anti-Nazi stance was still in very early stages at this point, but he was already respected and admired by his Allied foes for his ability to conduct a "clean" war in which the level of violence was at least partially mitigated by a certain amount of chivalry in the good treatment of prisoners, short truces for the recovery of badly wounded men, and a fear, shared by his Allied counterparts, of the atrocities sometimes committed by indigenous bandits, who occasionally attacked small units of both armies.

The German Spring Wind/Morning Breeze offensive was designed mainly to buy time for German forces in North Africa by pushing the front lines from Tunisia back into Algeria, which would give the Axis generals more time to consider whether the battles in North Africa should be extended or largely abandoned, with the always present reality that the

Axis forces could no longer hold all of their acquired territory stretching from North Africa to France to Scandinavia to Russia. As the Soviet Union prepared massive new offensives in the wake of Stalingrad, and an eventual Anglo-American invasion of northern Europe loomed on the horizon, it seemed unclear where a new fallback line in the Mediterranean Theater should be drawn. Just as the watertight bulkheads on the *Titanic* could buy time to launch the lifeboats but could not save the ship, an Axis offensive in North Africa in the winter of 1943 might deflect the Anglo-American allies for a time, but an Axis offensive was unlikely to produce any miracles. Yet, if an offensive strike was not at least attempted, the final outcome would be even more certain.

Erwin Rommel's personal career now increasingly reflected the Axis position in North Africa. The thrust and parry with Gen. Bernard Montgomery's British Eighth Army had left the Desert Fox sick and exhausted (a witches' brew of ailments would force him to return to the Reich after the Battle of Kasserine Pass to recuperate). Rommel was preparing to fight his last desert battle, and his window of opportunity was shrinking as the combination of Montgomery's slow-paced, leisurely pursuit of the German army across Libya and the presence of a huge American supply center at Tebessa, just west of Kasserine Pass, near the Algeria-Tunisia border seemed to be a perfect opportunity for a valedictory operation for a commander who would soon be tasked with the daunting responsibility of repulsing the looming allied invasion of northwest Europe.

As the Axis high command spent the month of January 1943 ferrying over a thousand men a day from Sicily to Tunisia to stage the planned offensive, the dangerously scattered American units settled in to await a spring offensive that was expected to trap the Germans between their own forces and the British Eighth Army that was still nudging the Germans westward from Libya to Tunisia. Correspondent Ernie Pyle, who would emerge as the most recognizable American war correspondent and would win a Pulitzer Prize before his death in the battle of Iwo Jima two years later, noted wryly that "almost all letters from home to the troops are full of sympathy because of the heat prostration they must be suffering," when in reality, the GIs were dealing with alternate bouts of cold rain and snow flurries, huddled against an icy wind that might rival that of Chicago. Pyle noted that he had encountered one lucky GI who had obtained an old-style kerosene stove once used to heat American one-room schoolhouses and now found himself deluged with offers to sell it at $450, an enormous sum in a time of nickel Cokes, ten-cent movie admissions, and two-cent daily newspapers. The soldier admitted that the device could be purchased at home for $3 but still preferred warmth over money that was relatively useless in a combat unit, as he insisted, "I would have been the same if I'd been offered $500."

As American and British units settled into what seemed to be a medium- to long-term stay in their defensive line along the Eastern Dorsal mountain range, they assumed that the Germans must be in the same hunkered-down mode, a mood that the senior American officer on the scene did little to disabuse.

The American commander who was about to face the Desert Fox in the first full-scale battle against the Germans was Lloyd Fredendall, a fifty-nine-year-old major general who would soon prove that an ability to train soldiers did not necessarily carry over into leading those men in combat. Much like Gen. George McClellan eighty years earlier, Fredendall was gifted with an enormous ability for self-promotion, and on the surface looked like a movie version of what an American senior commander should be. Like McClellan, Fredendall was short and stocky but adored by the press for his accessibility and newsworthy quotes. Unlike McClellan, who was an academic star at West Point, the New II Corps commander managed the dubious distinction of being thrown out of West Point twice for failing too many courses, then resurfacing at the equally demanding Massachusetts Institute of Technology, from which he did graduate. He received a commission in the Army two years after his more studious West Point classmates had graduated.

Lloyd Fredendall was probably the worst senior appointment in the US Army since Gen. John Pope was selected to relieve a competent but overly cautious George McClellan in 1862. In Pope's single significant battle, Second Bull Run, he became the only senior Union general to nearly lose his whole army in a single day, as he led the Army of the Potomac into a skillfully planned Stonewall Jackson/Robert E. Lee trap that just missed being fully sprung. Pope was summarily transferred to a frontier command where he was less likely to have any impact on the far more important Civil War campaign.

Now, in the winter of 1943, Lloyd Fredendall was entering a different sort of trap, fueled like Pope, with alternating overconfidence and hesitation that merged to produce a deadly formula in battle. The general ensconced himself in a Wild West–like gulch just under ten miles from the huge supply depot at Tebessa and began concocting plans for a major offensive that was intended to push all the way to the Mediterranean Sea and split the German army in two. Yet, ironically, as Fredendall was planning his "end the war in North Africa" offensive, he was using thousands of soldiers to construct a bombproof underground empire to make his huge command post invulnerable to air or artillery attack.

This labyrinthian lair now became the command center for one of the worst-led battles for the United States in World War II. Much like MacArthur's situation the previous year when he made major command decisions without leaving the confines of Malinta tunnel, the equally handsome, imposing Lloyd Fredendall simply believed that everything would come out well or blamed other persons or agencies if they did not. However, while MacArthur was using his bombproof lair to concoct plans that would simply delay the inevitable surrender of a Bataan garrison that was both starving and utterly surrounded by either Japanese soldiers or the sea, Fredendall's II Corps was merely marking time until the weather improved sufficiently to launch a spring offensive that would drive the Axis forces out of North Africa.

Ironically, at the same time that Rommel was planning a mid-February offensive against the Americans, Dwight Eisenhower, as Supreme Allied Commander in the Mediterranean, was mulling over his own attack plans to sweep the enemy northward toward the coast of North Africa. However, while the Desert Fox was finishing his plans, Eisenhower was attending the Casablanca conference that offered little time to hash out the details of his upcoming operations. When Ike finally visited II Corps headquarters, Fredendall's bluff optimism was countered by his intelligence officer's private concern of impending disaster. Col. Benjamin "Monk" Dickson was a West Point graduate who had attained minor notoriety at the Military Academy when his loudly proclaimed atheism caused a furor because he refused to attend mandatory chapel services. Dickson eventually found a military home as an intelligence officer and would gain substantial fame in late 1944 when, contrary to most other prognosticators, he insisted that the "defeated" Germans were actually planning a huge offensive in the Ardennes Forest. The 1965 film *Battle of the Bulge* featured Dickson as the lead character, played by Henry Fonda, and at the moment, in 1943, Dickson was probably General Fredendall's best asset. The II Corps commander largely ignored Dickson's warnings, and Rommel's worst fear that the American defenders would be fully prepared for the Germans' attack were never realized.

The battle that would soon be popularized as the "Battle of Kasserine Pass" was now about to begin against a backdrop of three roughly parallel mountain ranges that stood between the German army and the city of Casablanca, where Churchill and Roosevelt held their iconic conference. The Eastern Dorsal Mountain Range, Western Dorsal Mountain Range, and the Atlas Mountains all loomed over the drab, scrub-filled desert that had been fought over for twenty-five centuries. Although many of those earlier conflicts had been fought to the extermination of the losing army, Erwin Rommel's objectives were far more limited. Even Adolf Hitler had reluctantly come to the conclusion that the disaster at Stalingrad and an eventual Anglo-American invasion of northern Europe required the shifting of forces away from North Africa in the long term, even if substantial reinforcements were arriving from Sicily as a temporary measure to delay the Anglo-American advance into the continent of Europe.

Erwin Rommel's battle plan for this final Axis offensive in North Africa was to push significant Italian and German forces from their defensive position along the Eastern Dorsal Mountains in Tunisia into the Western Dorsal Mountains near the border at Algeria, and push an armored assault group through the Kasserine Pass and capture the huge Allied supply base at Tebessa, just inside Algeria, with the mountain of captured supplies providing the opportunity to create mischief all along the Allies' porous defense line in North Africa. The Desert Fox did not envision a strategically decisive victory as Montgomery's powerful Eighth Army would eventually cross from Libya into Tunisia and turn the odds back into the Allies' favor. The main purpose of the thrust toward Kasserine and Tebessa was to buy time by discouraging an imminent Allied offensive to push the Axis out of North Africa and then simply await developments.

While Lloyd Fredendall moved pieces around a mock battlefield tableau deep in his bunker, subordinate officers who were still above ground tried to make sense of scouting parties' reports that the German army seemed to be moving eastward, rather than withdrawing toward the Gulf of Gabes or the Mediterranean Sea. On February 14, 1943, the fourteenth anniversary of the legendary St. Valentine's Day Massacre in Chicago, General Hans-Jürgen von Arnim kicked off Operation Spring Breeze when two Panzer divisions rolled across the rough terrain of North Africa, pushed through the narrow Faid Pass, and roared into the town of Sidi Bou Zid, the first target on the road to the supply depot at Tebessa, fifty miles to the east. Looming over the town was the high point of Djebel Lessouda, currently occupied by a battalion of infantry from the 34th Division and a support force of three tank companies and a tank destroyer unit under the command of Lt. Col. John Waters. Colonel Waters's main claim to fame that morning was that he had married Gen. George Patton's daughter, which made him a minor celebrity in his unit. A second, similar force was positioned under Col. Thomas Drake south of Djebel Ksaira, and these two units were expected to delay a seemingly unlikely advance long enough to allow the garrisons of Sidi Bou Zid to join the fray.

While the temperature was a bit warmer than it was in Chicago in 1929, snow squalls erupted often enough to prompt the GIs to make the predictable comments on how their friends and relatives at home thought they were ensconced in a torrid desert. The desert would heat up shortly but not from a rise in temperatures. Somewhere above, in a gun metal sky, Luftwaffe Ju-88 bombers opened their bomb bay doors and peppered the ground while 88mm guns on nearby ridges spewed their own brand of destruction.

Lt. Col. Louis Hightower's unit pushed out of the town toward the looming hills with two companies of Sherman tanks and a dozen tank destroyers and came into the range of the lethal 88mm German dual-purpose guns that whittled the convoy of Shermans down from forty-four to seven vehicles as the survivors staggered back to town. Colonel Drake's command was even less fortunate. His combined infantry-tank force of nearly two thousand men was simply chopped to pieces with losses of virtually every vehicle, 75 percent of the men, and Drake himself, who was captured by a German major who had once been a lawyer in Chicago and offered the stunned new prisoner the full courtesy of a victor toward a valiant enemy. The prize capture of this stunning German victory was Colonel Waters, who when attempting to walk away from the burning wreck of an armored force encountered seven German soldiers who were astounded by their great good luck in capturing George Patton's son-in-law, a media coup that would continue to reverberate around America two years later when the general authorized a daring, botched armored raid designed to rescue his daughter's husband from a Bavarian prisoner of war camp.

While Fredendall moved pieces representing battle units on a large tabletop map deep in his personally designed bunker, more talented American commanders were attempting to make sense of the German offensive and plan countermoves to halt the enemy's progress. Gen. Orlando Ward, who commanded the excellent 2nd Armored Division, believed that survivors reporting events in the German offensive were exaggerating the power of the enemy forces and called for a counterattack using a tank battalion, a company of tank destroyers, a battalion of self-propelled artillery, and an infantry battalion mounted in half trucks. Their mission was to "clean out" German forces deployed around Sidi Bou Zid, which was roughly forty miles east of Kasserine Pass and ninety miles east of the invaluable supply dumps at Tebessa.

While bold action was certainly required as the American front began to collapse, General Ward's commendably aggressive plan almost immediately began to shred into pieces. First, the crucial infantry support battalions that were expected to accompany the tanks were centered around Colonel Waters's command, which was currently being dismantled by the Germans. The tanks would make their desperate charge without the riflemen. Second, the armored unit chosen for the operation had been called into action before the units completed tank versus tank training in the Mojave Desert, which was rapidly becoming the most important element of armored training experience.

This was a Battle of the Little Big Horn–type scenario, and the disaster in the desert was made even more deadly when two battalions of the 1st Armored Division whisked across open ground to contain the German threat to Sidi Bou Zid on February 15. The tanks swept forward in a V formation with minimal reconnaissance and sped into olive groves bursting with hidden German antitank batteries. The only small piece of luck for the American attacks was that the enemy 10th Panzer Division, so carefully hidden among the olive groves, did not include the unit's powerful new Tiger tanks that would become the scourge of Allied armor. The German tanks that were deployed, the much more numerous Panzer IVs, were on an equal level with American Shermans. However, the American tanks were in the open desert, and the Germans were carefully deployed in olive groves, and the result was predictable. Twenty Shermans were promptly turned into fiery wrecks, as a Luftwaffe spotter plane flew overhead and called in firing locations of the doomed formation. Dazed survivors clambered out of the burning wrecks and in many instances joined Colonel Waters and his men during two years of German captivity, which not only eliminated them from the North African chessboard, but also enabled the Desert Fox to leap ahead another thirty miles toward the vital American supply base at Tebessa.

While Ernie Pyle and other correspondents dodged enemy dive-bombers that had accompanied the German ground units, senior American commander Dwight Eisenhower began to have second thoughts about Lloyd Fredendall. He noted with sarcasm unusual for him that "Second Corps Headquarters has established itself in a deep and almost inaccessible cave a few miles east of Tebessa. The senior officers burrowed down there have exhibited a certain complacency illustrated by an unconscionable delay in perfecting defensive position in Kasserine Pass." He also noted that Fredendall had scattered much of the invaluable First Armed Division's tank units "into a large number of small contingents" that left division commander Orlando Ward with "nothing but minor detachments of light tanks."

Eisenhower soon learned the consequences of Fredendall's inability to place his men in strategically important positions. As Ike's jeep passed through the town of Sbeitla, firing began intensifying so rapidly that he sent two aides forward to provide covering fire as the general, waving a pistol, "formed the mobile reserve." Then, in the middle of such danger, Eisenhower's jeep driver fell asleep at the wheel and drove into a ditch leaving the senior American commander plenty of time to survey a retreating Army, at which point he was forced to admit, "It was too late to make changes in dispositions."

As the German offensive gobbled up desert territory, retreating Americans evacuated positions on the Eastern Dorsal Mountains and scurried through Kasserine Pass to reach at least temporary safety in the hills of the Western Dorsals.

As most units hurried though Kasserine Pass intending to put as much ground as possible between themselves and the advancing Germans, a garrison of sorts began to deploy in the hills towering over the narrow road below. The 19th Engineer Regiment, the 1st Battalion of the 26th Infantry Regiment, eight Sherman tanks, a handful of tank destroyers, and an artillery battalion equipped with horse-drawn World War I guns formed the nucleus of a rear guard under Col. Alexander Stark. General Fredendall had assigned Stark command with a slightly ridiculous exhortation to "pull a Stonewall Jackson there," referring to the Civil War general, who gloried in hitting an unexpecting enemy at a place of Jackson's choosing, striking with a highly mobile force of horse soldiers and almost as speedy "foot cavalry." Stark's assignment was actually closer to assuming command of the Alamo just before it was surrounded by the Mexican army.

One small piece of luck for the American defenders was that Rommel's assault force was also a hodgepodge "battle group" of reconnaissance companies, Panzergrenadier regiments, and Panzer battalions that had been temporarily cobbled together to seize the pass. Now a battle erupted between the jury-rigged forces. Just before Rommel's main assault was initiated at dawn on February 19, the Desert Fox received word that his assault force would soon become even more formidable with the imminent arrival of the 10th Panzer Division that was now en route.

The Germans received a nasty surprise when they encountered very little difficulty going on the floor of the pass, as the defenders were being reinforced by an additional tank destroyer battalion and infantry contingent. Then, in something out of an iconic 1950s "biker gang" film such as *The Wild One*, a large force of German motorcycle troops arrived on the scene and roared down the middle of the pass knocking out American strongpoints. The German were then followed by the "Centaurs" of the Italian Centauro Division, symbolized by the classic theme of half-horse/half-man creatures. By nightfall, the Centaurs were five miles into the pass and prepared to break out toward the mountains of supplies at Tebessa.

Yet Tebessa remained an unattained objective, despite Rommel's rampage through successive American lines. On the far side of Kasserine Pass, British and American artillery units were setting up a 1943 equivalent of Cemetery Hill at Gettysburg eighty years earlier. General von Arnim's promised complementary attack north of Kasserine never quite materialized, and the Desert Fox dithered just enough to allow Allied gunners to

Superb use of artillery by the American defenders prevented a temporary setback at Kasserine Pass from devolving into a major disaster.
LIBRARY OF CONGRESS

31

repulse any German attempt to push any great distance forward. One of the emerging heroes of the American artillery operations, a young colonel named William Westmoreland, was about to begin a two-decade-long series of promotions that would propel him to the senior command post in Vietnam two decades later.

Once the front had been stabilized, the military career grim reaper began its inevitable work. Eisenhower fired his intelligence chief, Colonel Mockler-Ferryman. Gen. Lloyd Fredendall was given hearty congratulations for his performance, secured a promotion to lieutenant general, and was sent back to the United States to command an army of clerk-typists. He would be replaced by Gen. George Patton and if nothing else, Patton would never be seen conducting a battle from an underground tunnel complex. The Desert Fox was congratulated for a victory that provided more options for a soon failing campaign. Four thousand American soldiers would be ferried to Rome as prisoners and marched into the Roman Colosseum as Benito Mussolini assumed his favorite role as twentieth-century incarnation of the Caesars, a role that had about four months to play. Erwin Rommel had fought his last desert battle and would soon be on his way to the far end of western Europe to confront the Allies in an even more daunting battle in Normandy. The Anglo-American forces had paid a price for overconfidence and bad intelligence, but reinforcements were pouring into North Africa so quickly that the losses would be made good in a matter of days. The shocking defeat at Kasserine Pass would initiate the removal of a number of clearly incompetent commanders, and the next time the Wehrmacht faced the Americans in combat, the Germans would be in for a rude awakening.

CHAPTER 3

Invasion USA

Battle for the Northland

THE FIRST INVASION OF AMERICAN SOIL BY A FOREIGN POWER SINCE THE War of 1812 had its origins in a massively complicated Imperial Japanese plan developed by the architect of the Pearl Harbor attack. Adm. Isoroku Yamamoto had spent the months following Pearl Harbor orchestrating a vast sweep across much of East Asia, which, by May 1942, had added most of the overseas Pacific possessions, formerly of America, Britain, and Holland, into the Greater East Asia Co. Prosperity Sphere. Now Yamamoto and his army colleagues believed that one final campaign would sweep the seas of the remnants of Western influence in much of Asia through a series of offensives designed to lure what remained of the American Pacific Fleet out of Pearl Harbor and into virtual annihilation.

The ensuing battle of Midway joined the Invasion of Normandy on D-Day and the Battle of the Bulge as the most comprehensively narrated campaigns involving American forces in the entire war. However, a less heavily discussed element of the geographically enormous Midway clash was Yamamoto's plan to add a new theater to the Pacific war right at the doorstep of the North American continent. On June 3, 1942, as the Battle of Midway entered its opening stages, Imperial Japanese Carrier Division 4, commanded by Rear Adm. Kakuta Kakuji, sailed into the strong winds of the North Pacific as carriers *Junyo* and *Ryujo* launched eighty-two planes on a mission to attack the American naval base at Dutch Harbor, Alaska.

One of the major reasons why these two valuable vessels would not be involved in the iconic final duel near Midway between three American and four Nipponese carriers was that Imperial Japanese authorities were determined to avenge the "personal insult" to the emperor that had been inflicted by Col. Jimmy Doolittle's bombers during their carrier-launched attack on Tokyo and other cities. A few weeks earlier, when Franklin Roosevelt insisted that the raiders had been launched from Shangri-La, the mysterious mountain realm from the hit film, *Lost Horizons*, some Japanese intelligence officers deduced that the raid had originated in Alaska, which was only 650 miles from Paramushiro Island in the Japanese-owned Kurile islands. This deduction gained added credibility when Imperial intelligence officers discovered that Doolittle himself was the son of an Alaska gold rush participant and had grown up in Nome. Therefore, the meticulously planned MI (Midway) operation included a substantial portion of the overall strike force tasked with grand invasions of Adak, Attu, and Kiska Islands in the adjacent Aleutian island chain.

This important companion piece to the occupation of Midway foresaw an essential use of the Aleutians as a step-off point for the invasion of the Alaskan mainland, in turn followed by a sweep southward along the American Pacific coast, possibly as far as Los Angeles. During the period between the Pearl Harbor attack and late spring 1942, American newspapers and magazines routinely carried stories about the expected Japanese assault on the West Coast, with the hugely popular *Life* magazine carrying a pictorial feature showing a possible Japanese invasion all the way down from Alaska to southern California, as posited by "unnerved" military experts and punctuated by artist drawings of barbaric-looking Imperial troops swarming into the most iconic buildings in Los Angeles.

Magazine and newspaper editors had a sound basis for their fear that this new Japanese offensive could be part of a broader plan to physically invade and occupy the American West Coast. On February 23, 1942, the Japanese submarine I-17 had surfaced near the amusement pier of the town of Ellwood, California, and opened fire with its deck gun with the primary target being a Richfield Oil Company refinery and storage facility which produced aviation fuel for the Army Air Force. Shells damaged both the production facilities and an oil derrick and knocked out part of the amusement pier, which quickly encouraged numerous local residents to flee as they expected an imminent enemy landing. Citizens from Los

Angeles to Santa Barbara began to flee from the coast, expecting a follow-up Imperial invasion, while the six other Imperial submarines that had been dispatched to menace the coast sank or damaged several merchant ships near the shoreline.

In essence, this raiding activity off the coast of California was the first step in an Imperial plan to keep the enemy so busy defending their own territory that they would not have the resources to attack the Japanese homeland. The combined operations against Midway and the Aleutians was the second step in the plan, and on June 1, 1942, two days after the last air raid on Dutch Harbor, Alaska, naval landing craft beached on the shore of Attu Island, and Imperial troops moved silently toward the main center of population, the small village of Chichagof. This settlement was home to forty Aleut Indians, nearly half of them children, and their teacher Foster Jones and his wife. Jones had closely followed reports of Nipponese atrocities against civilians in China and had taken the precaution of hiding a radio set and nonperishable food supplies in a remote canyon and was packed to make a run with his wife the moment the enemy landed.

On June 7, Japanese reconnaissance troops began breaking up into small parties to inspect Attu's forbidding interior, and in several places, they suddenly found themselves waist deep in snow. When a patrol closed on Chichagof, Jones made a run for his hideout but was shot moments later and became the first casualty in a six-month battle for the Aleutians.

Over on Kiska, twenty-five hundred Imperial troops swept inland, as the island's entire garrison, ten American soldiers operating the island's radio communication center, hurriedly burned their code books. Then, as the tiny force loped through the snow drifts, the invaders opened fire and wounded one American soldier in the leg before the defenders were surrounded and cut off. Then, in an act of compassion rare in the Pacific war, the wounded American was carried into a makeshift hospital facility, and a Japanese surgeon carefully attended to his injuries.

The appearance of Japanese ground troops on North American soil ignited panic-stricken headlines in most West Coast newspapers and prompted Adm. Frank Jack Fletcher, one of the heroes of Midway and now commanding officer of the Northern Sea Frontier, to fly to the

35

Aleutians, and after a brief tour, replace Adm. Robert Thesbald with Rear Adm. Thomas Kinkaid, a protégé of the emerging icon, Adm. William Halsey. Kinkaid would now begin to team up with his Army counterpart, Lt. Gen. Simon Bolivar Buckner, to expel the Japanese from their foothold in North America.

Buckner had one of the most interesting pedigrees of any senior American commander during World War II. The forty-five-year-old Kentucky native was the son of one of the most colorful generals of the Civil War. His father, Simon Bolivar Buckner Sr., was a West Point graduate who had cast his lot with the Confederacy, along with approximately half of the entire population of Kentucky, and was almost immediately commissioned as a general by fellow son of Kentucky, Jefferson Davis. In early 1862, in one of the first major battles after Bull Run/ Manassas, the elder Buckner and his thirteen-thousand-man garrison were forced to surrender the besieged Fort Donelson to a just emerging Union commander, Ulysses S. Grant. During the early stages of that conflict, victorious generals on both sides routinely offered surrender terms that allowed the opposing army to return home on parole, pending an emerging parole/exchange system in which units could return to their respective armies once they had been exchanged for a similar number of captured enemy soldiers. When Buckner requested terms from Grant, he was shocked to receive a terse reply demanding "Unconditional Surrender," which meant incarceration of the defeated garrison until individual exchanges could be worked out. Grant softened the blow somewhat to his fellow West Pointer by giving Buckner the entire contents of his own wallet to tide him over until an exchange could be arranged. Buckner accepted the money but made it clear that his adversary had broken the unwritten "rules" of the conflict by refusing to grant paroles.

Simon Buckner Sr. never fully reconciled with Grant but achieved a measure of revenge by being elected as governor of postwar Kentucky and becoming a serious candidate for the presidential nomination of the Democratic Party. He far outlived Grant, surviving in relatively good health until he was ninety-one, and in the meantime, at the age of sixty-three, fathered Simon Bolivar Buckner Jr.

The younger Buckner grew up as a living legacy of the Civil War by attending both Virginia Military Institute and West Point, with an appointment to the Academy from President Theodore Roosevelt. Simon Bolivar Buckner Jr. inherited his father's good looks, short temper, and intelligence, and his appointment as a senior commander of the part of the United States most threatened with an enemy invasion quickly made him a media star with cover status on national magazines and ultimate command of the Tenth Army, which would invade Okinawa, leading to his death in the final ground battle of the Pacific arena at Shuri Castle.

When Buckner took over the defense of Alaska, it seemed much more likely that the Japanese would invade North America rather than Americans invading the doorway to the Japanese home islands. Unlike the case in several Army-Navy joint operations, Buckner quickly established excellent relations with his Navy counterpart, and the two officers began to think in terms of expelling the Japanese from the Aleutians, rather than merely preventing Imperial forces from pushing outward toward the Alaskan mainland.

Buckner's naval counterpart, Adm. Thomas Kinkaid, did not have a father as illustrious as Buckner's, but his naval officer father had served on the USS *Pinta* while it was based in the Aleutians, and he had the good fortune of becoming friendly with a young Annapolis instructor named Ernest King during his days at the Academy. Much of Kinkaid's prewar career had been spent in diplomatic postings from Turkey to Italy and participating in the Geneva Disarmament Conference. He had also demonstrated an outstanding ability to secure the affection of his crew when during his command of USS *Colorado* in 1933, he allowed the families of crewmembers who could not afford housing in the Long Beach, California, community to actually live on the ship in newly constructed "family living spaces," while sending naval supplies ashore to his sailors' dependents who were remaining in town. Kinkaid's versatility caught the eye of Adm. William Leahy, who happened to be both Franklin Roosevelt's favorite card game partner and incidentally was also a member of the Joint Chiefs of Staff.

Kinkaid arrived at his new Aleutian command riding a generally positive record at Coral Sea, Midway, Guadalcanal, and Santa Cruz, which meant that he had actually participated in more significant naval battles than any other US admiral at that point in time. At a moment when a Japanese invasion of Alaska and even a possible drive down the West Coast was still very much a possibility, Buckner and Kinkaid were selected as "fighting commanders," capable of defeating a possibly disastrous enemy intrusion deep into American territory and daring enough to open up a "back door" for a future push toward the Japanese home islands from a whole new direction. Buckner and Kinkaid bonded almost immediately and quickly began implementing a plan that would put American forces on the offensive whenever the weather proved even minimally acceptable for military operations.

The first tangible product of the new Army/Navy offensive was on January 13, 1943, when an American strike force landed on Amchitka Island, which was literally in sight of the Japanese base on Kiska just to the north. Almost immediately, a duel for air supremacy over the island emerged as Imperial floatplanes regularly attacked engineers constructing a new airfield on Amchitka, while construction crews worked all night to repair the damage and to move forward the completion of the airstrip. Two weeks after the initial American landing, P-40 Warhawks rose from their newly completed strip and checkmated the enemy raiders. Within a few weeks, the Warhawks were joined with more powerful P-38 Lightning fighters and B-25 Mitchell and B-26 Marauder medium-range bombers, which turned the tables of air combat by regularly bombing Kiska.

Within two weeks of the American invasion of Amchitka, the American and Imperial garrisons of the Aleutians had settled down to a boring routine nourished by boring food and topped off with an enormous sense of isolation from the "real" war. Japanese soldiers on Attu and Kiska spent their free time studying English to all the better insult the American invaders when and if the Americans landed on those islands. Imperial service personnel from the northern home island of Hokkaido requested ski equipment from relatives and military quartermasters and used their frequent down time to utilize trails that were so challenging that they felt sorry for their companions at home who did not have access to such splendid slopes. One officer noted to his parents that "This island is essentially a huge ski lodge that members of my old ski club would envy."

However, early in February, the carnival atmosphere began to fade as, on the mountains of Attu, Japanese skiers stood watching what they believed was a Nipponese supply fleet closing on the shoreline far below. Then, to their collective shock, the "Japanese" ships opened fire on both Holtz Bay and Chichagof villages, while B-17 Flying Fortresses joined the fray. The two-hour bombardment killed two dozen members of the garrison, and then more men were added to the death toll as the ship, eventually identified as the cruiser USS *Indianapolis*, steamed seaward and ambushed a cargo ship carrying reinforcements and supplies. The *Akagane Maru* soon headed toward the bottom of the icy waters, and now, at least temporarily, the Japanese garrisons on Attu and Kiska were under siege.

In a sense, American and Imperial forces had now descended even farther into Alice in Wonderland's rabbit hole, as carefully planned decisions for strategic gains gave way to simply ensuring that the enemy did not seize total control of a bleak battlefield that offered almost no resources to the victor but did promise embarrassment and ridicule to the losing side.

Sizeable fleets, air squadrons, and ground forces were now confronting one another over a vast land and sea battlefront possession, which would add relatively little to each side's capability to defend its homeland. The concurrent battles in New Guinea and the Solomon Islands mattered, because possession of that region allowed Japan to threaten Australia and New Zealand and effectively made the Greater East Asia Co. Prosperity Sphere impervious to Anglo-American threat, while Allied success in that region would eventually put the enemy within striking distance of the Japanese homeland. A Japanese threat from the Aleutians into Alaska could theoretically threaten the American West Coast, and American expulsion of the enemy from the Aleutians could eventually provide a back door to Tokyo via the northern outer islands of the Empire, but as each side conducted their cost-benefit analysis, few leaders could say whether the opportunity would be worth the enormous effort such a campaign would entail.

In the early months of 1943, both American and Imperial decision makers concluded that, at least for the immediate future, control of the Aleutians did matter, and in early March Adm. Boshiro Hosogaya set in motion a plan to prevent the Americans from controlling the Aleutians. Hosogaya set sail from the home islands with a fleet including heavy cruisers *Nachi* and *Maya*, light cruisers *Abukuma* and *Tama*, converted merchant ships and light cruisers *Asaka Maru* and *Sakito Maru*, and a covey of five destroyers, with the intention of ending American control of the waters around the Aleutians. All of the Imperial aircraft carriers and battleships were fully engaged in the Solomons/New Guinea campaign far to the south, but so was most of the American Pacific Fleet, and Adm. Charles "Soc" McMorris was compelled to meet the enemy armada with a diminutive task force consisting of the cruisers *Richmond* and *Salt Lake City* and four supporting destroyers.

This compact squadron could blow an unescorted Japanese supply fleet to pieces but would be severely outgunned by the fleet that was now heading its way. The assumption that the enemy would not attempt to reestablish dominance in the Aleutians in the near future was proved erroneous on the morning of March 26 when the American fleet steamed southward almost two hundred miles south of Attu and closed to within one hundred miles of the Russian-owned Komandorski island group. As crewmembers lined up for breakfast, radar sets began detecting surface ships in the area which were initially assumed to be Soviet vessels that were still neutral bystanders in the Pacific war. Then the distinctive Imperial Pagoda masts began to take shape in binoculars, and the decks were cleared for action. The emerging confrontation was unique for a World War II naval engagement because neither fleet had access to any form of air support above or submarine support below, which pushed the impending action back in time to roughly the Spanish-American War of 1898. Now men in blue nautical uniforms would duel one another in a contest that had direct links to the age of Horatio Hornblower or Captain Kidd. A form of nautical minuet began to emerge as the fleets closed warily on each other.

The Japanese fleet gained a minor initial advantage as an Imperial spotter plane began to hover over the battle scene, while the one available American equivalent craft on the *Salt Lake City* was rendered useless when it was discovered that the vessel's catapult had not been charged for action. Engine malfunction quickly forced the recall of the Imperial spotter craft, and the two adversaries settled in for an old-fashioned gun duel.

When the two fleets had closed to within twelve miles of one another, the initial Japanese volley straddled cruisers *Richmond* and *Salt Lake City*, and as waterspout-soaked crewmembers stood at action stations, at a few minutes before nine o'clock in the morning, the duel finally erupted.

Admiral Hosogaya enjoyed an immediate advantage in a classic ship-to-ship duel that excluded airpower and submarines. Quite simply, thanks to a series of incredible American design blunders, Japanese cruisers carried torpedoes, and their American counterparts did not. This military gaffe may not quite have matched Union commanding general Winfield Scott in 1861 when he rejected Northern gunmakers' offers to supply the army with breech-loading and multi-shot rifles due to a fear that such rapid fire would cause soldiers to "waste ammunition," but sending cruisers to sea without torpedoes was hardly a winning strategy. Thus, when the Imperial cruisers launched their deadly salvos of "long lance" torpedoes, McMorris's small fleet had no equivalent counter-punch.

The Imperial fleet held a commanding advantage of deploying four cruisers to the American two and enjoying the capability of firing torpedoes from every ship, not just their destroyers. Equally important, Admiral McMorris's fleet was five hundred miles from the nearest American air base at Adak, while Hosogaya's fleet was only four hundred miles from a far larger base at Paramushiro. Yet, Admiral McMorris had more riverfront gambler instincts than his opponent, and he ordered his outnumbered, outgunned fleet to launch a high-risk attack against a more powerful fleet, and, in essence, Admiral Hosogaya blinked first.

A three-hour slugfest between two surface fleets hardly produced Trafalgar-like casualties. Fourteen Imperial sailors had been killed; only seven Americans shared this fate. At one point, the American flagship, *Salt Lake City*, was so immobilized that Admiral McMorris admitted that "the Japanese could have sunk her with a baseball." Yet, no baseball, let alone explosive shells, struck the vessel when it was dead in the water. Japanese ground forces still operated openly on islands that were American territory, but Admiral Hosogaya's timid climax to the Battle of the Komandorski Islands ensured that Imperial forces were certainly not going to expand their foothold even in the Arctic wasteland, let alone march triumphantly into Anchorage or Hollywood.

However, if a Japanese occupation of Hollywood had become a highly unlikely event, Hollywood was now invading the Aleutians in dramatic fashion. Col. Darryl Zanuck and Lt. John Huston arrived at Unmak and Adak armed with movie cameras and production teams with orders to transmit the realities of the Aleutians campaign to the American public. Huston was a popular actor who was also gaining fame as a producer/director after his smash hit two years earlier, *The Maltese Falcon*. During an extended stay in the Aleutians, Huston produced, directed, and narrated a Technicolor documentary with his distinctive, melodic voice adding just a taste of irony that massive forces of Americans and Japanese were engaging in battle for some of the most worthless land on the planet. Theater audiences were still not used to most feature films, let alone documentaries being shown in color, and yet, the technique served perfectly the displays of American individualism, as opposed to the rigidity of dress and demeanor in George Patton's North Africa forces half a world away. Officers and their men relaxed together, ate together, and fought together against a backdrop of astounding diversity in uniform and demeanor. Almost as if they were grizzled veterans of Robert E. Lee's Army of Northern Virginia, huge numbers of soldiers sported a wide range of mustaches and beards, even stroking them luxuriantly for the cameras. Headgear included World War I "pie plate" helmets, more modern "chamber pot" versions, berets, bush hats, cowboy hats, and baseball caps. When they lined up for meals, there was no front of the line or special seating for the officers; most just lolled on the endless grassland and smiled for the cameras.

The first half of *Report from the Aleutians* focused on the ground forces defending against a Japanese breakout toward the Alaskan mainland from their lairs on Attu and Kiska, and the audience at home was reassured by a vast array of machine guns and artillery covering every possible landing point on the American-held territory. American civilians were to be reassured that those buccaneers were not about to allow the enemy to occupy another square foot of American soil.

Yet in the second half of the film, the bravado and self-confidence of the ground garrison shifts over to the both businesslike and deadly work of the huge air armada being formed to take the war to the enemy-held parts of the Aleutians. Unlike the hundreds of bombers taking off from England to attack Axis targets in France and Germany, American bombers were taking off in the Aleutians in raiding parties of nine or ten. In what must have been a thrilling scene in American theaters, cameramen accompanied the raiders on their missions, and they jumped in horror as enemy aircraft guns pierced the flight cabin and crewmembers dropped from occasional hits. Yet the reality is that the Americans had turned from the besieged to the besiegers in the Aleutians as the enemy clearly could not contest the airspace against the vastly superior resources of the American Air Force.

Report from the Aleutians was a first-rate documentary from a first-rate director, but the film did not fully portray the ability of the Japanese forces to parry the American blows. While the less than two-hour flight from Adak to Kiska would be considered a "milk run" for American airmen based in Britain, the Japanese defenders had set up massive anti-aircraft batteries on their islands and began to develop fighter strips to challenge the intruders with their own aircraft. As the number of American military personnel in Alaska rose nearly tenfold in only a few months, a chain of bases appeared, ranging from nearly the Lower 48 ambiance of Ladd Field in Fairbanks and Elmendorf Air Base in Anchorage to a small Navy PBY base at Atka.

The Americans had clearly changed roles, and even if holiday cards and food parcels might take several months to reach the garrison, the men could listen to radio programs, play top ten tunes on record players, watch relatively new films, and enjoy occasional live performances from Bob Hope, Edgar Bergen, Errol Flynn, Ingrid Bergman, and Olivia de Havilland. While their fellow servicemen in the South Pacific were engaged in a constantly deadly hide and seek with Imperial forces, American troops in the Aleutians were engaged in a stalemate similar to the Union and Confederate armies encamped relatively close to each other during rain, snowy cold winter months when combat was not constant, but no one actually knew when the spring campaign would begin. By the end of winter in 1943, the American forces in the Aleutians had passed the two hundred thousand mark, and one antidote to the seemingly endless boredom was the unofficial word that the Aleutians would become the jumping-off point for an American assault on Japan from the north, possibly in conjunction with a Soviet army that might enter the fray after three Soviet ships were sunk by Japanese ships, and more than a hundred other vessels were stopped and searched by Imperial vessels. The Aleutians were closer to the Japanese home islands than the farthest American penetration so far in the South Pacific. And, if Russia shed its neutrality with respect to Japan, vast new opportunities existed for a very different end game against the forces of the emperor.

CHAPTER 4

The Road to Tunisgrad

As correspondent Ernie Pyle walked among the debris and destruction that was the aftermath of the German victory at Kasserine Pass, his attention soon focused on the bloated remnants of a jeep that had taken a direct hit from a German five-hundred-pound bomb. "Three soldiers were in the jeep, and they were blown to disintegration. Nothing was found of them to bury, but searchers did find scattered coins, knives and bits of clothing. One soldier had a pocket Bible and about half of the sheets were found. Another had a large wad of currency—bills just folded over once. Those bills were blown together with such force that it was impossible to get them out. The blast had vulcanized them." In some respects, Pyle was describing the site of a one-sided battle where there was no question who won and who had lost, almost a World War II equivalent of a Civil War correspondent describing the scene in the aftermath of Manassas/Bull Run in July of 1861, in which one army had clearly routed the other, and the Union had essentially to go back to square one, learning from the mistakes of that awful summer day.

Lloyd Fredendall had now joined Union general Irvin McDowell in that group of American generals who had suffered ignominious defeats in their first major command opportunity, but while the Union cause had to wait for the emergence of Ulysses S. Grant to turn defeat into victory, the tide would change much more rapidly in this new war as Gen. George Patton would make his presence felt only hours after Fredendall was exiled to a stateside posting.

Patton arrived to take over command of the defeated American forces in a specially modified M3A scout car equipped with police sirens and bristling with antiaircraft weapons. As the heir to legendary Confederate leaders in the Civil War, the native Virginian was equally fixated on his own path to destiny but also able to convey to his initially downtrodden troops that the War Between the States had been over for seventy-five years, and Hitler's minions were a threat to the entire planet.

One of the ironies of the Battle of Kasserine Pass was that the German high command was seeking only a temporary edge over the Allies in order to conduct an orderly retreat northward toward the ports of North Africa that provided vital sustenance for the Axis forces. Thus, a technically defeated American Army now found itself pursuing a retreating "victorious" Axis army. As Patton's forces pushed northward, the American GIs noticed two attributes of their German enemies. First, they left absolutely nothing of military value behind to be reused by the Allies. As correspondent Ernie Pyle noted, "Nothing was left behind that was repairable. Wrecked cars were stripped of their tires, instruments and lights. They left no tin cans, boxes or other usable materials. Mountain passes and paths around wrecked bridges were mined. They cut down every telephone pole along the highways and then snipped the wires."

Yet American soldiers marching through largely barren terrain also grudgingly admitted a certain chivalry among them not seen in the Pacific war. Hard-bitten soldiers were touched to find that otherwise bitter enemies had buried American soldiers with their own men. One observer noted, "The Americans are not segregated in any way." Their graves were identical to the Germans', except beneath the wooden crosses were printed "Amerikaner," and below that their GI serial number. Presumably their dog tags had been buried with them. War-toughened soldiers were heard to share a momentary brotherhood with their enemies as they noted, "They respect our dead the same as we do theirs. It's comforting to know that."

Now, in one of the ironies of the war in North Africa, an untested American Army that had been pushed into hasty retreat by the Desert Fox in the rain, sleet, and snow of winter was pushing the Germans toward the sea. Marching through knee-high grass, budding flowers, and seemingly perpetual sunshine, the Americans were attempting to trap the Germans into a Dunkirk in reverse. As the opening of the baseball season

George Patton was rapidly emerging in 1943 as the face of American military success in the Mediterranean Theater.

loomed back home, young Americans were wondering out loud how the enemy had achieved a seemingly easy victory at Kasserine Pass, but now they themselves felt the tinge of victory as they gradually took control of the roads, the fields, and even the sky above.

As the GIs trudged through the ripening fields, a young woman who had achieved near "pin-up queen" status among more than a few of them was viewing the new offensive from a perspective most of the "ground pounders" could only dream about when Margaret Bourke-White climbed aboard an American bomber to become the first woman to fly on an Air Force combat mission. Thirty-nine years old and a multiple-time divorcee, Bourke-White had achieved her pin-up status because her good looks and sense of adventure made most film stars seem dull in comparison. Her photography had scored the first cover of *Life* magazine in 1937, and she had shared a lifeboat seat with Dwight Eisenhower's personal driver, Kay Summersby, after their ship was torpedoed in the Mediterranean. She had also been the only foreign correspondent in Moscow when the Germans invaded Russia in 1941. The subject of two 1980s films in which Farrah Fawcett and Candice Bergen each portrayed her, Bourke-White now donned a flight suit to photograph American bombers as they pounded an Axis army gradually retreating toward the port of Tunis. She had been angling to photograph a bomber raid since Jimmy Doolittle's iconic raid on Tokyo, and now, insisting to her male crewmembers that she was too busy to be scared, the correspondent snapped photos of Axis forces in a retrograde movement to the sea. Moving about the aircraft wearing a portable bottle of oxygen, she photographed each crewmember in action, including bracing herself against a 200 mile per hour slipstream when she climbed into the radio-operator-gunner's hatch. As American P-38 Lightnings and German ME-109s dueled nearby and three enemy fighters began a long spiral toward the ground, the whole operation seemed to become a sort of aerial ballet, she insisted, as "The sound and movements were so rhythmic it was like music and so reassuring." The captain and crew of the plane were presumably breathing a sigh of relief when the feisty reporter descended from the plane back at base, but her photos reassured much of the American public that the embarrassing defeat at Kasserine Pass was in the process of being avenged.

As the arrival of spring changed the entire physical environment of the North African battlefield, Dwight Eisenhower and George Patton both emphatically noted that during the Kasserine campaign not a single American division had experienced the opportunity to fight as a whole unit, as German victories were almost exclusively over isolated bits and pieces of a still less than unified American force. This situation would now change as the 1st Armored Division and the 1st, 9th, and 34th Infantry Divisions would sweep toward the Mediterranean Sea as a fully integrated army that hopefully would emulate Gen. William Sherman's March to the Sea as spring blossomed over the African countryside.

On March 9, 1943, Erwin Rommel was recalled to Germany by personal order of Adolf Hitler. Der Führer was still reeling at the shock of the Soviet capture of a quarter of a million Axis troops at Stalingrad, and while still determined to retain at least a foothold in North Africa for the present, needed to avoid any chance of allowing the Reich's most revered general to be taken as part of the garrison if the German defenses collapsed.

That caution was well advised, as on St. Patrick's Day, March 17th, Maj. Gen. Terry Allen's 1st Infantry Division, supported by the 1st Ranger Battalion, rolled into the village of Sened, captured its important rail station, and then used their newly held ground as a jump-off point to attack the picturesque town of Maknassy, which now placed the Allies only forty miles from the sea. Now, for the first time, the Allied army could move northward toward Tunis with a right flank on a largely secured body of water that would allow early access to seaborn resupply whenever necessary.

The Battle for Maknassy would prove to be a key event in the entire battle for North Africa. Gen. Orlando Ward would command a twenty-thousand-man task force centered around his own 1st Armored Division, which fielded nearly three hundred tanks, and the 60th Infantry Regiment to provide ground troop muscle to the operation. Unlike much of the "desert war," Allies and Axis troops in this battle would clash against a backdrop of a verdant farm center covered with olive and citrus orchards and a town center featuring several blocks of stores and offices. However, the power of this imposing American assault force was somewhat diluted by a number of in-house feuds in the two main assault units. First, one of Ward's senior commanders, Combat Command B leader Brig. Gen. Paul Robinett, was alternating between disparaging Ward in front of senior American Army generals and among his own staff officers below, a problem that even Eisenhower was beginning to notice. Then his main infantry striking force developed its own issues when unit commander, Col. Frederick de Rohan, seemed to be entering a popularity contest for his men's affections against his junior officers. Then, just to ensure that the American offensive would be placed under an even larger cloud, Patton, in response to Ward's earlier statement of relief that few of his most useful officers had been killed in recent clashes, the never dull Virginian, Patton insisted that minimal officer losses was bad for the morale of enlisted men and issued an order: "I want you to get more officers killed."

That terse order would soon be fulfilled as the Battle for Maknassy opened with a huge American initial advantage of a reinforced regiment storming the heights above the town against a slim German garrison of 350 men. However, German commander Col. Rudolf Lang soon welcomed the arrival of eight Tiger tanks, and three surges up the heights were thrown back in succession. Ward's personal lead-from-the-front command style salvaged a potential victory when the German defenders abandoned the town for a ridgeline on the far side of Maknassy, and Ward proved his valor in leading a charge that nearly cost him an eye. However, Ward was soon relieved of his command, and the divisional casualty list mounted toward three hundred killed and thirteen hundred wounded in this most recent operation.

The battle for Maknassy Heights, and soon after, the battle for the town itself, made for superb propaganda material in German media outlets. However, this momentary setback for the Allies was being more than counterbalanced by a slow strangulation of the Axis garrison of North Africa by attacks on shipping from air and sea. The Axis garrison in North Africa required one hundred forty thousand tons of supplies to function as an active military force. Yet, Allied bombers, submarines, and surface ships had constricted the supply line across the Mediterranean to twenty thousand tons a month, a trickle that was even now shrinking more rapidly. The German defenders could hold a position for a time with their bravery and ferocity, but even the vaunted Tiger tank was extremely vulnerable from the sky, which was increasingly controlled by the Allies. As the battle for North Africa began evolving into an Allied drive to push the Axis forces into the sea, *Life* magazine utilized its large team of combat reporters to offer an analysis of the state of the war in the spring of 1943. "Death and glory are two reliable trademarks of war. The Germans are now collecting the death, the Americans, the glory. The fact is that the Americans in Tunisia have developed into a first class fighting outfit, already worthy to fight beside the superb British 8th Army and the British 1st Army, veterans of Dunkirk. The Americans seemed cooler, more casual, more workmanlike in action. They took war as a very interesting job in which they were determined to excel. In the tight spots, they had tremendous loyalty to one another and utter concentration on the job. The Americans' most notable specialty was in concentrating artillery fire quickly and heavily and moving it around fast, directing it from extremely advanced observation ports. The infantry proved again and again that it could meet and stop German tanks. True, there were flies in the coffee and the mosquito season was beginning in earnest, and the Americans were overdressed for the heat. The veterans of a half a dozen hard battles looked forward to the earned rest of victories before the invasion of Europe."

As spring in North Africa began to rout the chill and damp of the preceding winter, George Patton and Bernard Montgomery met to plan a campaign that, in Patton's brusque comment, "is intended to kick the Axis bastards out of Africa." In modern terminology, Patton and Montgomery might be described as "frenemies," who, in a war replete with leaders possessing vivid personalities would both score near the top of the list. Both men were quirky—Montgomery was an adamant non-smoker in a profession and time of overwhelming numbers of smokers, and Patton was a devout believer in reincarnation. Yet each general showed a humane side, displayed when Patton would kiss dead soldiers, and Montgomery would pass out candy, comic books, and even cigarettes to pleasantly surprised enlisted men. Now these two rather nonconformist leaders were tasked with throwing the Axis out of Africa so that the invasion of Europe could begin.

As the Allied spring offensive gained momentum, the Axis forces retreated northward toward the port cities of North Africa, which were becoming the lifeline necessary at least to temporarily delay the Allied advance and a bit later to serve as embarkation points in an increasingly likely abandonment of the African continent. The centerpiece of Axis defense of North Africa was the newly constructed Mareth Line that anchored a two-hundred-mile corridor from the town of Mareth on the Gulf of Gabes to the port of Bizerte on the Mediterranean Sea.

On the eve of the first day of spring, 1943, Montgomery's Eighth Army and Patton's II Corps sprang into action with an objective to drive the Germans into the sea. Ernie Pyle described the battlefield as "walking and climbing and crawling country. The mountains were largely treeless, easy to defend and bitter to take. But we took them." The Germans would take firing positions on the back slope of enemy ridges and deeply dig into foxholes. In front of them, the fields and pastures were saturated with thousands of hidden mines. Then the forward slopes were left open as a standing invitation to the Allies to risk an advance. Most American units passed up this invitation to slaughter and stayed put while dozens of artillery battalions pulverized the whole area with artillery, then attempted to use this covering fire to sweep around the ends of the hills and take them from the sides and rear.

This form of combat was neither the lightning strike of the Germans through France in 1940 nor the semi-suicidal "over the top" charges in World War I trench warfare. The German high command had now decided that occupying North Africa was a luxury that they could not afford, and the insistence of Hitler and at least some of his generals that the army could still bleed the approaching Allies until whisked away at the last moment was based on a grievous underestimation of Allied sea- and airpower. Hitler was continuing to gamble and would do so to the end of the war that the Anglo-American alliance with the Soviet Union would eventually disintegrate and that every day the Allies were held in check in North Africa was a day closer to that outcome. On the other hand, if evacuation was postponed for too long, there was a serious risk that a quarter of a million Axis soldiers, roughly the number captured at Stalingrad, would be eliminated from the order of battle at the same time that the Americans were activating a growing list of new divisions.

American command of the skies over North African battlefields often nullified the advantages of superior German tanks in combat. In this photo, American vehicles roll along a mine-laden road to Tripoli after the Allied victory.
LIBRARY OF CONGRESS

As the Allied forces tightened their ring around a steadily shrinking Axis defense line, American reporters began to tell their readers at home about aspects of the war that might not be fully appreciated in the newsreels seen in movie theaters. One magazine carried a photo essay on the aftermath of the Battle of Maknassy with heavy emphasis on shots of long lines of captured Axis prisoners. Another shot displayed a quartet of still smiling German prisoners linked arm in arm like a sports team. While noting that all of the prisoners insisted that they were twenty-one or older, "the captured Germans all look very young," a hint at possible manpower shortage in the Reich. Another article emphasized the energy put into convincing American soldiers that the natives were not their enemies. The commentary made little attempt to minimize the warning to young American soldiers that in this very different environment, any attempt to stare at, jostle, speak to in public, or remove the veil of a native female might result in "serious injury if not death at the hands of local men," a hint that the Germans were not necessarily the only threat in this part of the world.

A totally opposite gender role was suggested in widely publicized stories and photo essays on a new breed of flight nurse emerging in the desert war. A photo essay depicted nurse/officers assigned to special transport planes to provide intensive care while their patients were being flown to base hospitals. These "angels" were depicted neither in traditional white, starched nurses' uniforms and caps nor the baggy men's fatigues donned by the nurses trapped on Bataan. The new nurse was fitted out in footwear that looked like ski boots, tight trousers, and short Air Force flight jackets that almost approximated a young lady's casual civilian attire twenty years in the future.

The men who were closing in on the enemy along the Tunis front were described as "just guys from Brooklyn and Main Street, but maybe you wouldn't remember them. They are too far away now. They are too tired. Their world will never be known to you, but if you could have seen them just once, even for an instant, you would have known that no matter how hard people were working for them back home, they never keep pace with their infantrymen in Tunisia."

Now that spring was blossoming in Tunisia, there was a riot of color that formed a brief interlude from the dun-colored monotony of the rainy winter and the dun-colored monotony of the hellish summer still ahead. While people at home trekked to baseball games, tilled their gardens, and strolled on boardwalks, the military in North Africa became familiar with a newly emerging word—Bizerte. This town was the most northern port in Tunisia as Axis commanders devised ways in which their now increasingly besieged soldiers could be plucked from the beaches in a reverse replay of the encounter at Dunkirk three years earlier. Some lucky Axis soldiers had already left Africa by incurring what Americans called a "million dollar wound"—an injury that made them useless for combat but not crippled for life.

However, the Tunis-Bizerte rally port was unlike Dunkirk, in the sense that the Royal Air Force was able to maintain just enough control of the airspace above the evacuation beaches that most rescue vessels could safely embark for Britain. The British and American air barons were determined that this advantage would not be enjoyed by the enemy now that the tables were turned.

The British army battling in northern Tunisia numbered about two hundred thousand men, actually just a bit smaller force than the army that had to be evacuated from Dunkirk in 1940. However, instead of being supported by a French army that was in a final stage of disintegration in June 1940, the British were now paired with an invigorated American army of three hundred thousand men, while the two combined armies enjoyed nearly total control of the sea and air. As the American army struck from the west, the British army would push forward from the south and squeeze the Axis forces into the twin pockets of Tunis and Bizerte.

Allied minelayers planted mines in the sea lanes between Sicily and Tunisia so much faster than Axis minelayers could remove them that evacuation ships were hemmed into a tiny mile or two safe zone across the water that allowed Allied airpower to concentrate on that single tiny corridor. When the Axis leaders shifted to air transport, the Allies responded with fighter sweeps to shoot down the transports and bombing runs to knock out airfields in Sicily and Tunis. In one raid alone, seventeen of fifty German transport planes were shot down in a single sweep at the cost of two American fighters, and then a dozen more transports were destroyed when they landed in Sicily. Interceptor squadrons, such as the Black Scorpions, the Exterminators, and the Fighting Cocks, paired off with their British counterparts and tore into German transport flights that at this point even included huge, majestic six-engine transport planes.

On the ground, the roughly 150 surviving Axis tanks were now staring down the barrels of fifteen hundred Allied tanks, and Axis divisions were now reduced to roughly five thousand non-wounded men in each unit. Yet, even though the ring around the Axis army was inexorably tightening, politicians and newsmen in the United States began wondering out loud why a badly outnumbered German army had not yet been utterly defeated. Lt. Gen. Lesley McNair, chief of Army Ground Forces, now openly questioned the inability of the Allies to finish the game in North Africa. He had insisted in a radio address to all soldiers, "You are going

Allied control of the air over the North African battlefield would prove a decisive advantage in the outcome of the campaign. Here, Spitfires are en route to the Mareth Line area.
LIBRARY OF CONGRESS

to get killing mad—why not now?" The general was promptly dispatched to the war front to find out for himself what was "wrong" in an obviously successful campaign. A year later, McNair would become the highest-ranking American general to die in combat when, ironically, American bombers dropped their payloads too early and bombed his command post. In the spring of 1943, he merely created a human-induced firestorm with a controversial series of personnel decisions.

As British thrusts at the German positions in what was now effectively a siege line extending from Bizerte to Tunis temporarily petered out, the American 1st Division (known as the Big Red One) and 9th Division struck along enemy positions on their own end of the line. McNair, who had been an artillery officer and the youngest American combat general in World War I, quickly entered a verbal brawl with senior officers of the 1st Division, including Theodore Roosevelt Jr., who dressed down his superior for taking unnecessary risks. McNair ignored the warning, climbed to an artillery observation point, and was almost immediately hit by a shell fragment that lodged in his skull while another piece severed the artery in his neck. Even as he was being transported back to the United States for an extended recuperation, word was circulating among American combat troops, who had suffered over one thousand casualties in closing the ring around the Germans, that the high command in Washington was being less than supportive.

While generals bickered, GIs and British Tommies kept pushing the German defenders into ever smaller pockets of resistance. At dawn on May 6, 1943, a combined Anglo-American offensive geared into action from Bizerte to Tunis. The American 1st Armored Division began slicing through the last Axis-controlled roads between the two towns but lost nearly fifty tanks in the process. The assault units of the 1st Infantry Division poured across the Tine River and after an initial repulse swept sizable German units in front of them. Yet, in the midst of their victorious romp, the seeds for future crises were sown, as corps commander Omar Bradley noted the self-absorption of both Big Red One division commander, Terry Allen, and his men of the "Holy First." In turn, Allen viewed his superior as "a phony Abraham Lincoln" who was in over his head in combat operations.

For the moment, simmering feuds were forgotten as residents of Tunis and Bizerte tossed flowers at their liberators and Axis soldiers were marched into captivity. Ernie Pyle noted simply, "Germans were everywhere, it made me a little light-headed." Although a surprisingly large number of German generals had managed to conveniently develop maladies that required treatment back in Germany, a dozen of them stayed to the last and joined a combined two hundred twenty-five thousand German and Italian soldiers in a captivity that would take some of them as far away as Mississippi and Louisiana. Gen. Hans-Jürgen von Arnim, Rommel's archrival, would be faced with the humiliation of signing the surrender documents, but this was actually a blessing in disguise, as the Desert Fox would be forced to commit suicide the following year for his indirect support of the plot to kill Hitler, while von Arnim would live into the 1960s after a relatively comfortable internment at Camp Clinton, Mississippi, with twenty-four other German generals.

Exhausted but ebullient American troops in Bizerte, Tunisia, savoring an aquatic interlude after a hard-earned victory.
LIBRARY OF CONGRESS

On May 20, 1943, the Allies held a massive victory parade with a profusion of generals and ambassadors all celebrating the expulsion of Axis forces from an entire continent. Three thousand Americans would not be coming home, but, in turn, over one hundred thousand Germans and one hundred thirty thousand Italian soldiers were removed from the Axis order of battle, a loss equivalent to the toll at Stalingrad only a few weeks earlier. The Allies would soon sort themselves out, try to learn needed lessons from the campaign, and set their sights on the ultimate target, the continent of Europe before May days had passed.

CHAPTER 5

The Ice Warriors

THE AMERICAN NAVAL VICTORY AT THE BATTLE OF THE KOMANDORSKI Islands in late March of 1943 essentially placed the Japanese garrisons in the Aleutian Islands under a state of siege. The garrisons of Attu and Kiska would now be compelled to occupy the islands with whatever resources were already on hand, supplemented only by the minimal supplies or reinforcements that the high command in Tokyo could dispatch on an occasional submarine mission. Yet if the Japanese commanders in the Aleutians were now under enormous pressure to prevent the Americans from recapturing the Imperial-controlled islands, their American counterparts were under equally great pressure from the American government, news media, and general public to throw the Nipponese invaders out of American territory almost immediately. American forces would morph from defenders to invaders of their own soil, as an enormous conveyor belt of supplies and reinforcements moved through a supply chain that extended all the way from the remaining American-held islands to Anchorage and Fairbanks, down to the Lower 48 of mainland America.

Conditions at Ladd Field in Fairbanks and Elmendorf Air Base at Anchorage may have been primitive and spartan by the standards of stateside military bases, but their athletic facilities, service clubs, movie theaters, and access to female companionship appeared to be paradise at Aleutian bases such as Atka, which the unlucky denizens sarcastically dubbed "Atkatraz," after the California maximum-security prison. Yet the "inmates" of Atka were enormously envied by the personnel posted to outer Aleutian Islands such as Adak which, in turn, seemed sumptuous to the farthest American-held island on the chain, Amchitka. Those unfortunate personnel slept on sleeping bags on the floor and lived exclusively on canned combat rations due to the difficulty in ferrying supplies that far west.

By early May of 1943, senior Army commander Gen. Simon Bolivar Buckner had amassed a force of two hundred thousand personnel, and now agreed with his naval counterpart, Adm. Thomas Kinkaid, that it was high time to expel the Japanese from their foothold on American soil during the generously titled "good weather" of late spring and summer.

One of the external inducements for initiating the assault on Attu and Kiska in the very near future was that, for a brief period in the spring of 1943, it actually appeared likely that the Soviet Union would declare war on Japan and add its vast military and considerable naval resources to a Soviet-American invasion of Japan from Nippon's far north downward toward Honshu Island and the Imperial nerve center of Tokyo.

During this time period, with apparent support from the Japanese high command, submarines began routinely searching neutral Russian cargo ships and soon escalated to outright violence when three Soviet cargo ships were sunk by Imperial vessels with not a hint to the Soviet government that this piracy was in any way accidental. However, just as Josef Stalin prepared to order his ambassador to Tokyo to declare war on Japan, the Soviet dictator experienced one of his frequent mood changes and decided to postpone attacking Nippon until the Empire had been further weakened by its war with America and Britain.

With or without Soviet intervention, the first step in expelling the Japanese from the Aleutians, Operation Landcrab, was set in motion as an invasion of Attu was finalized. The centerpiece for Landcrab was the 7th US Army division commanded by Maj. Gen. Albert E. Brown. In one of the ironies that so often emerges in warfare, Brown's "Hourglass" division was undergoing training in the hellish desert areas of California in preparation for insertion into the battle of North Africa. Lt. Gen. John DeWitt, commander of the Fourth Army that had overall responsibility for the Aleutians, was somewhat shocked at the use of a desert-trained division as the major battle unit in an Arctic environment, and requested his superior to at least replace Brown with Gen. Charles Corlett, a veteran of the Aleutians operation. An emphatic denial of DeWitt's request sent the desert fighters, minus virtually all of their vehicles, to spearhead Landcrab paired with smaller Canadian units that would provide reconnaissance, air support, and part of the naval support task force.

While a few units in the Hourglass Division featured enlistees from portions of Utah that provided at least some experience in a cold, snowy climate, the vast majority of the American invasion force had been enlisted from the decidedly non-Arctic states of Arizona, New Mexico, and Texas with a diverse roster that included a significant number of Mexican Americans and Native Americans in its ranks.

Now on the eve of battle in late April, eleven thousand men who had been specifically trained for desert warfare were loaded on transport vehicles with many of the men informed by various sources that they were headed to Hawaii. They were on their way to one of the new states that would be added to the union just over a decade and a half later, but it would hardly be a land of pineapples and grass-skirted dancers. The Hourglass men might have gotten a hint of where they were headed if the quartermaster general's order that they should be outfitted with newly designed cold weather gear had not been rescinded by the operation planning staff that insisted that the extra weight of the Arctic gear might slow down the men in battle.

On April 30, 1943, the invasion force arrived at a port that might have sent shivers down the spines of men who had closely studied the American Civil War. The landing site was Cold Harbor, which bore the same name as the location of perhaps the bloodiest few hours in the Civil War when Ulysses S. Grant launched an ill-considered frontal assault on Robert E. Lee's heavily entrenched Army of Northern Virginia in the late spring of 1864 and lost over seven thousand Union casualties in a notably brief battle. Luckily for the twentieth-century Americans in the Aleutians, the horrendous weather prevented the invasion force from sailing for Cold Harbor for several days, so that the Imperial garrison on Attu was pulled off high alert when the anticipated invasion failed to materialize.

On May 11, 1943, after several postponements due to horrendous weather conditions, the American invasion force, comprised of battleships *Pennsylvania*, *Idaho*, and *Nevada*, and escort carrier *Nassau*, stuffed with thirty Wildcat fighters, all screened by fifteen destroyers, opened the military chess match that was an amphibious invasion. Col. Yasuyo Yamazaki commanded a garrison of twenty-six hundred Imperial defenders of Attu, a number considerably higher than American intelligence estimates of five hundred to fifteen hundred. The defenders were extremely well dug in, equipped with fur-lined uniforms and Arctic boots, and for good measure, had been supplied with particularly generous amounts of sake. The Imperial garrison was also equipped on invasion day with a piece of remarkably good luck. The American high command, convinced that they could somehow achieve absolute surprise with a huge invasion fleet, decided to forego the massive pre-invasion bombardment that the American fleet could throw at the defenders.

Compared to the sheer violence of the Allied landings at Normandy thirteen months later, the first hours of Landcrab seemed to be a game of blind man's bluff in frozen slow motion. American forces did not sprint along sandy beaches toward enemy machine-gun nests. Instead, they slogged in slow motion through knee-deep snow, and in the first firefight of the invasion, the men of the Northern Force collided with exactly four Imperial defenders manning a hopelessly weak beach defense position. The ensuing firefight produced two Japanese fatalities, two men escaping back to their main force, and a literally glacial American advance inland. Imperial forces then added to the irony of invasion day by finally firing an artillery barrage against the American troops landing at Holtz Bay after the invaders had already completely abandoned the beach in their march inland. The irony of this North American version of D-Day carried over to the other major American invasion force that landed to the south of their sister units at a site with the malevolent name of Massacre Bay. An unexpected shift of wind direction sent the temperature soaring as the sun made a rare appearance, but the pleasant sunshine also turned the already difficult terrain into a huge bog with brown mush replacing expected ice and snow. Luckily for this group of invaders, Colonel Yamasaki had not chosen to defend this particular beach.

Most of the drama that was the Battle of Attu was played out on the middle third of the bleak island. The enormous western third of the island, which was the longest portion of Attu ending at Casco Cove, and

The beachhead at Massacre Bay was the jump-off point for the long slog through Attu.
LIBRARY OF CONGRESS

the eastern section, that was the narrowest part of the island as a slim finger extending between the Bering Sea and the North Pacific Ocean, contained no defensive works and were largely ignored by both armies. Colonel Yamasaki simply did not have enough men to defend the entire perimeter of Attu and concentrated his forces in a wide arc that centered on Holtz Bay, Chichagof Village, and Chichagof Harbor and the passes that led to those targets from the multiple American landing beaches. The Imperial defenders began the battle with two significant advantages. First, unlike the upcoming Battle of Tarawa and the ensuing battles on the road to the Japanese homeland, the Japanese high command had informed Yamasaki that they fully intended to send a fleet of submarines to extricate the garrison after the defenders had severely bled the enemy invasion force. Second, the garrison held both the high ground and control of the passes through which invaders would have to navigate in deep snow, while the Japanese defenders blasted away from the high ground. The battle for Attu was not intended to be an Arctic version of the Alamo for the Japanese defenders; as the battle opened the defenders were still confident that they would either throw the Americans back into the sea or be evacuated once they had inflicted maximum damage on the enemy invaders.

Moments after midnight on May 12, 1943, the beginning of the second day of the battle for Attu, a flotilla of three Imperial submarines exited Kiska harbor to launch an attack on the American fleet off Attu. Torpedoes barely missed the battleship *Pennsylvania* and several escorting destroyers, and as the undersea craft pulled back to their home port, the American fire support flotilla opened fire on Imperial troops deployed on the high ridges overlooking Massacre Valley. An American forward observer on the scene noted with satisfaction, "Dead Japanese, hunks of artillery and pieces of arms and legs rolled down out of the fog." Then swarms of B-24 Liberators and P-38 Lightnings began their own brand of intervention in the battle despite heavy Japanese antiaircraft fire.

The American advance inland appeared to be progressing like a slow motion film. The invaders slogged, waddled, and crawled through snow much like home front children playing in a series of snow drifts. Those children, however, were not being fired upon, and as the invaders moved inland, medics followed right behind them focusing on a growing number of invaders who had been hit by the semi-invisible Imperial defenders.

As the American invaders trudged through muck, mire, and snow from both the northern and southern landing beaches, they frequently confronted the paradoxical environment in which they were fighting an enemy from a hugely different culture on a battlefield nothing like their counterparts in the Central and South Pacific had encountered. However, unlike those comrades in arms, they were fighting on American soil, and they frequently entered houses with linoleum floors, curtains and glass windows, equipped with sewing machines and battery-operated radios that would not have been out of place in New York, Iowa, or Oregon. Yet these houses were all eerily silent and empty, as their owners had been forcibly removed to Japanese internment camps from which half of these former occupants would never return.

Now the liberators themselves were beginning to die, not in the massive death spree of an Antietam or The Somme or the invasion of Normandy, but in a steady but gradually rising trickle of fatalities as Japanese shells and bullets found their marks. The Japanese defenders alternated between ferocious firefights to the death and fallbacks to new defensive positions on a higher ridge, while the pursuers would often crawl on hands and knees in their quest to make contact with the enemy.

The person responsible for the southern half of this tightly choreographed minuet between forces advancing from two directions was Col. Edward Earle, who directed multiple battalions as they struggled up a combination of valley floors and mountain ridges in more of a never-ending series of stumbles rather than an actual walk. The Japanese defenders used their superior positions on the even higher ridges they occupied to pour mortar and machine-gun fire on the invasion force. In what was seen as a decisive favor of the Nipponese gods, fog hid the Japanese defenders and their guns, while the invaders remained in plain sight below them. As the advance ground to a halt, Colonel Earle, using commendably brave but perhaps ill thought out judgment, went forward on his own to locate both his advance scouts and, possibly, the location of the enemy. Imperial defenders found the colonel before he discovered them, and a follow-up American patrol discovered his body, as well as his unconscious aide sprawled below a hovering mist.

The next day, as battleships *Pennsylvania* and *Idaho* pounded enemy positions on the high ground above Holtz Bay, Maj. Gen. Albert Brown, the 7th Division's commanding officer, made his own reconnaissance of the battlefield, presumably with a larger security force than his subordinate had employed the previous day. The general soon came to the conclusion that the Nipponese defenders held a phenomenally strong defensive position in the mountainous, snow-covered terrain where incessant fog masked their movements, while negating much of the airpower that the invaders were employing. Aerial photography during one of the rare clear sky periods during the battle would reveal a battlefield that featured large numbers of open, horseshoe-shaped defensive positions, each one sited to support one or more similar configurations in a vast array of interlocking support bases. The defenders' position was enhanced by the surprising reality that even though Attu had been an American possession for decades, the American invasion force could never seem to find accurate maps of the Aleutian battlefield. Soldiers wasted uncounted hours climbing up the wrong hills due to faulty maps or getting lost in the valleys below. One of the responses to this navigational fiasco nearly initiated an even further escalation in an already ferocious Pacific war when American artillery units began employing phosphorous shells to mark enemy positions for advancing troops. As colored mist began to descend on suspected enemy positions, the Japanese defenders assumed that the invasion force had broken the unspoken agreement that neither side would employ poison gas on the battlefield. In reality, the colorful mist settling over the ground was non-toxic phosphorous designed to mark artillery targets and not a return to the horror of World War I poison gas attacks. However, the at least temporary elation of the Japanese defenders that they would not die of a gas attack was countered by radio transmissions that an attempt by the Imperial navy to reinforce and resupply the Attu garrison by submarine missions had failed, and the defenders could expect no help in holding the island.

On the other hand, American control of the seas surrounding the battlefield did not seem to offer huge tangible advantages to the soldiers clambering and crawling through the muck and snow of Attu. The lack of American combat experience in cold weather battles and erratic advances in producing Arctic combat gear were now creating an astoundingly high 80 percent frostbite or trench foot casualty rate in some combat units on Attu. A disturbingly large number of soldiers were being sent home after undergoing amputation of one or even both feet, as the invaders slogged through holes filled with frigid water or spent entire nights in flooded foxholes. Many of the front-line frostbite victims had to endure being carried slowly down hillsides by their comrades, slipping and sliding down icy paths on their way to hospital facilities. The Japanese defenders found these situations provided excellent opportunities to inflict heavy casualties on the invaders, as more and more combat troops were assigned to stretcher bearer duties.

The Battle of Attu proved to be a grueling contest between Imperial and American forces, and the constant harsh climate proved to be an adversary for both sides. Here, GIs carry a wounded comrade on a stretcher.
LIBRARY OF CONGRESS

The officers planning the re-conquest of Attu envisioned a three-day campaign, and, as the battle dragged on well beyond that timeframe, the 7th Division commander, Gen. Albert Brown, saw his career fading before his eyes. The general's request for reinforcements during an increasingly stalemated battle was met with his relief in favor of Maj. Gen. Eugene Landrum. General Landrum's childhood in Florida hardly provided an ideal stepping stone to command in the Arctic, but he had at least served as the commander of the Aleutian island of Adak's garrison, which largely compensated for his lack of snowball-fighting experience in his younger years.

If General Brown had encountered an interesting transition from his boyhood in the Deep South to command of an Arctic battle, the opposing army also contained an individual who had lived in two very different worlds. Master-Sergeant Paul Tatsuguchi had grown up in Japan and had moved to California to attend college and medical school and serve an internship and residency in American hospitals. He had then married a member of his church who shared his bi-national experience, and the couple eventually returned to Japan with mixed feelings about their possible reception in a homeland in which they were now largely outsiders. Their concerns proved valid when Tatsuguchi was drafted into the Imperial army and became virtually the only practicing physician who was denied a commission as an officer. Now Dr. Tatsuguchi was trapped on a frigid island in the middle of a fight to the death between two nations that he seemed to admire equally. His diary, which was retrieved and published by an American sergeant and became a media sensation in the United States, revealed the emotional rollercoaster that was the experience of both armies in Operation Landcrab. Even as the American invasion wavered between success and failure, Tatsuguchi, like his fellow defenders, awaited external intervention from a reinforcing fleet that would turn the tide of the battle.

So far in the Battle of Attu, the Japanese defenders had slowed the American advance to a crawl but at a cost of losing a third of the Imperial garrison in the process. Now, perhaps eighteen hundred still battle-worthy Nipponese defenders were locked in combat with over twelve thousand American invaders. The Imperial units continued to gradually withdraw to a new defensive position stretching from Holtz Bay to Chichagof Harbor while tacitly ceding the rest of Attu to the American invaders. Yet, as the battle continued, neither side was aware that Adm. Mineichi Koga, the senior officer in the Imperial navy, had decided that Attu was worth defending and was assembling a relief force including four cruisers, a seaplane carrier, and a convoy of transports and cargo ships that would throw men and supplies onto the embattled island.

Up to this point in the war, it seemed that it was American admirals who were more likely to abandon support for besieged garrisons. Only days after Pearl Harbor, Adm. William Pye, the temporary replacement for disgraced Adm. Husband Kimmel, initially responded to the widely publicized defense of Wake Island by a vastly outnumbered garrison of four hundred Marines by sending a relief force including priceless aircraft carriers. Yet in a last-minute change of heart, the rescue fleet was recalled as it neared the battle zone, and the American garrison was overrun and only saved from a massacre of every prisoner when the emperor ordered the victorious Japanese assault commander to call off the mass execution as a "Christmas gesture" to the American public. A few months later, the 1st Marine Division, fighting a larger Imperial garrison on Guadalcanal, was also abandoned by its naval support fleet when the senior naval officer set sail for safer waters after four Allied cruisers were sunk off nearby Savo Island.

Now, during the battle for Attu, it was the American invaders who were gaining the upper hand, as the Imperial high command dithered about whether the island was worth the risk of holding tight. Since the Imperial high command had been able to successfully evacuate nearly all of their able-bodied surviving soldiers from Guadalcanal eight months earlier, the Battle of Attu was the first time American forces had clearly besieged a virtually surrounded Japanese force. Even now, in the spring of 1943, the American high command could not fully appreciate the permanent status of non-person that befell any Imperial warrior who dared to surrender instead of killing himself. While German soldiers fought ferociously even in enormously one-sided battles, they were still required by their superiors only to fight to the "last bullet" and were allowed to surrender if they could inflict no more damage on their enemies, as was shown only weeks earlier when tens of thousands of Hitler's men were marched into the dubious safety of Soviet prisoner of war camps after the surrender of Stalingrad. If Nazis could be persuaded to surrender, it seemed logical that Japanese forces could be enticed into capitulation, especially since it seemed that Nippon had emerged as the most technically advanced society in Asia. Thus, American planes dropped thousands of leaflets over the Japanese-held portion of Attu that were effusive in their praise of Japanese prowess in battle and congratulated the defenders for "soldierly conduct worthy of the highest military traditions." The Imperial defenders were encouraged to send a senior officer and up to four staff officers to a designated point in Chichagof Valley where guides would escort the surrender party to American headquarters after which every member of the Japanese garrison would be "entitled to the privileges due prisoners of war according to the rules of land warfare." The pamphlets insisted that "German and Italian forces have already taken advantage of this offer" with broad hints that if life in a prisoner of war camp was not exactly a vacation, their fellow Axis internees were well fed, provided with ample activities, and were, most importantly, virtually guaranteed to survive the war. Yet even American-educated, Christian subjects of the emperor, such as Sergeant Tatsuguchi, could not force themselves to adapt a concept of surrendering to perhaps fight another day, in the way that Italian and German Axis partners were capable of doing.

Yet whatever "fraternal" feelings were kindled by German propaganda about their "honorary Aryan" Nipponese allies, the Japanese defenders of Attu simply could not conceive of life without victory. The Japanese warriors knew that no one could win every battle without fail and thus, when defeat approached, suicide was the logical choice to avoid the humiliation of surrender or captivity. For the defenders of Attu, the line between "suicide" and "killing" was now rather blurred. Medical personnel, such as Sergeant Tatsuguchi, were now ordered to "assist" their no longer combat-effective patients into death by whatever means thought most appropriate.

Now, much like the three hundred Spartan warriors who were holding the pass at Thermopolis against Xerxes' Persian hordes twenty-four centuries earlier, the Imperial units that could no longer successfully defend a position morphed into attack units and charged into surging American forces. The Imperial troops smashed into Landrum's still tentatively advancing Americans. Japanese ground forces looked skyward to see a squadron of Mitsubishi bombers attempt to support their army comrades in a rare display of Imperial airpower. However, twin-engine P-38 Lightnings suddenly joined the fray, and at a cost of two American aircraft, nine Japanese bombers crashed into the snow or sea below.

As the Japanese attempt to thwart the American advance began to peter out, some unconscious or semi-conscious Imperial troops were snatched up by the Americans. Startled American intelligence personnel suddenly realized that since Imperial soldiers never expected to be captured alive, they had never been trained how to resist interrogation or to refuse to provide information to their captors. Now, confronted with superior officers, even if serving in an enemy army, the prisoners who never expected to return alive to Japan simply cooperated to the fullest extent with their "new superiors."

Scattered units of the Japanese garrison fell back to Colonel Yamasaki's final defense line, Chichagof Harbor. In turn, General Landrum began the massive task of concentrating his southern and northern assault forces into a compact whole that could eventually roll over the badly decimated Imperial garrison. However, Yamasaki had no intention of passively waiting for a now imminent final American assault. At midnight on May 29, there were still perhaps eight hundred Imperial troops capable of some form of combat, and a half-hour into the new day, these men moved up the valley from Chichagof Harbor, taking special precautions to avoid slamming into the primary American battle line. The main target was the

The American assault on Chichagof Ridge in July tested the endurance of even the most intrepid US fighters.
LIBRARY OF CONGRESS

American rear echelon that would be assumed to be much more lightly defended. Sprawled back onto high ground named Engineer Hill was a collection of field kitchens, hospital facilities, and administrative centers. A silent wave of men armed with an eclectic collection of swords, bayonets, grenades, and pistols, a large portion of the still living Nipponese defenders of Attu clambered up and down hills until the wave coalesced near Engineer Hill. The assault force poured into initially poorly defended targets, including a field hospital where the attackers promptly bayoneted the largely helpless patients, and at least two headquarters structures where typewriters were more available than rifles.

The attackers grabbed all of the cigarettes, candy, and food cans they could carry, while dispatching every American they encountered. However, the price of this booty was exceptionally steep for the attackers, as Colonel Yamasaki, waving his sword to encourage his men to move on to more critical targets, slumped dead from an American bullet. Meanwhile, American defenders dragged an antitank gun into position during the frenzied attack and sent deadly shells into the packed-together attackers. At a total cost of seventeen dead and thirty-five wounded, the survivors of Engineer Hill had taken the Japanese commander and 350 of his men off the chessboard of war.

The American survivors of the banzai charge linked up with other units to capture Chichagof Harbor and town on the afternoon of May 30 and effectively ended organized Japanese resistance on Attu. At a cost of 550 Americans killed, twelve hundred wounded in action, twelve hundred cold weather casualties, and nine hundred men sidelined by disease or accidents, an American flag once again waved over this small segment of American territory. While the number of men killed in action was only half as high as in the upcoming Battle of Tarawa, the percentage of all casualties as a part of the entire invasion force would only be exceeded by the bloodbath of Iwo Jima. Just as at Iwo Jima two years later, raising the American flag over a battleground had not come cheaply.

Now the center of attention shifted even closer to the Alaskan mainland as preparations began to eject the Japanese from the even more strongly defended island of Kiska. While Emperor Hirohito gave a rare public reprimand to his army and navy commanders after the loss of

Attu, exclaiming, "Isn't there some way or some place were we can win a real victory over the Americans?", the Imperial high command dithered between reinforcing or evacuating their single remaining stronghold in North America. As bombers and warships pummeled the island, Imperial submarines attempted to evacuate nearly one thousand men from Kiska's garrison but lost almost half of the men and three of the submarines in the process. A combined Canadian-American invasion called Operation Cottage was scheduled for August 15, 1943, centered around a combat team that included the Alaskan Regiment, the 87th Mountain Combat Team that had been training for combat in Italy, the 13th Royal Canadian Infantry Brigade, and the exotic combat force nicknamed the "Devil's Brigade," officially known as the First Special Service Force, which was a joint Canadian-American unit. Now, thirty-five thousand men belonging to units with such colorful names as the Rocky Mountain Rangers and the Winnipeg Grenadiers would join with former Alaskan prospectors and Montana cowboys to chase the invaders out of North America.

On August 15, 1943, Operation Cottage sprang into action against a backdrop of rain, ice, fog and an eerie silence on the target island. As the troops stormed ashore, they found half-eaten meals and very deadly booby traps, the still-living canine mascot of the island's pre-occupation weather team, and mocking written taunts from the now absent Imperial defenders. The incredibly dense fog and mist and the search for an enemy that "had to be somewhere" initiated a deadly firefight between Allied units. Nipponese booby traps exploded at regular intervals and a much more potent explosion in the harbor badly damaged an American destroyer. A now evacuated Imperial garrison had almost by remote control killed nearly one hundred Allied soldiers and sailors and wounded more than two hundred others. *Time* magazine writers concocted a new term for the "battle of Kiska," a JANFU—Joint Army Navy Foul Up—as Japanese radio broadcasts noted the ability of the Nipponese to produce enemy casualties even thousands of miles from their physical presence.

On the other hand, the Imperial forces had been thrown out of their toehold in North America, and over five thousand Imperial personnel had died for little long-term gain. Ships and men that could have made a difference at either Midway or Guadalcanal had been frittered away in

The unforeseen Japanese evacuation of Kiska proved to be a pleasant surprise for the Allied landing forces. This Canadian member of the joint American-Canadian landing force aims a machine gun left behind by retreating Japanese soldiers. LIBRARY OF CONGRESS

a distant sideshow. Yet the United States had rescued the Aleutians by deploying nearly one hundred fifty thousand men, hundreds of planes, and dozens of ships to expel the Imperial invaders and only then decided that the road to Tokyo did not begin in Alaska, which may or may not have been a wise decision. The enemy had been thrown out of American territory, but as the Pacific offensive veered toward Japan, islands much smaller than the Aleutians would be turned into battlegrounds that dwarfed the Aleutian operation casualties. Looming an enormous distance to the south of Attu was the island of Tarawa, which would provide a whole new definition of violence and loss in the Pacific war.

CHAPTER 6

Up Periscope

WHILE THE AXIS POWERS AND THE WESTERN ALLIES BATTLED FOR control of the seemingly endless sea of sand that dominated the landscape of North Africa, combat in the real seas of the globe was reaching its own level of crescendo. The United States and the United Kingdom and its dominions were the only combatants fighting a truly global "world war," as Germany and Italy focused on the Atlantic and Mediterranean Theaters, while their ally, Japan, focused on the Pacific and, to a lesser extent, the Indian Ocean. By early 1943, American naval forces with significant Australian and British support were effectively in an extended offensive stance in the Pacific Theater but faced a daunting challenge in the Atlantic, as German submarine wolfpacks continued to threaten to cut the sea lanes connecting the American cornucopia of industrial production that allowed still semi-besieged Britain to continue to confront the Wehrmacht until massive reinforcements arrived from the New World.

During the previous year, the U-boats of Grand Adm. Karl Donitz's powerful undersea fleet had decimated Allied shipping all the way from the western approaches to Britain to the resort beaches of the American Atlantic and Gulf coasts. The naval contest between the Kriegsmarine and Allied naval forces would be a battle for the supremacy of the sea link between North America and Britain, an umbilical cord that, if severed, would allow Hitler to dominate the continent of Europe indefinitely.

The conflict that was increasingly described as the Battle of the Atlantic was, at the beginning of 1943, a contest seemingly on the edge of imminent disaster for the Allies. During the previous year, Allied convoys were losing five ships a day to enemy submarine attacks, as 1,664 vessels that had plied the ocean on New Year's Day 1942 were now at the bottom of the sea. While twenty-four-hour-a-day operations in American and British shipyards had produced seven million tons of new vessels, eight million tons had been lost to submarines at a steep but acceptable cost to Germany of eighty-seven U-boats. The German submarine flotilla of ninety-one combat-ready boats on January 1, 1942, was now up to 250 vessels with more on the way.

The all-volunteer German U-boat service began 1943 infused with excellent morale, based on perceptions that crewmembers were serving on a winning team that was giving the far larger Allied navy a run for their money. Generous amounts of leave time while boats were being refitted allowed the submarine personnel to fully absorb their status as heroes in large cities and hometowns. Submarine skippers had their pictures on trading cards, much like American baseball players, and in turn, encouraged a relaxed discipline that was a far cry from most of the German

The German U-boat fleet emerged as the most serious threat to transporting Americans to England for an eventual invasion of the continent. Here is an artists' rendition of the lethal undersea weapon.
LIBRARY OF CONGRESS

Wehrmacht. On the other hand, U-boat crews suffered astoundingly high casualties on missions, as more than half of the submarines in service in 1939 were now on the bottom of the Atlantic Ocean in a period before Allied anti-submarine warfare was functioning properly.

Yet, at the beginning of 1943, Admiral Donitz was in the enviable position of commanding a service that was seen as a winner that would continue to add luster as the Luftwaffe failed to prevent Allied air attacks on German cities, and huge numbers of Hitler's soldiers entered prisoner of war camps at Stalingrad and Tunisia. In a unique irony, Adolf Hitler, who loved airplanes and fast motor vehicles and hated anything to do with the sea, promptly approved his submarine chief's request for eight hundred new submarines and forty thousand more crew members, although Air Chief Hermann Goering managed to sabotage a further request for naval control of the long-range renaissance bomber Condor squadrons.

As 1943 began, a huge conveyor belt–like operation was shifting into first gear—the dispatch of a massive American Expeditionary Force to Britain in the first step toward an invasion of the European continent in 1944. American naval authorities were convinced that because most of the American Expeditionary Force would be transported by new, fast "attack transports," the troops would be relatively safe from the U-boat menace, since the transports were faster than the submarines and would be protected by significant escort units. The convoys carrying American GIs to North Africa battlefields faced far fewer U-boats than were stationed in the North Atlantic. A grim reminder that the North Atlantic experience just might be different occurred during two significant tragedies in early 1943.

On January 29, 1943, a small convoy sailed from the Canadian port of St. John. The center point of the small fleet was the US Army troopship *Dorchester*, carrying 750 soldiers to Greenland to reinforce the garrison of that island. Escorted by three Coast Guard cutters, *Tampa*, *Escanaba*, and *Comanche*, the small fleet steered a nominally evasive course toward its destination but did not follow a full-scale zigzag pattern. As the small convoy crawled eastward at 10 knots, U-boat 456 carefully noted blind spots in the defense pattern, and at 4:00 a.m. on February 3, 1943, launched a spread of torpedoes that doomed the *Dorchester* to a rapid sinking. Much like the *Andrea Doria* collision off Long Island in 1956, the rapid extreme list to one side effectively rendered half of the lifeboats on the *Dorchester* useless. *Dorchester* crewmembers failed to fire illumination shells, and panicky soldiers rushed the remaining, badly overcrowded usable lifeboats. Life rafts dropped into the sea hit men swimming below, and like the *Titanic* situation three decades earlier, large numbers of soldiers felt it was safer to stick with the ship than take a chance in the sea. In one of the most widely publicized actions in the war, the four chaplains aboard, a rabbi, Catholic priest, and two Protestant ministers, gave away their own life belts to other soldiers and huddled together to drown in the final plunge. Much like the *Titanic* in 1912, the water below was at the freezing level that would reduce survival time in the sea to moments, but the three Coast Guard vessels were actively rescuing as many swimmers as possible. Even with the onsite presence of rescue ships, only 229 of 906 persons aboard *Dorchester* survived, creating an even higher fatality rate than the *Titanic*. Three days later, the grim scenario was repeated as the USS *Henry R. Mallory* wended its way to Iceland carrying four hundred reinforcements for that island's garrison. The *Mallory* attracted the attention of an entire German wolfpack that promptly closed in for the kill. Massive torpedo hits reduced the *Mallory*'s lifespan to a mere thirty minutes. Ten lifeboats were launched in a panicky operation that dropped the boats too rapidly, causing nine of them to capsize. Only two hundred of the five hundred souls aboard would see the next dawn, so that within seventy-two hours, two disasters had, combined, caused nearly two-thirds the deaths of the iconic *Titanic* disaster. The appalling casualty rate on these two American troop ships was still relatively low, compared to the stupendous losses on some merchant vessels. The British tanker *Cardella* left port with forty-seven crew members, and forty-six went down while the attacking U-boat picked up a single survivor. The American freighter *Van Rensselaer* left port with a crew of seventy-one including an armed contingent of sailors. The ship was tracked by U-456, which fired torpedoes but did not interfere with the attempts to lower lifeboats from the doomed ship. Nevertheless, most of the boats promptly capsized, and only twenty-five swimmers survived to reach a passing life raft.

Honoring the **FOUR CHAPLAINS**

FIRST DAY OF ISSUE

A PRIEST, A RABBI AND TWO MINISTERS WHO GAVE THEIR LIVES THAT OTHERS MIGHT LIVE

FLEETWOOD

ARMY TRANSPORT DORCHESTER TORPEDOED BY SUBMARINE, FEBRUARY 3, 1943

After the *Dorchester* was torpedoed and sunk by a German U-boat in February 1943, this interfaith quartet of chaplains joined the many victims of the dangerous voyage to land American forces in Great Britain.

Now a cold fear ran in planning offices in London and Washington. If the U-boats could sever either the personnel or supply components of the transatlantic connections, the invasion of France could be seriously jeopardized. Yet with the cross-Channel invasion looming, one American naval officer remarked in shock and disgust, "We are just like a housewife flapping her apron to chase the chickens out of the hatches"; there seemed to be more noise than workable solutions.

The first step toward addressing this crisis was the gradual realization that there was no "silver bullet"—a single neat solution to the U-boat menace. Yet as 1943 moved toward spring, at least three somewhat unglamorous responses began to crystalize. The first of these three was the "ugly duckling" stepsister of the iconic B-17 Flying Fortress. When American bomber commanders called for long-range bombers to attack an enemy far from the battlefront, the B-17 Flying Fortress emerged from Boeing Corporation engineers and quickly became an iconic aircraft in American popular culture. Yet Boeing's enormous production facilities could not keep up with demand, and the Consolidated Aircraft Company was invited to develop a second long-range craft. Consolidated produced a plane called the B-24 Liberator which was faster, flew farther, and carried more bombs than the Fortress but could never evoke the popular enthusiasm its rival did. Critics insisted that the B-24 was hard to fly, accident prone, and in a visual sense, ugly. However, the plane was very available in large numbers, and the Army Air Force was happy to enter the field of long-range convoy support that might justify the enormous expense of the aircraft. Like prehistoric pterodactyls circling their prey, the Liberators became the bane of a U-boat shipper's existence, as the plane's array of anti-submarine weapons struck time and again, while also signaling other anti-submarine forces to join in the hunt.

The seagoing "ugly duckling" counterpart to the B-24 Liberator was an equally less than glamorous craft—the "escort aircraft carrier." Given a nickname midway between cute and dismissive, these crafts were called "jeep" carriers, combining the ubiquitous Army land vehicle and the strange, multispecies character that inhabited the cartoon and comic book world of Popeye the Sailor. These "baby" flat-tops were a far cry from their fleet carrier cousins that now occupied the role of the chessboard kings of nautical warfare. They began their existence as freighters or tankers and were then outfitted with a flight deck superimposed on the top, which allowed enough deck space for a dozen or so aircraft including convoy scout planes, divebombers, torpedo planes, and fighters. These vessels had essentially the same speed as their merchant ship cousins but added a huge new dimension to the anti-submarine game, as the U-boats had far too little on-deck firepower to counter more than one or two attacking aircraft when they surfaced, while the carrier planes could land and take off in relays to maintain a near constant air umbrella over the merchant ships.

The third member of the game-changing "ugly duckling" trio introduced for anti-submarine warfare was another junior-size version of a more familiar warship. This was the "destroyer-escort," which was the nautical equivalent of a postwar compact car. If even standard-size destroyers were small, cramped, and uncomfortable with poor handling in storms, the destroyer escorts took all of these issues to new levels. While conventional destroyers performed many tasks, destroyer escorts were developed with the primary purpose of sinking enemy submarines. Their lighter surface armament was compensated by massive anti-submarine arrays, including additional radar sets and depth charges. They often hovered around the flanks of convoys and utilized their high fuel capacity to outwait their undersea adversaries that were forced to surface at some point.

This new trio of anti-submarine weapons were decidedly unglamorous. There would be no *Memphis Belle*–like film centered on the seagoing Liberator or iconic books about the escort carriers and destroyers. Yet they became extremely unwelcome guests in the lair of the U-boats, helping to create a nightmare scenario for the German defenders of occupied France. During the first six months of 1943, 629 Allied merchant ships were sunk during their ocean passages. By the same period of time in 1944, that number had plummeted to a mere sixty-seven vessels, none of them troop carriers. Hitler's gamble to starve Britain and annihilate an American Expeditionary Force before it could arrive on the far side of the Atlantic Ocean devolved into utter failure. But on the other side of the globe, an equally intense naval conflict was still moving toward a longer-term climax in a major reversal of roles for the personnel of the US Navy in the Pacific war.

During the peak of the German U-boat offensive against the eastern and Gulf coasts of the United States, U-boat crewmen would use their periscopes to view the amusement parks, boardwalk rides, and beach bathing of American civilians in a form of second-hand experience of the normal peacetime life the Germans had led before the war. Then, in an example of the almost polar opposite, during the deployment of forces in the Pacific Theater in the spring of 1943, *Life* magazine published a full-page picture of the most sacred spot in Japan, Mount Fuji, taken from an American submarine sitting just off the coast. The accompanying commentary made it clear to Americans that just as the German "happy times" were ending, American citizens could expect that this was only the first installment of an American blockade of Japan. In this new alternative world of undersea warfare, it would be the American submarines that would "run silent, run deep," as they began to make it impossible for the Japanese merchant navy to transport the booty of their stolen empire back to the resource-starved home islands. Now it would be the American crews who experienced the emotional seesaw of reveling in the victory of sinking enemy ships and then enduring the unique terror of being trapped in a fragile, cigar-shaped vessel being pounded by depth charges by enemy surface vessels.

In many respects, Japan in World War II occupied a strategic situation similar to Britain in the Battle of the Atlantic. Like Britain, Japan was essentially a series of islands endowed with too few resources to prosper without an infusion of goods and materials from an extended empire. Just as British officials feared the consequences of a total cut-off of necessary supplies by the U-boat campaign, Imperial Japanese officials worked far into the nights attempting to provide adequate protection for their now huge transport fleet that was clearly vulnerable to American, British, and Australian submarine attack.

During the first year of the Pacific war, the survival of the Empire was aided somewhat by the fact that the American undersea fleet was still dominated by twenty-year-old "S" boats that were clearly unsuited for this new brand of warfare. The roughly one hundred boats available to American submarine units were slow, noisy, and could remain underwater for relatively brief intervals. However, by 1943, the boats were being replaced by the new Gato-class vessels that represented the cusp of underwater craft engineering at the time. Almost exclusively named after a variety of marine life forms, they became the new home for the twin dolphin insignia of a submariner. While their service did not produce quite the appalling fatality rates of their German counterparts, 25 percent of their sailors would never return from the sea, an outcome never far from each crewman's thoughts.

Yet like their German counterparts, there were definite compensations for the Americans' exposure to enormous danger. Top graduates of the US Naval Academy eagerly volunteered for submarine assignments, while first-tier Hollywood stars vied to be selected to portray the real submariners in first-tier films depicting their adventures. In one of the most schizophrenic lifestyles of combat personnel in World War II, submariners spent part of their time ensconced in beachfront hotels in Hawaii and Australia, attracted significant female attention, and dined on luxury food, all interspersed with long cruises on tiny vessels with no privacy, minimal comfort, and a very high risk of dying at the bottom of the sea.

While the Gato-class boats were an enormous upgrade in comfort from the old S boats, life for their men in no way matched the shore experience of lounging in beachfront hotels appropriated from civilian use for the comfort of submariners. Seamen rotated in eight-hour shifts on shared three-tier bunks, were permitted a twenty-second shower once a week, and often stood or sat on the floor at meals, as the tiny dining area was usually equipped with limited tables and chairs. On the other hand, the frequent spit-and-polish aspects of some surface ships simply did not exist, as T-shirts, blue jeans, and flip-flop sandals negated the need for inspections of enlisted men, even if officers maintained a slightly more formal attire much of the time. The food was considered excellent as long as it did not spoil, and unlike many surface vessels, officers and enlisted men ate exactly the same cuisine and shared an informality among ranks.

Unlike the iconic naval battles of Midway in 1942 and Leyte Gulf in 1944, the year between produced no Trafalgar-like mass fleet action between the American and Japanese navies. However, in order to protect assets from its ill-gotten new empire, the Japanese were obliged to transport their stolen resources from the Prosperity Sphere back to the Nipponese home islands with minimal loss in transit.

The American most responsible for ensuring that this transfer did not succeed was Adm. Charles Lockwood. Lockwood was a Virginian who graduated from Annapolis in 1912, and after brief stints in battleships, transferred to the fledgling undersea service with a posting on the rather undramatically named submarine, A-2. During World War I, Lockwood commanded Submarine Division 1 of the Asiatic fleet and afterward alternated undersea assignments with plush postings, such as naval attaché to Britain, which ultimately became a springboard after Pearl Harbor to the post of Commander, Submarines, Southwest Pacific. A few months later, even more responsibility was added to his portfolio, as Adm. Robert Henry, commander of all submarines in the entire Pacific, died in a freak plane crash near San Francisco.

Soon after Lockwood arrived in his new headquarters at Pearl Harbor, the submariner began to acquire a nickname from his men, "Uncle Charlie," as he appropriated civilian beachfront hotels for exclusive use of submarine crews of every rank. Returning crews back from patrols were greeted at the docks with huge crates of ice cream, then ushered toward meals centered around choice cuts of meat and fresh vegetables and socially rewarding down time before the next cruise.

While the crewmen readily accepted their welcome cornucopia, their officers were confronting Lockwood with a far more serious matter. The American torpedoes were proving far inferior in destructive capability to their Japanese counterparts. The Imperial Type 93 "Long Lance" torpedo carried triple the explosive charge of its American equivalent, was extremely reliable, and could close on a target at 40 miles per hour. American weapons specialists had been working desperately to produce some counterpart of the Japanese weapons for use in American submarines and believed that they had hit paydirt with the Mark 14. The American torpedo was still a bit slower than its Japanese counterpart but used a revolutionary new targeting system based on a magnetic field detector that could massively expand the potential damage to any enemy vessel. Unfortunately, the Mark 14 had been subjected to testing only in the Atlantic Ocean, while most American submarine attacks on enemy shipping would be in the Pacific. Skippers of dozens of submarines spent most of eighteen months wincing and raging in anger as a perfect hit on a Japanese vessel simply slid under the target with Nipponese commanders often unaware that they had even been attacked. It eventually became clear that Pacific waters were not the same as the Atlantic Ocean, and by 1943, conventional detonators were beginning to replace the experimental models. Yet just as the detonation issue began to be resolved, a new "gremlin" appeared. In a poorly considered nod toward preventing cost overruns, the relatively expensive, sturdy firing pins that made torpedoes explode were replaced with cheaper metal components that initiated an explosion on a far more erratic basis. The American submarines patrolling the vast Pacific Ocean in 1943 were operated by extraordinary young crewmen and superb officers who knew their business. Yet they faced both ill-advised budget cutting by their superiors and a Japanese adversary that represented a fierce seagoing people who were not about to cede control of the Pacific trade routes to their now clearly deadliest existential enemy, the United States.

By the spring of 1943, an average of one new submarine a week was arriving in the Pacific area of operations, and they brought with them the cutting-edge technology being developed by American research activities. One of the biggest game changers was the new high-definition centimetric radar that had been used by American aircraft in the battle for the Atlantic to spot submerged U-boats. Now the captain of an American submarine could spot a Japanese target as far away as six miles at night, compute the target's course and speed, and then run ahead in an "end around" to strike the enemy from an unexpected direction. Since neither Imperial submarines nor most escort ships carried radar equipment in 1943, the opportunity for enormous victories was now rapidly approaching.

The arrival of these new technical upgrades in early 1943 came at a perfect time for the news media publicizing the submarine campaign in the Pacific. A number of boats and officers now received publicity worthy of a film star or baseball player, and one of the first recipients of this media hype was the *Wahoo* and the photogenic tandem of its skipper Lt. Comm. Dudley Morton and executive officer Lt. Richard O'Kane. Morton, who was nicknamed "Mush" for his southern drawl, was described as "built like a bear and as playful as a cub" and had been a high-profile football star while in college. Now he was another kind of quarterback who talked and joked with enlisted men and inspired a crew that, in turn, revered their captain. O'Kane was his senior officer's equal in promoting enthusiasm with an equally aggressive but jocular nature. The *Wahoo* was now about to set sail on an experimental mission devised by the senior commander of submarines in Brisbane, Rear Adm. James Fife. Fife suggested to his star officers a naval experiment in which captain and executive officers would switch traditional roles. Instead of the captain manning his usual post at the periscope during an attack run, Fife suggested that O'Kane actually view the action and pass the information on to Morton, who would then be free to more calmly review the data and make a cooler judgment about what to do next.

In mid-January 1943, the new game plan was put into action when the *Wahoo* arrived off the north coast of New Guinea near the island of Wewak. Amazingly, the island did not yet appear on US Navy charts, but a young machinist mate produced a school atlas he had just purchased on leave in Brisbane and another crewmember with an interest in photography improvised an enlargement of the area on a chart. Using the very 'low-tech" equipment, the boat crept toward the shoreline in what one crew member described as the atmosphere of a "fraternity raiding party" and closed on the heavily wooded beach.

The action quickly intensified as an Imperial destroyer sighted the *Wahoo* periscope, which Morton had ordered to be kept on the surface to entice an enemy vessel to make an attack run. As the destroyer closed in, the *Wahoo* fired torpedoes, and moments later, an Imperial warship was consigned to the shallow bay from which it had attacked.

Two days later a small Imperial flotilla of two freighters, a tanker, and a troop transport loaded with reinforcements for another Japanese base ventured out of the same port and encountered the patiently waiting *Wahoo*. The *Wahoo* officers nodded in a delighted shock that the enemy ships made no attempt to zigzag, and torpedoes were soon streaming on their deadly missions. All of the vessels were hit, and soon hundreds of Imperial troops were flailing in the water, hoping to clamber aboard rafts that dotted the sea. In a provocative response to the increasingly disturbing stories of Japanese barbarity to American prisoners, Morton ordered the boat to surface and opened fire on the swimmers with deck guns, an action he made no attempt to hide in his official report.

The *Wahoo* and both "Mush" Morton and Richard O'Kane would soon become household names on the American home front, but the duel between submarines and surface ships continued unabated, and within a year *Wahoo* would join its victims on the bottom of the Pacific, with Morton and his crew. O'Kane, who received command of his own submarine, would finish the war in a brutal Japanese prison camp after his boat, *Tang*, was hit by one of its own torpedoes leaving all but the captain and three servicemen dead. Yet, by the end of 1943, the Battle of the Atlantic had largely been won by the Allies, and the Japanese home islands were beginning to experience the economic privation that the powerful American undersea fleet was now inflicting upon Nippon.

CHAPTER 7

The Dawn of "Husky"

WHILE ALLIED FORCES WERE CLOSING THE RING AROUND THE ENOR-
mous Axis garrison defending Tunis, almost the length of an entire
continent away, an olive drab van rolled onto a naval pier in Greenock,
Scotland, and a Royal Navy officer aided by two nondescript helpers grap-
pled with an unwieldy four-hundred-pound metal container embossed
with a "Handle with Care—Optical Instrument" sign and a notation that
this item was a "special shipment." The small party and their bulky cargo
were headed toward the submarine HMS *Seraph*, which was preparing for
an exceptionally long voyage. The next night, Lt. S. E. Jewell guided his
boat out of the lock and initiated one of the most important submarine
voyages in World War II.

The *Seraph* was not about to engage enemy shipping; in fact, precautions were made to stay clear of any vessel whether Axis or Allied. In
essence, the captain and crew were engaged in a glorified disposal service,
and there was only one item slated to be dumped overboard. Lieutenant Jewell was already a veteran of cloak and dagger operations, as several
months earlier he had secretly debarked American general Mark Clark
near an isolated beachfront villa outside the Algerian capital Algiers, so
that Clark could negotiate a secret deal with Vichy French officials to allow
the Allies to land in the initial phase of the liberation of North Africa.

This time, Jewell and his crew were bound for Spain, and after an
eleven-day cruise, the craft arrived in the Gulf of Cadiz off the southern
Andalusia coast of Francisco Franco's Fascist but neutral Spain. Amazingly, the mysterious container, subject to constant guessing on the part
of the crew, contained a human passenger who had no need of fresh air.

The passenger was a recently deceased resident of Britain who had died of respiratory failure, according to some reports, while serving an extended prison term.

This "non-person" eventually designated as "the man who never was" in a highly successful postwar book and film, was about to become a major actor in one of the most successful Allied espionage campaigns of the war. Spain had been ruled by Gen. Francisco Franco since his Nationalist faction, supported by such varied patrons as the Vatican, Fascist Italy, and Nazi Germany, had defeated a "Republican" government supported less generously than Franco by the Soviet Union, and private anti-Fascist volunteers from much of Europe and the United States.

Substantial German assistance gained minimal reward when Franco refused to join his fellow Fascist states in a war with the Allies, even when Hitler sweetened the pot with a proposed joint invasion of British-held Gibraltar that Spaniards longed to return to their rule. A dejected and furious Hitler remarked after a phone conference with Franco that he would rather have four teeth pulled than face the "Maximus Leader's" brand of negotiations even one more time. Franco, who would rule for another three decades and was welcomed into the NATO fold during the Cold War, did feel enough obligation to his Fascist partners that he routinely passed on information gathered from his agents when they intercepted Allied mail or communications. This concession to the Axis was the heart of the "Mincemeat" plan.

The mystery corpse was rowed relatively near shore by the *Seraph* raft, fitted with appropriate but fake identification, and dropped overboard wearing a life jacket. In a sequence of events that would put even a good spy novel to shame, the corpse, which had been preserved during the voyage with dry ice, was dressed in the uniform of a Royal Navy officer, who also happened to have a briefcase affixed with the Royal Seal of Britain on it when the body was pushed overboard with a rubber life raft, now fully inflated, also dumped a thousand yards closer to the Spanish port of Huelva. As was hoped and expected by Allied intelligence forces, the body was spotted by a fisherman, taken to shore, identified by Spanish police as Maj. William Martin, Royal Marines, and in the spirit of fraternal Axis relations, promptly loaned to German intelligence before the

British embassy was notified. German intelligence officers quickly scored a bonanza of information as, "Major Martin was carrying information on the impending Allied invasion of Sardinia that was identified by false documents as the necessary prelude to a later invasion of Sicily." There was even a hint that Greece would be invaded simultaneously with Sardinia, leaving Sicily as a target well into the future. After the German intelligence authorities had closely examined the corpse and documents, the British embassy was duly informed of the tragic death of one of their men in uniform and permitted to acquire the corpse for proper burial.

Without firing a shot, the Allies had gained a huge espionage success, as, while Sicily was not ignored in Axis defense plans, reinforcements that would have significantly improved the German position on Sicily were now rushed to points that the Allies had no intentions of attacking in the near future.

The enormous success of Mincemeat, much like the Allied ability to convince the Germans that Normandy was not the primary target for the Overlord operation, did not guarantee success of Operation Husky but did provide an important potential game changer in an operation that was hardly a guaranteed success.

The Allied high command was able to convince the enemy that Sicily was merely one of several targets for invasion, but the senior commanders still believed that even an unreinforced Axis garrison on Sicily would be a deadly menace to the seaborne invasion forces unless Axis power was somehow diminished before the landing on the invasion beaches. One possible solution to this dilemma was to attempt the most massive Allied airborne assault to this point of the war. Much of the hope for success of a pre-invasion airborne operation rested on two colorful officers from the opposite sides of the Atlantic Ocean. The higher-ranking of these two men was Lt. Gen. Frederick Browning. "Boy" Browning had experienced the not unduly stimulating upbringing of the British upper crust and had elected to make a career of the army rather than dive into the thrust and parry of a business career in London. While he enjoyed a solid string of promotions that would lead to the rank of general, his major public relations coup occurred in 1932 when he utilized a military leave to explore the southern coast of Britain on a holiday. That holiday would turn into a publicity bonanza for Browning when he met and married rising star author Daphne Du Maurier, who was recuperating from appendicitis. A number of her best-selling books were turned into films, two of which, *Rebecca* and *The Birds*, were directed by Alfred Hitchcock.

By 1941, "Boy" Browning was a major general and a pioneer in the emerging combat arm of parachute and airborne assault. He commissioned popular artist Edward Seago to design one of the most famous insignia of the war—an emblem of the warrior Bellerophon riding Pegasus as a symbol of the daring of the winged warriors of World War II.

Browning was now paired off with an equally high-profile American officer who had grown up in circumstances as far removed from the British general as could be conceived in 1943. Col. James Gavin was a thirty-six-year-old paratroop commander who looked almost as young as the men under his command. Born of at best uncertain parentage in Brooklyn, he was deposited in a Convent of Mercy orphanage at age two, adopted by a Mount Carmel, Pennsylvania, couple, and by age eleven had multiple newspaper routes and a job sweeping floors in a barbershop. Gavin was determined to avoid the major career in his town, coal mining, and he ran away from home to gain slightly less dangerous jobs in New York City. At seventeen, Gavin enlisted in the Army, serving in Panama while reading extensively in military history in his minimal free time. A year later, he passed the entrance examination for West Point, while lying about his age on the application to cover his dubious initial enlistment. As a young officer, Gavin was attracted to the newly emerging parachute forces, which he compared to the "foot cavalry" of Stonewall Jackson. After authorship of several field manuals, Gavin was seen as a rising star and given a series of rapid promotions that ended in regimental command in the 82nd Airborne Division.

Gavin and the Seventh US Army commander George Patton were each noted for their hot tempers and strong opinions, and the Seventh Army commander's strong "suggestion" that the paratroops should land in Sicily at night brought a rebuff from Gavin. While Gavin won the military debate as Patton reluctantly acceded to the substantial risks, the risk of a night drop was quickly replaced by 35-mile-per-hour winds over Sicily that in many respects were even more of a danger than lack of daylight.

Yet, as events proceeded, the American paratroopers would still face less danger than the Allied glider forces that would constitute the other aerial invasion of Sicily.

The first Allied service personnel who penetrated into the Nazi-dominated continent of Europe were the Red Devils of the 1st Airlanding Brigade of the British 1st Airborne Division. Just over two thousand men of the all-volunteer force passed over the southern tip of Sicily, Cape Passero, at 10:00 p.m. on July 9, 1943. Their mission was to land outside the city of Syracuse and capture the vital Ponte Grande span over the Anapo River until follow-up infantry units could move off the invasion beaches and take over responsibility for the contested bridge.

These British glider assault personnel already enjoyed a major psychological edge over their American counterparts. Assignment to American glider units was usually a consolation prize for men who had failed to successfully complete the Spartan training course experienced by American paratroop candidates, and the US glider troops often saw themselves as the "second team" behind the more glamorous paratroopers. Their British counterparts, on the other hand, were primarily men who actually volunteered to be glider assault personnel and were treated as full partners of their higher-profile paratroop counterparts. In many respects, these glider men seemed even more daring than their paratrooper cousins, as they would actually crash-land on the battlefield, which was even more dangerous than arriving by parachute.

The basic assault plan for the Red Devils was to arrive over a series of three landing zones at 10:00 p.m. the night before the ground/seaborne invasion, with eight mammoth Horsa gliders landing on both sides of the targeted bridge, and seize the span before the defenders could fully react. The Ponte Grande was the gateway to an attack on the port of Syracuse, about one thousand yards from the target which spanned the Anapo River which, in turn, emptied into Syracuse Harbor. The center of the whole operation was a mere company of the South Staffordshire Regiment, which would rely on surprise and confusion to snatch the bridge from the enemy.

Now began a road to disaster. Operation Ladbroke was centered around the belief that the single assault company would be supported by a massive contingent of two thousand support troops that would essentially block any reinforcement of the bridge garrison. In a series of mishaps and bad luck that rivaled the *Titanic* disaster, the assault plan began to unravel. An ideal wind speed for successful glider landing reasonably near the intended target ranged in the area of 5 to 15 miles per hour. Yet, as the aerial flotilla crossed the Mediterranean, wind indicators rose steadily until they reached 35 miles per hour. This dangerous situation was enhanced as an expected minimal Axis antiaircraft gun reception was far more intense than predicted, and glider pilots were forced to alter their course as two aircraft crashed toward Sicily due to antiaircraft hits. This unexpected intensity encouraged the pilots of the powered tow planes to leave their formation to avoid the dense flak throttling their aircraft.

This deadly combination of unfortunate events simply tore apart the entire operation. A total of just under 150 gliders left Tunisian bases and crossed the Mediterranean. Nearly seventy of these craft were at the bottom of the sea a few hours later with over 250 Red Devils now ensconced in watery graves. Most of the remaining craft were either towed back to Tunisia with their passengers still aboard or released their gliders so early or so late that the assault troops were scattered over more than twenty miles of southern Sicily, at least initially, in groups too small to make an impact on Axis defenses. A small ray of humor relieved the unremitting story of horror when one glider landed on the main airstrip of Malta, where the pilot was chided for blocking access to the strip.

The American paratroop force was plagued by the same weather issues as the C-47 transports lumbered over the Mediterranean. Col. James Gavin, the young commander of the 505th Parachute Infantry Regiment, was now leading his men into battle saddled with two nicknames, "Slim Jim" and "Jumping Jim," but he would have gladly traded all present and future nicknames for a modest drop in the wind velocity. Unlike their British counterparts who crash-landed onto a battlefield, the American paratroopers would glide earthbound on the strings of a parachute which would make a particularly enticing target for Axis forces on the ground. Contingents of eighteen men each overloaded with equipment waded onto the transport planes in a wide variety of moods from loudly talkative to comforted in their own silence. Gavin himself may have been enjoying the irony that his plane was delayed on takeoff, as a young soldier clambered aboard just before takeoff to personally deliver a huge duffel bag filled with prisoner of war tags that would have to be filled out by the colonel, a tag for each prisoner his men captured on the ground. The monotony of a long flight across the sea was instantly relieved when a red light signaled its passengers to bail out just as enemy antiaircraft shells and their tracer bullets lit up the sky.

Colonel Gavin was the first man to jump, the first man to reach solid ground, and initially, an "invasion force" of one person. Passwords and countersigns began to echo through the night air, and moments later, the colonel was employing the Italian language that he had reluctantly studied in high school to interrogate the first Italian prisoners of the operation. German propaganda officers had showered their increasingly reluctant Italian allies with a storyline that suggested that American paratroops were recruited primarily from the ranks of convicted murderers on death row, sprinkled with ex-convicts offered huge bonuses to use their criminal talents against the enemy. Thus, Italian soldiers captured during their first long night of the Battle of Sicily were shocked and relieved when the American invaders were generally polite, many spoke at least some Italian, and the worst atrocity inflicted on the captives was that some paratroopers confiscated the defenders' belts so they could not run away while they were holding up their pants. Much as did their British allies, the American paratroopers, still hugely scattered, fumbled their way along dark roads and waited for sunrise for the opportunity to harass the defenders from the rear, while hoping and praying that the planned invasion would swell Allied numbers enormously.

As Allied airborne troops groped their way through the darkness and tried to make sense of their situation and tasks, an enormous Allied fleet steamed into position to support the more traditional invasion from the sea. The island that Allied ground units were about to invade was roughly one hundred miles wide from the western port city of Marsala to the urban center of Messina, with a hundred-mile-long eastern shoreline gradually dropping off to a mere twenty-five-mile coast in the far west. This ten-thousand-square-mile near-appendage to the Italian mainland had been fought over by Spartans, Athenians, Romans, Vandals, Goths, Saracens, and Normans in earlier centuries with Spaniards, Germans, and Britons entering the fray in more recent times. Once the Italian states were able to largely unify as a nation, Sicily promptly became a second-class part of the new nation, and the island continued to experience that status under Mussolini's Fascist regime. Mussolini's promise to significantly improve the living standards of Sicilians had proved a hollow bargain, and if and when the Allies actually did land, most Sicilians had privately decided to keep their heads down and see who actually would win the battle.

The single most important Allied objective was the major port city of Messina on the northwest coast, which faced the Italian mainland across a narrow three-mile channel that was crossed frequently by a fleet of ferry boats. Only slightly less important than Messina were another port city, Marsala, on the far western tip of the island, Palermo on the northern coast, Catania, almost exactly in the middle of the long eastern coastline, and Syracuse, forty miles down the coast from Catania.

While the Allies fully intended to occupy the entire island, the invasion landings would be concentrated along a ninety-mile-long beachfront extending from the port city of Licata on the Gulf of Gela on the southern coast around the port of Syracuse at the northern end of the Gulf of Noto. As the invasion forces moved inland in an ever expanding sweep through the entire island, the Americans would serve as the flank guard for a giant scythe-like offensive that would eventually push the Axis garrison all the way to Messina with its back now on the channel between Sicily and mainland Italy.

The best case Allied scenario was some form of a reprise of "Tunis-grad," in which the entire Axis army would be obliged to surrender or face utter destruction. However, while the Axis garrison in Tunis had its back to a wide sea in which supplies and reinforcements were obliged to cross a large body of water complicated by Allied control of the air and sea, a worst-case scenario for the Axis forces in Sicily still had the enormous advantage of mainland Italy and its huge rail and road system beckoning in clear sight just across the narrow channel. On paper at least, the Axis garrison of Sicily looked extremely formidable on the eve of Operation Husky. The Italian garrison on Sicily included nearly two hundred thousand army defenders with an additional fifty thousand air force and naval personnel with ground troops divided between two corps that included a total of four regular infantry divisions, but like the British after Dunkirk, the Italian defenders of Tunisia had lost a huge inventory of armor during the defeat, and the defense of Sicily relied on a hodge-podge of roughly one hundred captured French Renault tanks bordering on obsolescence, and less than fifty even more obsolete Italian Fiat tanks. None of these vehicles could match up against most Allied equivalents, and, thus, the main weapon against American and British armor was two dozen Semovente tank destroyers.

In any other category except numbers, the Italian garrison on Sicily had little chance to throw Allied invaders into the sea. However, at the time of the planned Husky invasion, Adolf Hitler had intervened, and, with the permission of Mussolini, deployed two excellent German divisions to the island. One of these units was the 15th Panzergrenadier Division, which was a compilation of several other battered German units with an excellent core of veteran troops, but a very modest armored array of just over fifty tanks. This army unit was then paired off with one of Luftwaffe commander Hermann Goering's favorite air force ground divisions, not so modestly designated "Panzer-Division Hermann Goering." This was one of the Luftwaffe chief's pet units, a form of extended honor guard that was a composite of airborne soldiers, armored units, and grounded aircrews, all centered around an impressive armored contingent of nearly 120 tanks, including seventeen of the state of the art Tiger tanks for which the Allies had no effective counterpart. The German high command, eager to dissuade Mussolini from surrendering to the Allies, placed almost sixty-eight thousand ground troops and over six hundred combat planes at Mussolini's disposal to throw back an Allied invasion of Sicily, a major contribution considering the enormous casualties now being suffered on the Eastern Front. Axis propaganda reveled in the status of Sicily as the "Italian Gibraltar."

The Axis propaganda machine may have been far more optimistic than conditions in the summer of 1943 warranted, but they were correct in noting an enormous advantage they enjoyed in this upcoming battle that had not been the case in North Africa. Unlike the Tunisian experience, the Axis garrison on Sicily could be reinforced promptly from the

Italian mainland that loomed in clear sight two miles away from the Messina docks and beaches. While Sicilians may have conceived of themselves as somewhat of a tribe apart from their counterparts across the narrow straits, most Italian soldiers still viewed the island as an integral part of the motherland, even if much of the Sicilian population was less convinced of the benefits of this relationship.

Whatever the exact political status of Sicily, most Allied service personnel generally viewed "Husky" as the first invasion of Hitler's European lair, and even if none of the Americans and relatively few of the British soldiers had been involved in the evacuation of Dunkirk three years earlier, this was still seen as a return to the continent, if not exactly *the* return envisioned by the leaders, busy planning "Overlord" for the next spring. The victory at "Tunisgrad" had made up for much of the embarrassment at Tobruk and Kasserine Pass, but the leaders from the North Africa campaign were still, at least temporarily, in command, and Eisenhower, Patton, Montgomery, and others were happy to play this next round out in Sicily until the hoped-for call to oversee Overlord arrived in the relatively near future. The invasion of northwest Europe might have indeed been beckoning in 1944 for the senior commanders, but in the summer of 1943, the Sicilian operation was about the best command on offer.

Allied planners had minimal interest in the natural resources or production capabilities of Sicily; the island was quite simply the gateway to the Italian mainland and had to be captured before the long march up to Rome could begin. Augusta, Catania, and Syracuse emerged as the first major objectives and Gen. George Patton's Seventh Army would effectively be tasked with being a flank protector for Gen. Bernard Montgomery's Eighth Army as it conducted a huge sweep outward from the initial landing beaches that was intended to push the entire Axis army into a retreat toward the northeastern coast and a last stand at Messina. Operation Ladbroke, the pre-invasion airborne assault, had, at great cost, succeeded in capturing the vital Ponte Grande bridge that the seaborne assault forces would require to move farther inland. Allied ground forces were about to experience their own terror as the first landing craft motored its way to the strand.

In the predawn half-light of a Mediterranean early summer morning, an enormous armada of 3,266 ships, ranging from battleships to PT boats, edged into position along the southern beaches of Sicily. Over eighty thousand officers and men were involved in what at that point was the largest single fleet movement in naval history. While British and American ships dominated the crowded sea, vessels from Canada, India, Holland, Poland, and Greece dotted the water with most of the vessels not directly involved in fire support preparing to return to North Africa for more men and supplies before the day ended.

Unlike the invasion of Normandy the following year, when dozens of air bases in Britain allowed the invaders to totally dominate the skies above the sea and landing beaches, on this long hot summer day in 1943, dozens of German and Italian aircraft dueled their Allied opponents over sand and sea. One American naval officer noted with some dismay the power of the Axis air force as, "We had our own large-scale raid—36 planes. They dropped bombs all over the harbor area but only one hit. Bombs came within fifty yards of us, and concussion knocked down men in the shell handling room. At night, German flares lighted the whole harbor, and every plane darted in and out of rain squalls to maximize attack opportunities."

While the British landing beaches stretched along the east coast of Sicily from Syracuse to Pachino, the American forces would be landing along the southern coastline, primarily from Scolitti to Licata, with all of these beaches fronting the sea of Gela. The landing sites, Joss, Dime, and Cent beaches, would prove to be more heavily fortified than their British equivalents, and this was particularly true of the target for the 1st Infantry Division, Dime Beach, which encompassed the strategically placed town of Gela.

The flank of the men of the Big Red One was covered by Col. William Darby's Force X, which was comprised of the 1st and 4th Ranger battalions and a company of combat engineers that utilized stealth and speed to capture one of the first towns in Axis-occupied Europe. Much like one of his chroniclers, Ernie Pyle, Colonel Darby was an outspoken iconoclast who would not survive the war, and like Pyle, would be the central character in a significant 1950s film: Pyle in *The Story of GI Joe*, and Darby in *Darby's Rangers*. The then thirty-two-year-old colonel had essentially conceived the concept of an American equivalent to the British commando Special Forces when he read the book and then saw the subsequent Technicolor film of Kenneth Roberts's *Northwest Passage*. Roberts's best-selling account, which resulted in nineteen editions, was the chronicle of Major Robert Rogers and his Rogers' Rangers unit. Darby wanted to form the first true Special Forces unit in American history.

Darby had received permission to cobble together a unit of volunteers, who then trained in a remote corner of Northern Ireland and impressed senior officers to the extent that elements of the Special Forces unit were assigned to Operation Husky.

Four summers earlier, defending British soldiers had fought house to house, street to street in Dunkirk to cover the evacuation of their comrades on the nearby beaches as the British Expeditionary Force was extracted from a continent about to be dominated by the Axis powers. Now, at the opposite end of Europe, American invaders were fighting house to house, street to street, to liberate the first town in that occupied continent. Like the Tommies before them, in a cat and mouse hunt, they alternately changed roles from rooting out snipers from upper floors of houses to using bazookas and satchel charges to disable Italian tanks rushed into the battle to expel the Yankee invaders.

Soon the tables were turned in Gela, as the Italian infantry units defending the town were reinforced with armored forces detached from the elite Centauro division that had fought so well in North Africa. Elements of the 501 Battaglione equipped with captured French Renault R 35 tanks fought their way through the narrow streets of the town. The American engineers were equipped with bazookas and began stalking the Renault tanks up and down the curving streets, while Rangers, who were not equipped with bazookas, improvised homemade satchel chargers and threw them down from the windows of upper floors of American-controlled houses. Then, in the kind of daredevil action that would lead to Darby's death two years later, the Ranger commander dashed back to the invasion beach, found an operable 37mm antitank gun, and carted it back to Gela, where the weapon turned the tide of the battle as Darby personally sought out targets.

Although at great cost to British airborne forces, the first day of Operation Husky had seen the landing of a massive and growing Allied force on Axis soil. However, the German high command had no intention of allowing an Allied force to land uncontested, and the true intensity of the duel for Sicily would be revealed the next morning when the Panzers finally lurched into action along the beachfront.

CHAPTER 8

Climax on Sicily

SUNDAY, JULY 11, 1943, DAWNED AS A STIFLINGLY HOT DAY AFTER THE
Allied invasion of Sicily. The invaders controlled only a tiny sliver of the
island running from the southern beaches inland to the small community
of Gela, where American troops could still hear the Mediterranean surf
pounding a short distance away. American newspapers and magazines
displayed maps of a roughly two-mile-wide occupation zone that was
now crowded with vehicles moving slowly inland against a panorama of
wrecked Allied and Axis vehicles giving the impression of a sprawling
junkyard. Badly damaged amphibious tanks bobbed up and down in shallow water, while engineers prodded the sand with their detection equipment exposing some of the thousands of deadly mines Axis troops had
buried in anticipation of an Allied invasion. Now some of those German
minelayers were marching with hands over their heads toward waiting
evacuation craft often clad in what one British journalist insisted, "Were
neat and clean uniforms that look like the Home Guard in England."
Two of the names bandied about the most often were Maj. Gen. Terry
"Terrible" Allen and his senior assistant, Brig. Gen. Theodore Roosevelt
Jr., who dueled for pride of place in their ability to push the front lines
ever farther inland. Allen claimed to one correspondent, "Hell, we haven't
even started to fight. Our artillery hasn't even been overrun yet," while
Roosevelt chimed in that, "I won't go back into the sea."

These two frequently noteworthy officers were soon joined in Gela's
Cathedral Square by Gen. George Patton, equipped with his trademark
pearl-handled revolvers and an expensive Leica camera dangling around
his neck. Patton had nothing but praise for Col. William Darby and his

Ranger units, but was less than enthused about the activities of Allen and Roosevelt. Patton later recounted that he "talked to General Roosevelt about the failure of the 1st Division to carry its objectives, which he insisted was based on the fact that the Big Red One had attacked German positions without either their antitank guns or their artillery." Patton's mood was not improved when he looked out to sea and saw a Liberty cargo ship literally blown in two from a German bombing raid. As he turned away from the doomed ship, he saw a landward disaster already in the making. Noting the activity as, "The most stupid thing I have ever seen soldiers do," he watched clueless soldiers dig new foxholes adjacent to multiple piles of five-hundred-pound bombs and seven tons of high explosive shells. He stormed over to the perpetrators and insisted that, "If they want to save the Graves Registration burials that was a fine thing to do, but otherwise, they had better dig somewhere else." Just as the seemingly clueless diggers began to react to Patton's warning, an opportunity for another form of meaningless death presented itself when two British Hurricane fighter bombers streaked in at low altitude and strafed the American beachhead, essentially doing the work of the Luftwaffe for them.

Allied planes actively attacking enemy positions seemed initially to be in short supply, and a series of massive low-level German raids sank the destroyer *Maddox*, cargo vessel *Robert Rowan*, and hospital ship *Talamba* in quick succession. Luckily for the Allies, even daring raids by Axis planes failed to place a massive dent in an Anglo-American fleet as an enormous array of ground and ship antiaircraft guns shot down over 150 of the intruders, forcing the German high command to pull most of their most vulnerable aerial units back to the Italian mainland.

The massive Anglo-American invasion of Sicily and the failure of the Axis defenders to drive the invaders right back into the sea set in motion a series of events that permanently nullified the benefits of the earlier Axis victory at Kasserine Pass. Soon after the Allied landings in Sicily, Adolf Hitler and Benito Mussolini held a conference in Venice where the Duce pledged eternal fraternity with his fellow Fascist dictator, while Hitler called off his now fizzling Eastern Front offensive at Kursk in order to rush additional Wehrmacht reinforcements to Italy. Yet there was a darker side to the Führer's seemingly selfless gesture to Mussolini:

The new German reinforcements targeted for Italy were, to a large extent, to be utilized to forcibly occupy the ancestral homeland of the father of the Fascist movement. Whether the Allies or the Germans were now in Sicily and mainland Italy, Benito Mussolini's days as a master of his own country were seemingly numbered.

As the Duce and Führer began hedging their bets against a split between the two primary members of the Axis alliance in Europe, the two senior ground commanders of the Allied invasion force were planning a massive offensive not only to fully occupy Sicily but also to trap a major portion of the Axis garrison on this arid, yet steamy island. In the opening phase of an Anglo-American contest to capture and occupy the major cities of Sicily, Montgomery and Patton were beginning to develop strategies to beat their rival to the most valuable parts of Sicily, almost as if engaged in an enormous game of Monopoly in which some locations were significantly more valuable than others with the "Boardwalk" on their "board" clearly the city of Messina, the port that faced the Italian mainland across a three-mile channel.

Unlike the Monopoly board where the two most valuable properties, Boardwalk and Park Place, are essentially adjacent to one another, Messina and the second most valuable location, the capital city of Palermo, were on opposite sides of the island with forbidding mountainous country interspersed with narrow dangerous roads, looming in the middle distance almost taunting the Anglo-American invaders to accept the challenge of attempting to make forward progress in a land that still seemed to belong to the deities of classical Greece and Rome.

In an amazing irony, two of the most egocentric yet talented generals of World War II were deposited on the same forbidding island to seek glory with the consolation that their operations would not be impeded by extreme cold, torrential rain, or dense jungle. Sicily was hot, dry, and mountainous, and defended by a large force of Italians who were just about ready to end their attempt to establish a new Roman Empire, and a smaller number of energetic Germans who would measure their success in their ability to stall the Allied invasion for so long that their inevitable capture of Sicily no longer looked like a marvelous victory to the British and American governments.

Despite massive Allied air cover, a number of Allied cargo ships became victims of relentless German divebombing attacks, like this one during the invasion of Sicily.
LIBRARY OF CONGRESS

As the massive Axis counterattack against the Allied landing in Sicily began to lose steam, British and American forces began to push out from their narrow beachheads near Gela to the much more valuable targets of Catania that sprawled on Sicily's east coast almost exactly halfway between Cape Passero on the very southern tip of the island and Messina near the northern tip, and also Palermo, the ancient capital of multiple invading cultures that attempted at least partially to subsume Sicily into their particular empire or state.

Gen. Harold Alexander, who had been given the unenviable task of harnessing Patton and Montgomery to the same team, carefully orchestrated a plan that would allow an Allied breakout from their Gela beachhead with a steady expansion of territory until the defenders were pushed into such a small enclave that they would be forced to surrender.

The main spoils of war in Operation Husky were a string of Sicilian air bases that in Allied hands would allow longer-range attacks against mainland Italy than could be accomplished from the current forward base at Malta, and the capture of the Sicilian ports of Palermo, Catania, and Syracuse, all capable of handling over one thousand tons of cargo a day followed by a march on Messina, which could handle five thousand tons of shipping a day and would be the launch pad for a drive toward the Italian mainland. Less than seventy-two hours after the Germans launched their offensive intended to throw the Allied invaders into the sea, British and American forces had pushed forward far enough to establish a battle line that extended roughly one hundred miles from the south central seacoast town of Palma di Montechiaro to the east coast shore town of Priolo on the Gulf of Augusta, just north of Syracuse, and the original landing site of Gela now becoming the center point of the line. General Alexander had to alternate between unleashing and tethering Patton and Montgomery, as both army commanders eagerly pushed toward the first major piece of the contest, the historical capital of Sicily, the city of Palermo.

Patton's front man for the emerging race was Maj. Gen. Lucian Truscott, commander of the 3rd Infantry Division. Truscott was almost literally a battered old war horse. He was nearing fifty but looked twenty years older, spoke with a rasp that sounded like he had swallowed acid, and perhaps he had—he ostensibly had ingested an entire bottle of carbolic acid as a child when he mistook the contents for soda pop. He had established a career as a third grade school teacher before the Army offered a better career path. Truscott rivaled William Darby for colorful demeanor, even if he looked old enough to be Darby's grandfather, and he instituted a new hyper-fast marching style called the Truscott Trot that covered ground at a speed nearly 50 percent higher than similar infantry units.

Joining General Truscott among the emergent American heroes of the battle for Sicily was a young man who, unlike Truscott, actually looked much younger than he really was but had emerged from the same hardscrabble background that was common in much of rural America before Pearl Harbor. Audie Murphy was born in 1925 on a farm near Kingston, Texas, and long before he neared full adulthood had falsified his birth certificate to enlist in the Army at seventeen. The Sicilian campaign became one long background resume for a future film star, as he alternated between sniper duty, clambering into burning enemy tanks to turn the machine guns on the crew, and eventually emerging as a hugely popular sergeant and then lieutenant with a subsequent Medal of Honor and the distinction of starring as himself in his postwar film biography *To Hell*

The Anglo-American invasion of Sicily marked the first step in the fall of Fascist Italy. A US Army jeep can be seen from the ruins of a Roman amphitheater in the vicinity of Syracuse.
LIBRARY OF CONGRESS

and Back. Since General Truscott had, at sixteen, claimed to be eighteen to enter a college teacher training course and then falsely claimed to be a high school graduate with a year of college when he applied for officer candidate school, the battle for Sicily would be well populated with tall tale folk heroes in William Darby, Lucien Truscott, and Audie Murphy, with a huge inventory of plot lines for postwar films about their exploits.

Patton was rapidly gaining a band of larger-than-life subordinates to help win his race with Montgomery, as the two Allied armies alternately sped and crawled toward the ancient capital city of Sicily, the metropolis of Palermo. Patton exhorted his men to minimize stopping for any reason as British and American forces began to outflank the German defenders and sped toward the seaside of the Gulf of Palermo. While Patton technically followed Allied orders by assigning Gen. Omar Bradley's II Corps to act as a flank guard for the advancing British/Canadian 30th Corps, he also created a special assault force designated the Provisional Corps and assigned Maj. Gen. Geoffrey Keys to make a run to beat the British into the Sicilian capital city. Keys's composite of the 504th Parachute Infantry Regiment, the 2nd Armored Division, William Darby's Force X Rangers, and the fast-moving "Truscott Trot" members of the 3rd Division reached the outskirts of Palermo on July 22. Luckily for the advancing Allied units, Palermo's defenses were designed to repel an enemy attack from the sea, not to challenge an invader from the mountainous land side. At a loss of roughly three hundred casualties, Patton won his race with Montgomery as the Italian garrison suffered three thousand casualties and an enormous surrender tally of fifty-three thousand defenders, not counting thousands of other defenders who were simply encouraged by American officials to "self-demobilize" and go home. Six days later, American engineers completed a herculean effort to remove scuttled Italian vessels from the harbor and put the port on a 30 percent operational level which would be enough to support Patton's push toward the ultimate goal of Messina.

The Allied advance through Sicily was alternately exhausting and exhilarating for British and American ground troops. *Life* magazine's correspondent, Jack Beldan, accompanied Darby's Rangers on their "walk in the sun," and noted the special agony of clambering up and down a seemingly endless succession of hills as, "The men advanced stumbling, crawling and gasping toward the crest of each hill after noting the remains of retreating Italian defenders." As the Americans closed in on the town of Butera, German officers attempted to form Italian soldiers into a defensive line along the main street of the town. While the Italian defenders attempted to surrender to the Americans, the German "advisors" opened fire as their allies staged a running retreat. By dawn the next day, Butera had changed hands from a German-occupied town to an American-occupied town, and famished American soldiers were downing plates of half-eaten spaghetti in household dining rooms where Germans had started the meal.

The liberation of any Italian community, from Palermo to Enna, brought with it a wide range of surprises based on whether the Germans had decided to run or fight. When the American forces reached Enna, a huge crowd of Italians suddenly opened their ranks to a young woman who, speaking unaccented American English, quickly became the spokesperson for the entire population. The woman noted that she had left her home state of West Virginia a decade earlier to help care for elderly relatives in Sicily, and she now pleaded for American rations to feed her fellow Italian citizens who had been reduced to three slices of bread and two ounces of macaroni a day when the Germans appropriated most of the local supplies for their own use.

As the American troops shared their rations with the townspeople and made it clear that they were not the rapacious monsters described in Axis propaganda, the entire mood of both sides began to change. Fear turned to frivolity when the town mayor was offered a stick of chewing gum by an American soldier and subsequently swallowed the whole piece, as he had no idea what chewing gum actually was.

While the Germans were in no hurry to write off all of Sicily in the immediate future, the high command had little interest in fighting to the last bullet for the island. Wehrmacht snipers, booby traps, harassment fire, and air raids were designed to slow down the Allied advance across the island. The Germans fought a slowly backpedaling campaign as the Axis and Allied forces dueled on ground that was always a bit closer to Messina than the previous engagement. German combat units spent most of July gradually retreating in a northwest direction toward Messina, while artillery batteries challenged the Allied advance with a parallel diminishment of Allied naval support as the battle shifted toward the Straits of Messina. Yet, while the battle line shifted daily at a relatively modest formal advance for the Anglo-Americans, the political reality of Sicily and the rest of the Fascist Italian state was beginning to change much more rapidly.

Members of the senior leadership of the Fascist inner circle were now shocked at the prospect that the Allies would most likely storm into mainland Italy in the very near future. Members of the Grand Council issued a directive to Mussolini that he was expected to attend a "frank and open" session of the body. Much of the membership slammed a stunned Duce when they insisted that entry into the current war was "ill advised," and after an emotional twelve-hour debate, the Duce was stripped of his office by King Victor Emmanuel and replaced by Field Marshal Pietro Badoglio, who issued a tepid pledge to Hitler that Italy had every intention of remaining in the Axis alliance while authorizing the initiation of secret peace talks with the Allies.

Now the German defenders and their remaining Italian allies glanced ever more frequently over their shoulders at the harbor of Messina, while dodging bombs and bullets from forty squadrons of Allied attack planes that seemed to rule the skies.

The Axis presence in Sicily was beginning to evaporate as Allied units were gathering up over three thousand (mostly Italian) prisoners a day, while American corps commander Gen. Omar Bradley issued orders that in most cases the new prisoners were to be immediately paroled to save the need for feeding them. As the Italian lines collapsed, even the most prestigious German units, such as the Hermann Goering Division, began to abandon carefully constructed defensive positions to retreat back to a hopefully more secure line of defense.

Yet, as the Germans watched with professional distaste as the Italian units simply evaporated one after another, there was every confidence in the Wehrmacht ranks that they were not to be sacrificed wholesale as little more than pawns, though they did believe that high command orders that anyone who panicked or retreated without orders would be shot. With that in mind, their best play was simply to assume that the high command had some plan to extricate these invaluable men from a less than supremely valuable island.

While Hitler dithered between ordering a withdrawal from Sicily or a last-ditch defense of the island, the senior field commander, Gen. Hans-Valentin Hube, began to implement a plan that would prevent Sicily from becoming a Wehrmacht graveyard as had happened in Tunisia. The withdrawal from front lines back to Messina and then across the straits to mainland Italy would be unhurried, measured, and worthy of the German genius for detail. Hube, with strong backing on the part of theater commander Field Marshal Albert Kesserling, issued an evacuation plan on August 2 that would begin a retrograde movement from behind a new defensive line called the Tottorici Line. The battered and mauled 15th Panzergrenadier Division would become the first German division to be evacuated back to Calabria on the mainland while German demolition experts initiated a frenzy of destruction to delay the Allied advance.

One of few remaining Axis advantages in the later stages of the battle was control of a defensive line centered on the storied high ground of Mount Etna, which loomed above the battlefield like a classical era god watching tiny humans battle among themselves.

Montgomery suggested to Patton that the British Eighth Army's XXX Corps hook left around the towering mountain, while Patton's Seventh Army would push along the coastal highway at its base in order to trap the enemy in the middle. While Patton insisted to his unit commanders that the capture of Sicily was "a horse race in which the prestige of the United States Army is at stake; we must take Messina before the British," the German high command viewed the looming heights as simply one more natural obstacle that could delay the Allies long enough to extricate the German army.

The Patton-Montgomery rivalry was now beginning to pick up a new head of steam as two personally brave commanders began to lose track of who was actually the real enemy they were fighting. Both commanders could be insufferable to anyone caught in their ever-growing orbits. During his schooldays, Montgomery had once settled an argument by attempting to set his rival on fire, while Patton had added spice to a visit to a field hospital by slapping and threatening to execute two soldiers who showed no visible wounds but were actually quite ill with malaria. Montgomery's gaffe was probably less career threatening, as the incident occurred before he entered the military service. Patton, on the other hand, was censured by influential newspapers and congressional personnel and was fortunate to only lose command of a major unit on D-Day, when a

Members of the American invasion force on Sicily were merely the latest in a long list of invaders of this ancient island. Here, a US soldier (left) mimics the pose of his Italian counterpart as depicted in a World War I memorial in Brolo, Sicily.
LIBRARY OF CONGRESS

significant number of prominent Americans were demanding that Eisenhower send his maverick general home in disgrace.

While General Patton attempted to salvage his career after the hospital slapping fiasco, General Hube, who would die in an Eastern Front plane crash the following spring, continued to implement his gradual fallback, as Axis units leapfrogged ever closer to Messina and its vital ferry terminal. As the Germans retreated eastward toward the sea, a new temporary stop line was created near the towns of Adrano and Troiana that sat astride one of the major roads into Messina. The Hermann Goering and 15th Panzergrenadier Divisions now stood outside this key position, and August 1943, began with an American thrust to push the defenders aside. The action erupted when elements of the First Army Division, aided by units loaned to the Big Red One from other units, smashed into a German defensive line that was far stronger than initially anticipated. Patton's close friend, Col. Paddy Flint, led advance units into what emerged as a clever German trap. Flint was a colorful showman who entered the battle bare-chested, except for a black silk scarf that he insisted was his best good luck charm. This former horse cavalry officer was then transformed into a latter-day George Armstrong Custer as he stood upright blasting away with his M-1 rifle as he dared the Germans to kill him. German bullets may have missed this particular target, but Paddy Flint's command was significantly whittled down and fortunate to survive as a fighting unit.

The opening days of August now produced a grim slugging match as the Germans backpedaled toward Messina's ferry docks, while a diverse Allied assault force, including Canadians, North African Goums Mountain troops, and other special troops dueled with ever resilient Germans who were determined not to lose their only path back to the Fatherland.

One of the most high-profile casualties of the drive toward Messina was a general who could match Paddy Flint in the drama department. Terry "Terrible" Allen was the embodiment of the First Infantry Division claim to unique status in the American Army. Allen was a devout Catholic in a predominantly Protestant senior command; he married a beauty queen, drank too much, and had aged enormously in his relatively short time in senior command. Allen then managed to look a gift horse in the mouth when he angrily rejected an offer of a temporary return to the United States to train an entire Army corps for future operations.

Allen had reached the point where he felt that he was the living embodiment of the Big Red One and was cheered on by his senior lieutenant, Brig. Gen. Theodore Roosevelt Jr., who was also cantankerous and looked a decade or two older than his real age. This pair now seemed to be fighting in their own private army and were aging far more rapidly than most of their counterparts, with Roosevelt destined to die of a heart attack soon after he landed on D-Day the following June. Ironically, just as Allen achieved the fame of appearing on the cover of *Time* magazine for his exploits in Sicily, he was on his way home for at least a temporary session in a personal hell of stateside duty.

While American senior officers attempted to finesse the banishment of Allen and Roosevelt, two of the most famous generals in the Army, a German nobleman who had been spared from Adolf Hitler's disgust for German generals emerging from the nobility was about to secure the Führer's admiration on the docks of Messina. Baron/General Gustave von Lieberstein, commander of the 2nd Landing Flotilla, was emerging as the key player in a Dunkirk-like evacuation called Operation Instruction Course. This commander, in league with Col. Ernst Baade, commander of the Messina Straits, was appointed on July 26, 1943, to evacuate the entire Axis army from Messina to the Italian mainland glistening in the summer sun two miles across the strait. The baron's ultimate weapon in this task was the Siebel Ferry, a craft designed to shuttle loads of up to twenty-five railway cars along three routes across the three miles of water that separated Sicily from the mainland. Ironically Fritz Siebel had been tasked to develop the ferries for the more offensive-purposed Operation Sea Lion, the planned German invasion of Britain in 1940. Now the German military was getting an opportunity to try out Siebel's craft in an evacuation instead of an invasion.

The ferries were powered by souped-up aircraft engines and comprised of a series of pontoons built around a central cabin on the craft. While the top speed of 8 knots was hardly in the same league as a power boat, the crafts were extremely buoyant, difficult to sink, and would now become the centerpiece of a plan to save the German garrison on Sicily from the fate of their counterparts in Tunisia.

One of the ironies of Operation Instruction Course, beyond its decidedly nonmilitary codename, was that in this particular case the Führer neither authorized nor forbade the evacuation. Thus, Baade, with total support from senior German field marshal Alfred Jodl and Kesserling, simply did an end run around the Führer's inner circle and initiated a German version of the Dunkirk evacuation. As a massive array of almost five hundred German antiaircraft guns kept Allied planes too high to easily destroy a fairly elusive target, the initial plan of a nighttime-only evacuation was expanded to twenty-four hours a day, and over a thirteen-day period from August 3 to August 16, 101,000 Axis soldiers, ten thousand vehicles, two hundred cannons, fifty tanks, and seventeen thousand tons of supplies were ferried to the relative safety of the mainland. German losses were far less than those suffered by the British at Dunkirk three years earlier, as only seven German craft went to the bottom of Messina Strait with minimal loss of personnel. As Patton's Seventh Army forces began to close in on Messina, the last remaining German defenders of the 29th Panzer Division simply seemed to evaporate in front of them. In the predawn hours of August 17, a reinforced platoon of Company L of the 7th Infantry Division, moved tentatively toward the looming buildings that marked the outer edge of Messina. Patton arrived later in the morning and held an official surrender ceremony in the center of the city just as British tanks arrived on the scene with groceries contributed from their commander to Patton for winning a "jolly good race." At the same time, two miles across the straits, Hans-Valentin Hube was receiving his own congratulations from German officers for his role in evacuating most of the German garrison from what might have ended up as another Stalingrad or "Tunisgrad." The Anglo-American Allies had knocked Italy out of the Axis, and at least temporarily, Benito Mussolini was under house arrest by his own soldiers. The American Army had lost just over two thousand men killed and six thousand wounded in Operation Husky, with a relatively similar casualty total among the British units of its Eighth Army. The Mediterranean Sea was now primarily an Allied lake, the German progression in the Soviet Union had been reversed, and the Axis had effectively been winnowed down to a dual alliance between Japan and Germany, neither of which had any significant ability to assist the other as they were squeezed from multiple directions. As the German high command planned the evacuation from Sicily, Adolf Hitler called off his massive summer offensive, Operation Citadel, that had been launched around Kursk, as even he began to realize that the Wehrmacht was simply not powerful enough to annihilate the vast alliance that had grouped against him.

The Allied Mediterranean campaign was about to shift from the island of Sicily to the peninsula that was mainland Italy, which was technically

The Allied capture of Messina was greeted by most Italians as a liberation, not a conquest. This photo shows villagers returning to their homes after the Germans' departure.
LIBRARY OF CONGRESS

no longer home to an enemy power. Yet those tens of thousands of evacuated German soldiers still felt that the war was far from lost, and the main prize of Rome still loomed hundreds of miles and numerous mountain ranges and surging rivers away from the Anglo-Americans, at that moment briefly enjoying the fruits of victory in the seemingly unending Sicilian sunshine.

CHAPTER 9

Whirlwind over the Reich

ALMOST IMMEDIATELY AFTER THE SHOCK OF PEARL HARBOR TURNED into a largely unanimous sense of rage and desire for revenge on the part of the American people, the old ghosts of World War I temporarily dominated the conversation about the new conflict. American Army personnel were still called "doughboys," not "GIs"; the "soup bowl" British-style helmets were still standard headgear in the opening battles; and large numbers of combat soldiers still carried 1903 model Springfield bolt-action rifles. Fighters were still designated as "pursuit" planes, and battleships were still referred to as "dreadnoughts," while Gary Cooper won plaudits playing World War I hero Sgt. Alvin York.

Yet in one crucial aspect, this "Great War" reference point was notably and crucially absent. When the United States entered hostilities against Germany in 1917, their French and British allies still controlled two-thirds of France, along an extended trench line, and newly arriving "Yanks" could be transported from ports to the battle line in a still largely Allied-controlled French nation. The Americans could become acclimated to the conflict in relatively safe rear areas and, in turn, be pulled back from combat for rest and recreation. However, in this new war, the German enemy controlled the Continent all the way to the English Channel, and until a massive Allied expeditionary force could land in northwest Europe, the only way in which the German war machine could be compromised was through the use of long-range bombers operating over enemy territory for most of their mission with little aid expected until they were back on the British side of the English Channel. Thus, until the planned 1944 invasion of mainland Europe could be initiated, the only significant offensive operations that could be launched against the heart of Hitler's stolen empire would be dependent upon massive numbers of American multi-engine long-range bombers joining the already operational British bomber offensive on German-occupied northwest Europe.

By early 1943, British and American "bomber barons" were forming an alliance that would attempt to prove that a massive routing of material and personnel by heavy bombers and escorting fighters might, in a best-case scenario, so badly damage the enemy ability to conduct war that ground troops would merely be needed to accept the surrender of the German army already pulverized from the sky. The American Army Air Force and the British Royal Air Force were now united in a joint campaign to demonstrate that ground combat was simply a mopping up operation after the sky warriors had effectively cleared the board of enemy combat forces. Yet, this transatlantic alliance did not erase a still significant professional debate between the Royal Air Force and the US Army Air Force as to exactly how this reality could be best achieved.

The major significant contested issue between the allied air services had immediate consequences for the prosecution of the war. Early in the conflict, the Royal Air Force Bomber Command had attempted daylight bombing raids on Axis targets, and the losses had been staggering. This early disaster had prompted a shift to nighttime "area bombing" that centered around the theory that at least some bombs dropped under the cover of darkness would hit at least some worthwhile enemy targets. When the American Amy Air Force entered the fray, the Yanks brought with them the highly touted Norden bombsight, which utilized a primitive computer system to provide technically such accuracy that an American bombardier could drop bombs from huge heights directly into a "pickle barrel." These claims were hugely exaggerated, as true "smart bombs" were still decades in the future, but since the British war leaders were delighted to finally have the fabulous manufacturing potential of the United States behind them, the Allies simply passed on a debate about the value of daylight and night bombing and announced the intention of "round the clock bombing," a phrase that even the skeptical Josef Stalin liked immensely. In theory, the Third Reich and its occupied territories would be subject to both daylight and night bombing, therefore stretching both interceptor squadrons and antiaircraft batteries to near constant combat. The first significant target city for this new concept of aerial warfare was the German port city of Hamburg, which housed enormous shipbuilding enterprises, tank factories, and aircraft assembly plants with an especially prominent position in naval construction in a factory complex that had already built the mighty battleship *Bismarck*, and dozens of U-boats. Because the naval construction factories would be much more difficult to relocate than the bomber or tank factories, the city was honeycombed with antiaircraft defenses centered around over four hundred guns from standard antiaircraft batteries to huge 128mm flak tower weapons, all supported by twenty-four searchlight batteries crammed into a city the size of Boston.

On Saturday afternoon, July 24, 1943, these massive defense batteries would be put to their ultimate test as 871 British bombers droned overhead in the opening round of a potential Allied "knockout blow" against the port city. Because the city had so far escaped serious Allied bomber raids, more than a few residents believed that their community's close ties with Britain and its historical and cultural significance had made it a low priority for Allied attacks. Yet now Lancaster bombers were clearly overhead, dodging flak batteries and the first waves of Luftwaffe fighters in an hour-long procession dropping their lethal cargoes and generally successfully dodging the antiaircraft batteries as only three of their fleet sputtered in a downward spiral toward the city.

In the often *Alice in Wonderland* environment of World War II aerial missions, on the other side of the North Sea and English Channel, American aircrews were enjoying films, drinks, and female companionship while their British counterparts were fighting for their lives. Gen. Ira Eaker, the dynamic thirty-seven-year-old commander of the American bombardment fleet, was determined to prove that the British abandonment of daylight bombing was a mistake. Eaker and the vast assemblage of men serving under him in Britain actually experienced a very different war than their RAF counterparts. The British allies and the Italian and German adversaries all served in totally independent air organizations that took no orders from their respective nations' armies or navies. Yet in the United States, neither the Army nor the Navy had any great desire to release one of the most glamorous branches of each service from some level of control by the nation's ground and sea services. A barely tolerable compromise had been approved by Franklin Roosevelt in which the "Air Corps" would be redesignated the Army Air Force for the duration of the current war and would then receive total independence a year after the final peace had been established. In turn, the Army Air Force would be permitted to utilize the services of famous fashion designers to produce glamorous uniforms; the organization would be allowed to snatch away the highest score achievers on the service entrance intelligence tests and could grab for the service such high-profile personalities and glamorous actors as James Stewart and Clark Gable. Hollywood was now churning out exciting Air Force–centered fare such as *Bombardier*, *Aerial Gunner*, and *Air Force* in which top stars donned Air Force uniforms while squiring the silver screen's most alluring actresses in films that mixed action, recruiting messages for the Air Force, and romantic entanglements galore.

While home front American civilians thrilled to the stylized plots of the steady wave of Air Force films, Arnold, Eaker, and their staffs were now almost totally convinced that precision daylight bombing was the "secret weapon" that would defeat Germany without the need for a bloody and problematic amphibious invasion of the European continent. Thus, the Royal Air Force plan for a series of American daytime raids on Hamburg would provide a perfect opportunity to prove the value of precision day bombing against the same geographic location.

So, while the crews of the RAF bombers rested by day, two combat wings of American heavy bombers droned over the North Sea, forty minutes ahead of the main American attack force. They flew within fifty miles of the German coast, feinted toward the city of Kiel, and then abruptly changed course as enemy fighters responded to the thrust. Then, 323 Flying Fortresses, droning over the sea after a rare early afternoon lift-off, made landfall a bit farther down the coast and appeared over Hamburg. These planes had taken off from airfields in Wales (which many geographically challenged American aircrews believed was actually a part of England), and then reaching the Continent, swooped over Heligoland, Cuxhaven, and eventually the southern suburbs of Hamburg. This complex series of feints was made even more elaborate when still another American bomber force approached German-occupied Denmark and set off attack warnings over a large segment of the Reich's air defense system. The average American bomber spent only twelve minutes flying over the actual city of Hamburg, but the powerful 30mm cannons deployed by Luftwaffe interceptors damaged seventy-eight of the 109 raiders, including sixteen of seventeen aircraft in a single unlucky squadron. Yet, as the most unlucky of these intruders spiraled downward, both attackers and defenders exaggerated losses and gains, with the Germans chuckling at the tendency of the intruders to hit either grazing cow herds or the empty sea and the Americans celebrating the sinking of the under construction thirty-six-thousand-ton cruiser *General Artigas*, along with serious damage inflicted on a number of armament factories and a construction yard for U-boats.

While the Anglo-American air assault on Hamburg was publicized as an excellent example of the destructive power of the day/night "round the clock bombing" that, at the moment, was being advertised to Josef Stalin as the Western Allies early contribution to the projected two-front assault on Nazi Germany, a combination of American civilians and military officers were cooking up the possibility of adding an entirely different dimension to the aerial assault on the Third Reich by striking directly at the enemy's fuel production facilities. Tanks and planes without fuel were effectively useless artifacts, and a disproportionate amount of energy/petroleum was produced in an increasingly reluctant partner of the Axis Alliance.

Operation Tidal Wave soon emerged as a daring plan to dramatically reduce enemy fuel supplies. The genesis of this plan emerged from a decidedly nonmilitary source. Harry Hopkins, presidential advisor and semi-permanent White House guest, spent much of the war period in rapidly declining health that, if nothing else, gave Franklin Roosevelt's closest advisor ample time to ruminate about daring operations that might significantly shorten the war. In 1943, one of Hopkins's major issues was the desirability of launching a highly publicized raid on the German war machine that promised the same headline-grabbing impact as the April 1942 air raid on Tokyo.

Hopkins sat for hours chain-smoking and planning in his office down the hall from the president and carefully noted that the Romanian city of Ploesti ran neck and neck with Titusville, Pennsylvania, as the initial source of petroleum refining, and unlike the Pennsylvania town, had grown into the single most important fuel producer in the entire German empire. The Romanian government was technically an ally of Germany, mainly because of fear of an expansionist Soviet Union, and the German units stationed in Romania were relatively low profile and at least outwardly correct in their behavior toward the population. However, much of the populace still had positive feelings about Britain and the United States and hoped to merely survive the war and look forward to a better life in a postwar world.

The hope of simply keeping the war outside Romania began to fade when a team of American Army Air Force analysts came to the amazing conclusion that a successful surprise air attack on the Ploesti petroleum production complex would destroy over one-third of the entire oil supply of the Third Reich and shorten the war by a minimum of six months. The concept of this operation gained increasing traction, and when the possible operation was discussed as an even more daring ground-level assault that would leave enemy interceptors striking against empty air after the intruders were initially identified on radar scopes, the plan received final approval.

Initial enthusiasm for Operation Tidal Wave might have been tempered if Allied planners had received additional intelligence on two key aspects of the Ploesti oil refining operation. First, there was no single refinery in the town. There were actually more than a dozen refineries scattered throughout the town and far into the foothills of the adjacent mountains ringing the city. In an era when "smart" bombs were still decades in the future, there was little likelihood of causing fatal damage in a single raid.

The second complicating factor could only have been appreciated by Allied planners if they had access to Scottish census records of several generations earlier. The Luftwaffe officer who had ultimate control over the protection of the Ploesti oil fields against Allied attack had the very un-Germanic name of Col. Douglas Pitcairn and was descended from a prominent Perthshire Scottish family that split apart in a Catholic-Protestant religious feud soon after a member of the family was the naval officer who had first sighted Pitcairn Island, the landing place of the mutinous HMS *Bounty*, in the South Pacific. The feud over religious doctrine prompted Colonel Pitcairn's direct ancestors to emigrate to Germany, and Douglas returned to Britain as a Luftwaffe fighter pilot in the air battle over London in 1940. Now this carnival of irony was about to extend even further during the summer of 1943 when Pitcairn would match wits with his primary American adversary, Gen. Uzal Ent, commander of the 9th Bombing Command in the Air Force, the scion of a German family that had left Germany due to a recurring religious persecution for its own beliefs. Now Pitcairn's army of antiaircraft batteries and interceptor planes would be matched up against American heavy bombs with colorful squadron names such as Liberandos, Eight Balls, the Traveling Circus, the Pyramidders, and the Sky Scorpions, all preparing to swoop down the foothills of the Carpathian Mountains for a final sixty-mile sprint toward the vital airfields and Pitcairn's cleverly organized welcome. Ironically, Pitcairn's counterpart in the American Army Air Force, Brig. Gen. Gordon Seville, had as much confidence as his Luftwaffe rival that the mission would turn into a disaster. The plan essentially called for a twenty-seven-hundred-mile mission by three hundred bombers needing perfect navigation just to arrive over their targets, which were seven oil refineries scattered over a broad landscape and yet requiring pinpoint timing and accuracy, a mission that Seville called "ridiculous and suicidal."

The mission began to face serious obstacles before the first bomber even took off. Due to the growing needs of the Sicilian campaign, the bomb groups were slated to be transferred to Operation Husky and General Ent asked his supervisors to at least permit a high-altitude mission. General Eisenhower then joined the growing legion of doubters and requested General Brereton, Ninth Air Force commander, to cancel the mission. The request was promptly refused.

On August 1, 1943, 187 heavy bombers assembled for the launch of "Tidal Wave." Eleven pilots quickly aborted before takeoff, and the remaining aircraft followed General Ent into the air. As the Liberandos droned toward Romania, aircraft waggled their wings signaling engine problems, until only 164 aircraft remained when the attack force arrived over Romanian airspace.

Douglas Pitcairn and his staff had assembled one of the most powerful antiaircraft arrays in Europe, centered around three hundred antiaircraft guns, many of which had been cleverly hidden or disguised. Guns were positioned under innocent-looking prop haystacks in fields, deployed on water towers and church steeples, and even placed on a high speed "flak train" bristling with guns and able to keep pace with the low-flying bombers. Raiders that made it through this kind of ground fire would then be pounced upon by 120 Luftwaffe fighters supported by two hundred Romanian counterparts.

The initially planned seven-air-group attack was reduced to only one bomber group that actually managed to arrive over the target on its assigned course and on time. The 98th Bomb Group was commanded by Col. John Kane who, thanks to the enormous popularity of the "Buck Rogers" newspaper comic strips and recent movie serial starring superstar swimmer Larry "Buster" Crabbe, was automatically nicknamed "Killer Kane" after Rogers's cinema and comic strip archenemy.

"Killer" Kane searched futilely for the other groups and then took careful note of what appeared below. The group commander dodged the aerial balloons equipped with cables capable of slicing off aircraft wings, barely missed two-hundred-foot smokestacks, and watched in terror as his left wing caught fire. Now the flames of crashing planes intermingled with the fires belching from at least some of the oil refineries, and soon the dry late summer fields were catching fire from the Liberandos that had crashed during the attack. Fifty-five of the surviving raiders limped to marginal safety with severe damage while five hundred crewmembers would receive Purple Hearts, either in Allied hospitals, after release from Axis prison camps, or posthumously. "Killer Kane" would join three other raiders in receiving the Medal of Honor, and General Brereton insisted that the raid had knocked out 60 percent of Ploesti's oil production capabilities. Yet in a final irony, the shortage of transportation assets to ship the fuel had forced officials to shutter 50 percent of their production facilities, which now reopened quickly to make up the shortfall. The Third Reich had no shortage of slave laborers, and ten thousand of these unfortunate "guests" of German aggression were quickly transferred to Ploesti to repair the damaged factories, while the carnage among Tidal Wave raiders discouraged any imminent follow-up missions. Yet new bombers and crews were still pouring into Britain, and Anglo-American attention now shifted to the concept of destroying the German fighter plane industry before the intruders even left the factory to attack the Allied bomber streams.

One of the key proponents of this new targeting system was an Anglo-American soldier/airman named Col. Richard Doyly Hughes. Hughes had experienced a true transatlantic upbringing as he was born in Salt Lake City to a visiting British couple, was educated in British boarding schools and Sandhurst, served as an officer in the British army in the Great War, and then moved back to America just in time for the Great Crash of 1929. By 1943, Hughes had the distinction of holding concurrent commissions in both the American Army Air Force and the Royal Air Force, and despite his slightly irregular status, had spent much of his time seeking some fatal weak spot in the Luftwaffe air operation. As the generally recognized leading expert on targeting enemy resources, Colonel Hughes had been strongly opposed to Tidal Wave as too complex and under strength in the proposed number of raiders. Now, this unusual hybrid airman wearing an American uniform filled with British decorations carefully studied his maps of Germany, crunched long lists of numbers, and came to the conclusion that Allied bombing missions would be exponentially more successful if only German fighters could be destroyed while they were being constructed instead of in aerial combat. Amazingly, while Allied fighter plane production was scattered all over British and American factory complexes, the Germans had centered over half of their fighter production and vital ball bearing and engine manufacturing in only three cities, Regensburg for the planes and Wiener-Neustadt and Schweinfurt for the ball bearings that were essential parts of every engine. If Tidal Wave had failed to utterly destroy the enemy aircraft fuel production, the next priority was to destroy the planes themselves before they ever took to the skies. All of the production facilities were centered in southeastern Germany and Austria, two regions that had seldom experienced previous air attacks and, therefore, had relatively few interceptor squadrons.

The Anglo-American air strategist quickly gained an important ally in Col. Curtis LeMay, commanding officer of the 305th Bomb Group. LeMay was just beginning to gain recognition as an outstanding innovator in the area of bomber attack formations, while, at the same time, caricatured for the ever-present cigar clenched between his teeth which actually covered a paralysis of key facial muscles that would otherwise droop. A generation later he would emerge as the hugely controversial orchestrator of nuclear and conventional attack plans at the peak of the Cold War, urging John F. Kennedy to launch a preemptive first strike at the peak of the Cuban Missile Crisis and satirized as Jack D. Ripper in Stanley Kubrick's dark comedy, *Dr. Strangelove*. Even in 1943, LeMay had already acquired an ever-lengthening list of sarcastic nicknames, such as "the Demon," "Bombs Away LeMay," and "The Big Cigar." Yet on the morning of August 17, 1943, the controversial bomber enthusiast was leading a force of newly arrived B-17 F bombers in one of the most complicated attack missions up to that point in the war. The 4th Bomber Wing was on its way to attack the Messerschmitt fighter production factory in Regensburg, which would immediately ignite a massive Luftwaffe attempt to tear into the Allied planes on their way back to England. However, the new planes were equipped with special extra fuel cells embedded into the internal wing tanks which gave the aircraft enough fuel to be able to fly to North Africa, a direction which the enemy defenders would never expect.

The second surprise for the German defenders was that the American First Bomber Wing would follow LeMay's force by a mere fifteen minutes, take exactly the same route to Regensburg, and then, at the last possible moment, change course for Schweinfurt, just as the enemy interceptors ran low on fuel. As a final diversion to limit the ability of the Luftwaffe fighters to focus on the Regensburg and Schweinfurt raids, a massive force of both British- and American-crewed B-25 Mitchell and B-26 Marauder medium bombers would launch a raid on German coastal fighter airfields with the raiders escorted by a huge wing of 150 British Spitfires.

The battle of Regensburg-Schweinfurt would go down in aerial combat history as one of the most evenly matched, hard fought aerial battles in World War II. In essence, just enough of the Allied attack plan worked to result in a multidimensional aerial barroom brawl that saw planes explode across the landscape in huge numbers. The first major glitch in the Allied plan occurred when the follow-up 1st Bomber Wing assault force took off from Britain five hours late and failed to initially divert the enemy planes from attacking the earlier arriving 4th Bomber Wing. Three hundred Luftwaffe interceptors covered the skies above the American intruders and waited for the short-range escort fighters to run low on fuel and return home. Then, twin-engine, rocket-firing ME-110s swooped down as one row of planes followed the next unit below them down to the attack. As twenty-four Flying Fortresses spun earthward in a final plunge, far below German technical personnel turned on artificial fog generators to reduce visibility of the four vital ball bearing factories. Explosions erupted throughout the town, and, amazingly three factories were actually hit by American bombs that badly damaged building exteriors but largely failed to destroy the far more valuable machine tools that actually produced the ball bearings. Yet the mixed results of the aerial battle were proven out over at Regensburg, where key elements of the assembly process were actually hit badly enough to cost the Luftwaffe three weeks of fighter production or nearly one thousand ME-109 planes. Ultimately, at a cost of thirty-six destroyed fighters, the German Air Force shot down sixty Flying Fortresses with six hundred extensively trained crewmembers now dead or in Luftwaffe prison camps.

Yet, despite appalling losses to American aircrews, the Regensburg-Schweinfurt raid did result in the deaths of two of the most talented adversaries that the Allied air forces had encountered. First, the aerial duel included the most prestigious and successful German fighter group, JG 26, led by Major "Wutz" Galland, the brother of chief of fighters, Adolf Galland, who eventually became the chief of the West German air force during the Cold War. "Wutz" Galland flew into an aerial joust with American ace Herbert Zemke, who was piloting a P-47 Thunderbolt which was as rugged and heavy as his opponent's two engine ME-110. As Galland's squadron flew low looking for American bombers, his unit was hit from above by Zemke's squadron, which blazed away and landed fatal hits on the German commander's plane. Then, as reports of the damage to Regensburg fighter production facilities streamed into Berlin, Hans Jeschonnek, the dynamic young chief of staff of the Luftwaffe, badgered by Hermann Goering's charges of weakness, committed suicide.

Thus, by 1943, despite sometimes crippling losses and ever-lengthening killed in action lists of young British and American pilots and aircrew, the Allies were extending some measure of revenge for the tens of thousands of British citizens who had died under the bombs of Hitler's Blitz in 1940-41. A late summer article in *Life* magazine focused on the Allied bombing of Hamburg as the first major step in an aerial offensive on the Third Reich that would only grow in intensity as the year continued. Titled "Hamburg in Ruins, Germany's Biggest Seaport Is Destroyed," the article noted with grim satisfaction, "Hamburg has ceased to exist as a town. Hamburg means a journey between corpses which lie everywhere in the street and even hang in the trees, thrown there by the blasts." Citing both Allied air force sources and the reports sent by observers from neutral countries, this article insisted, "In six days the Allied air forces dropped a total of 8,000 tons of bombs—a greater weight than has ever been dropped on any city in history. A Swedish reporter has reported that steam shovels are being used to dig mass cemeteries. A Swiss account notes, 'Suddenly the sirens howl—the trams stop abruptly. For 90 minutes the bombs drop uninterrupted in the city's center, harbors and beaches. After the alert the sky is red as far as they eye can see. At 9:00 AM it is still night because of the enormous dust and smoke clouds which are hiding the sun. The streets are flooded. Already the sirens howling to announce a daylight attack; this is Sunday morning. The devil's concert begins in the shipyards. The electricity, water and gas supplies are all cut off; entire blocks from 400 to 500 flats crumble.'" American airmen had paid an enormous price to make "round the clock" bombing a reality. Yet, as both graveyards and German prisoner of war camps filled at an ever-growing pace, an aerial siege on the Reich had now begun.

CHAPTER 10

Death of an Admiral, Birth of a Legend

As the Imperial Defenders of Buna were making their last stand and the skeletal, malaria-ridden Nipponese troops on Guadalcanal were being evacuated or urged to commit suicide, the architect of the initially successful Japanese sweep across the Pacific was closeted on his flagship *Yamato* winning small amounts of money from his staff officers playing chess and poker. Adm. Isoroku Yamamoto was over fifteen hundred miles from the decision-making center of the Empire in Tokyo, and while his American adversary, Adm. Chester Nimitz, could take advantage of his residence in a sprawling house overlooking Pearl Harbor to take long walks, play horseshoes, and fire on a pistol range, the Imperial navy commander had to limit himself to more cerebral exercises.

By the spring of 1943, most of Yamamoto's thoughts centered on responding to the growing crises in the Pacific war caused by the loss of Guadalcanal and the one-sided defeat in New Guinea that were clearly throwing Imperial forces into a pattern of extended retreat. Japanese intelligence sources had discovered that the American high command seemed to be preparing an offensive to move from newly conquered Guadalcanal up the chain of the Solomon Islands to either invading or neutralizing the key Japanese air and naval base at Rabaul on the northern tip of the island of New Britain. This base, captured by Imperial forces in the first weeks of the war, featured an enormous protected harbor and a vast complex of six airfields that could launch war planes vectored to threaten communications between the United States and Australia. In turn, as long as Rabaul was firmly in Imperial possession, an American offensive to retake the Philippines would face the danger of a massive flank attack.

As the last of the famished and exhausted Imperial defenders on Guadalcanal were evacuated from the beaches of the island, Yamamoto and his advisers concluded that the immediate imperative was to delay an inevitable American march toward Japan long enough to either force the enemy into a compromise peace or prepare the home islands for a last major confrontation with the enemy. A major element in the delaying operation was Operation I-Go, the transfer of over 350 Imperial war planes from the carrier fleet to land-based airfields in preparation for a massive attack on a wide selection of enemy targets.

While I-Go was technically an offensive operation, the plan was being implemented to simply maintain territory the Imperial forces already held, not to recapture recently lost territory. Yamamoto believed that an enormous concentration of airpower would possibly cripple Allied air operations in the short term, delay the initiation of upcoming Allied ground offensives, and cover the transfer of far-flung Imperial army units into the key central Solomon Islands battlefield. Thus, in short order, the Combined Fleet's four remaining operable carriers were stripped of their air squadrons to join forces with Imperial Army air units to create a massive armada rivaling the strike force that hit Pearl Harbor sixteen months earlier.

On April 1, 1943, memories of the excitement on December 7, 1941, stirred Nipponese personnel as 350 aircraft were concentrated for a new "victory" operation. The air offensive began with a fighter sweep by nearly sixty Zeros over the American-held Russell Islands, a tiny speck of dry land between Guadalcanal and New Georgia. The center point of the tiny cluster of islands was Renard Airfield, which became the operations center for an eclectic mix of forty-one fighters, including Wildcats, Warhawks, and Lightnings. The fastest planes, the P-38 Lightnings, provided top cover to protect the slower interceptors that still could not match the superb "Zekes," as the Nipponese planes dove into their attack patterns. As drained fuel tanks ended the joust for both sides, the Zeros flew back to their bases with wildly exaggerated victory claims when in reality the encounter had produced nothing more than a drawn engagement with each side losing nine planes.

Six days later, on April 7, a far more powerful Imperial air armada of nearly 230 aircraft targeted the vast fleet of American ships either docked at Guadalcanal or cruising near the shoreline. The attack force swooped downward in two successive waves to be met by seventy-six American interceptors, of which only the twelve Lightnings could be considered an even match for the Zeros. The disparity in the speed and maneuverability of the two fleets allowed the Imperial intruders to score a modest victory against Allied shipping, as the raiders sank the American destroyer *Aaron Ward*, the New Zealand corvette *Moa*, and an oil tanker, but the outgunned and outnumbered American fighters shot down twenty-one attack planes at a cost of only seven of their own forces.

The highly exaggerated Japanese claims of ships sunk and enemy planes shot down convinced Yamamoto that I-Go was functioning well beyond expectations, and over the next four days, Imperial planes struck targets all across the coastline of New Guinea, hitting Oro Bay, Milne Bay, and Port Moresby with nearly two hundred planes on each mission. In each raid, the Imperial attack forces had air superiority of anywhere from two to one to nine to one, yet only five Allied planes were shot down at a cost of forty Japanese aircraft from the attack forces with a grand total of two Allied merchant ships sunk in the process. However, authoritative reports and figures were not a strong point in a Japanese military in which saving face trumped reality. As Imperial intelligence officers ticked off enemy losses "confirmed" by their vaunted airmen, the tally reached even more giddy heights; the last phase of I-Go netted an "official" total of one Allied cruiser sunk, two destroyers capsized, twenty-five transport ships destroyed, and 175 Allied fighters shot out of the skies. Victory celebrations erupted anew in the Imperial homeland, Yamamoto was saluted for his reprise of Pearl Harbor, and "victory disease" reigned again.

While the I-Go operation generated a military impact far below that of Midway a year earlier or Leyte Gulf a year later, Admiral Yamamoto's "great offensive" would not only emerge as a hugely underwhelming Imperial triumph but ultimately caused the death of the architect of the Pearl Harbor attack. Yamamoto had determined that the I-Go operation was so important that he should orchestrate the great offensive from as near to the action as possible.

Ensconced in a breezy cottage atop a hill overlooking the town of Rabaul, the admiral sorted through action reports of each day of the operation, met with local army and navy commanders, waved farewell greetings to departing attack squadrons, and found time for occasional rounds of poker. As each day of the operation brought new reports of one-sided triumphs over the enemy, the admiral decided to join in the celebratory mood by flying to a number of the bases from which the operation was launched to personally thank his men for their courage and valor. Unfortunately for the admiral, American cryptographers at Pearl Harbor were essentially reading his mail, which provided the American high command with a vital moment by moment itinerary of the most hated man in the United States.

Surprisingly, although the vast majority of American civilians would have supported almost any assassination attempt on this most reviled of Axis villains, the military leaders who would actually make the decision were more hesitant to act than most of their nonmilitary countrymen. During the American War of Independence, Gen. George Washington refused to directly retaliate when at least some portion of British general William Howe's staff approved a possible assassination plot against the American commander by a small group of turncoats at Valley Forge. Civil War Union and Confederate commanders, who often communicated directly through various truce lines, would have been repulsed at the death of their adversary counterparts in anything but fair and open battle, often sending their best surgeons to tend to their wounded enemies. Even in the European Theater of the current war, the assassination of the person who was likely the most daunting opponent of the Anglo-American armies, Erwin Rommel, would have been deemed ludicrous, given his relatively chivalrous behavior and positive mention by Winston Churchill in a speech to Parliament.

Compared to most previous wars in which the United States had been engaged, the war in the Pacific was enormously uncharted territory in the area of what was considered "appropriate" behavior in this less than rule-oriented activity called warfare. Only four decades earlier, when Japan emerged as a potential global power in its decisive defeat of the seemingly far more powerful Russia, President Theodore Roosevelt had expressed his admiration for the extremely lenient treatment of Russian prisoners captured in that war. In 1905, the code of Bushido centered around leniency and chivalry on the part of an Imperial warrior or samurai. By 1943, as chilling reports of Japanese atrocities against American soldiers and Filipino civilians in the Philippines were just beginning to filter back to the United States, the traditional relative immunity of an enemy commander from a planned assassination was rapidly evaporating.

Ironically, just as the moral issue of targeting Yamamoto for death was crumbling, critics of an assassination attempt argued that their primary enemy should be spared on the very different grounds that he was making such poor decisions that victory would be more likely if he stayed alive. American victories at Midway, Guadalcanal, and more peripheral locations seemed to be tied in some respects to poor decision-making on the part of Yamamoto. Perhaps this iconic enemy would continue to serve the American cause by extending his streak of poor decisions.

Ultimately, morale trumped combat strategy in the decision process, as Admiral Nimitz's aides compared the impact of the Imperial admiral's demise to the death of the now seemingly irreplaceable admiral from Texas, and an aerial "hunting party" was duly assigned to the controversial mission. The agents of the demise of the "most wanted man" by Americans would initiate their deadly mission at the same small piece of real estate that had become a virtual obsession for Admiral Yamamoto only six months earlier The iconic battle of Guadalcanal had largely been ignited over possession of a primitive Japanese airfield that was captured and then held by the American 1st Marine Division.

In April of 1943, Henderson Field, codenamed Cactus One, was still a major center for operations in the Solomon Islands. The field housed a variety of Army Air Force, Navy, and Marine aircraft but only one high-speed fighter plane boasted a fuel capacity that could reach Yamamoto's inspection tour locations and have its crew return alive. A midair attack on the admiral's transport plane would require a thousand-mile roundtrip from Guadalcanal, and the only single pilot attack craft that could manage this distance was the Army Air Force P-38 Lightning. The Lightning was not the fastest combat plane in the skies, but it featured extended range, and, for pilots flying in the vast Pacific region, the comfort of two propellers meant a fair chance of arriving home even if one engine failed. Now eighteen of these silver aircraft would converge on a single spot over Bougainville and confront the architect of the Day of Infamy.

The central figure in this newly arriving airgroup was Maj. John Mitchell, commander of the 339th fighter squadron. Mitchell was a twenty-eight-year-old Mississippian who had graduated from the University of Chicago and yet served as an enlisted soldier in the Coast Artillery. He had arrived at Guadalcanal at the peak of the battle for Henderson Field when enemy lines had crept to within two hundred yards of the base and was flying missions in the notoriously underpowered P-39 Airacobras. Now he and his seventeen fellow pilots flew P-38 Lightnings that featured high maintenance needs, huge fuel consumption, and balky heating systems, but were flying gun platforms equipped with a fearsome array of four machine guns and a 20mm cannon that combined could rip apart most enemy planes in record time. Major Mitchell would now command Operation Vengeance, and everyone involved knew that the "vengeance" part of the mission was for the nearly three thousand Americans who had died at Pearl Harbor.

Major Mitchell had alternated flying missions with ground duties hosting such visiting dignitaries as congressman and future president Lyndon Johnson and Air Force chief Henry "Hap" Arnold, but now the most important mission of his life was about to commence. Flying only thirty feet above the endless sea below, the assault force flew in radio silence communicating only with hand gestures. At 10:00 a.m. on a gorgeous April 18 morning, eighteen American raiders and eight Imperial aircraft converged just above the water's edge at Bougainville Island. Security concerns mandated that the two senior Japanese officers, Yamamoto and his chief of staff, Matome Ugaki, would fly in separate "Betty" bombers. The pilots of the six escorting Zeros kept a wary eye for a still very unlikely appearance of enemy interceptors. The two transport bombers flew so close to one another that Ugaki and Yamamoto could view one another from their seemingly wing tip to wing tip aircraft. Then, as the brilliant green jungle canopy of Bougainville came fully into view, aerial gunners opened their ports on the Bettys, Zeros dove close to provide cover, and an aerial melee crashed into action.

Ugaki Matoma was the more fortunate of the two admirals on this morning. His plane flew over the coastline at Cape Moira in a seaward direction as two Lightnings shot the wings of the aircraft to pieces. The dying craft struck the water and headed to the bottom of the sea just slowly enough that the admiral and three other personnel could clamber out rapidly enough to avoid drowning. Yamamoto's plane was headed inland as the Lightnings took turns spraying machine-gun and cannon fire into the perishing craft, yet the architect of Pearl Harbor was already dead before the crash, as an American bullet had hit him in the temple as he joined the entire complement of the aircraft in death.

Imperial Japan in 1943 was an odd amalgamation of a human-deity-worshipping throwback and a modern police state. Isoroku Yamamoto was very much the epitome of this seemingly impossible merger of the two realities. He adored baseball and poker, read American magazines, and drove across much of the United States in his own Ford. Yet he at least tacitly tolerated a culture of barbarism in which sailors under his command at the Battle of Midway rescued downed American pilots, tortured them for information, and then threw them back overboard tied down with weights. In Japan, Yamamoto's likeness would adorn every living room in an almost sacred corner; in America, his likeness was featured on dartboards and the bottom of urinals. Members of the royal family greeted the box containing his ashes when his remains arrived in Tokyo, yet his funeral march was Western classical music. And, in a final irony, his last great offensive would significantly impact an American naval officer who would convert a near-death experience into a trademark for one of the most magical eras in American history.

Among the many American witnesses to Admiral Yamamoto's ultimately failed last offensive was a junior lieutenant in the American Navy who, ironically, would also die from a bullet piercing his skull at a moment of an otherwise glorious, balmy day. Lt. (JG) John F. Kennedy, a twenty-five-year-old Harvard graduate and already a renowned author, happened to be watching the sky from the deck of LST 449 off the coast of Guadalcanal when nearly seventy Japanese bombers suddenly swooped down on the ship and its companion vessels. Nine enemy raiders targeted the slow, awkward vessel on which Kennedy was a passenger, and as the bombs straddled the ship, its captain was thrown across the bridge, suffering a near fatal broken neck. Young Kennedy was essentially standing on top of a bomb, as his ship was carrying a huge supply of ammunition that would virtually evaporate the vessel if a bomb scored the right hit. Kennedy was at least fortunate enough to be near an antiaircraft gun and had the satisfaction of helping to load one of the ship's few weapons. Kennedy's first day in combat climaxed in a grim fashion when one of the enemy raiders was hit by fire and plummeted into the water close enough that the future president noted the extreme youth of his now helpless enemy antagonist. Then, as a symbol of the total war he was entering, when LST 449 swung over to rescue the downed pilot, he began firing his revolver at his would-be rescuers.

Just under eighteen years later, on January 20, 1961, when the former Patrol Torpedo boat commander was finishing one of the most iconic presidential inaugural addresses in American history, the celebratory parade included a full-sized model of Kennedy's now iconic PT-109, while Warner Brothers studios were already discussing a film version of his exploits in that tiny craft.

In many respects, much of the initiation of the Kennedy legend from "Camelot" to Dallas would emerge during a few months in 1943 when a young man who had already won acclaim for his writing skills about the origins of World War II would now fully participate in the conflict at the cusp of danger and violence that it had created. The birth of the Kennedy legend that centered around the danger and valor of serving in one of the most vulnerable vessels in the American Navy actually began with the exploits of another young naval officer who would emerge as the future president's mentor when Kennedy decided to pursue a different path to adventure than his older brother Joseph.

The first step in the genesis of the association of the future president of the United States and a tiny craft, often referred to as a "mosquito boat," began in the spring of 1938 when the rumblings of a possible war in Europe energized Congress to appropriate $15 million to construct a "torpedo boat" for use by the US Navy. These sleek but diminutive craft were only seventy feet long and powered by 1,200-horsepower super-charged Packard automotive company engines. The design was quickly upgraded to a seventy-seven-foot craft that carried four torpedo tubes, two twin .50-caliber machine guns deployed in small gun tubs, and two .30-caliber light machine guns mounted on pedestals. While few naval leaders could

John F. Kennedy's command of PT-109 would become an iconic part of the 1960 presidential election campaign.
JOHN F. KENNEDY PRESIDENTIAL LIBRARY AND MUSEUM, BOSTON

imagine the actual circumstances, the Patrol Torpedo boats would become the primary strike force in the first ship-to-ship battles between the American Navy and its soon to be deadly enemy, the Imperial Japanese navy.

During the last weeks preceding the attack on Pearl Harbor, the American War Department belatedly decided to reverse its standing policy to regard the Philippine Islands as expendable and rushed reinforcements to the archipelago. One of the major reinforcement convoys that made the tedious five-thousand-mile voyage from Pearl Harbor to Manila Bay included a battalion of light tanks, a squadron of crated P-40 Warhawks, and a squadron of six PT boats led by Comm. John D. Bulkeley. While Japan and the United States were still technically at peace, Nipponese expansion in Indochina, Formosa, and the Marianas effectively surrounded the American Commonwealth that was due to receive total independence in 1946. While the American War Department had initially decided to annex the soon to be independent islands, planners conducted a complete turnaround and now believed that if war could be avoided until summer 1942, the Philippines could be held with the arrival of massive aid. Unfortunately for American planners, the Japanese struck far earlier.

A massive series of air raids from Imperial possessions hours after the Pearl Harbor attack caught most of the three dozen modern bombers and one hundred first-line fighters on the ground for refueling, and by nightfall on December 8 (December 7 at Pearl Harbor), Gen. Douglas MacArthur's air umbrella for his ground forces was down to about twenty serviceable fighter planes, now outnumbered twenty to one by their Imperial counterparts. Since the American initial defense plan was based on some facsimile of parity in the air, Douglas MacArthur ordered the implementation of a backup plan that entailed a retreat into the jungles of Bataan peninsula across Manila Bay from the capital, with the prospect of eventual relief from Pearl Harbor. Unfortunately, the relief force MacArthur envisioned was expected to be protected by ships that were now sitting on the bottom of Pearl Harbor and by planes that were now burning wrecks on Hawaiian airfields. No help would be forthcoming for MacArthur, and the new mandate was for personnel in the Philippines to delay the enemy and buy time until an eventual surrender or destruction.

Along with the Battle of the Bulge in the European Theater, the Battle of Bataan became the iconic Alamo-like stand for the American public in World War II. The American press wildly inflated both enemy numbers and enemy losses in the grueling battle between roughly twenty thousand Americans and about one hundred thousand barely trained Filipino recruits and a smaller but superbly equipped enemy force. Once the roughly thirty submarines stationed in the islands were ordered to evacuate, the major naval presence during the siege was Bulkeley and his tiny squadron. While minor damage inflicted against larger enemy vessels was hugely exaggerated, Bulkeley and his men would become national heroes near the end of the grim siege.

While Douglas MacArthur had earned the dubious title of "Dugout Doug" from many of his men on Bataan when he deigned to leave his heavily tunneled headquarters on nearby Corregidor Island exactly once to visit the front lines, he somewhat compensated for this neglect by insisting to Roosevelt and Army commander George Marshall that he would not leave his post and assumed he would die fighting in a final battle in the dank halls of his headquarters. MacArthur and Franklin Roosevelt loathed one another, but the commander-in-chief envisioned a scenario where his general was captured unconscious by the Japanese and then paraded around the subject nations of the Greater East Asia Co. Prosperity Sphere in a cage like a valuable zoo exhibit. By the time MacArthur reluctantly acceded to his president's demands, the enemy had captured almost the entire territory between Corregidor Island and the last American-held airstrip at the southernmost tip of the Philippines.

One of the most heavily publicized escape stories of World War II emerged as Bulkeley and his surviving PT boats ferried MacArthur and his family from the Corregidor docks down to a dusty, ramshackle airfield where two Flying Fortresses waited to fly the dignitaries to Australia. A few weeks later, Commander Bulkeley, who had received a farewell promise from MacArthur that he would attempt to evacuate the naval officer before the Philippines fell, had that promise honored as Bulkeley clambered aboard one of the last American planes to leave the Philippines.

John Bulkeley soon emerged as one of the first heroes of the Pacific war. Hollywood tapped first-tier actor Robert Montgomery (father of Elizabeth Montgomery of *Bewitched* fame) to play Bulkeley in a film version of the bestselling book *They Were Expendable* and participated in a huge parade through Manhattan kicking off a drive to raise $3 million for the Army and Navy Emergency Relief Fund. A personal welcome home by Mayor Fiorello La Guardia included performances by Jimmy Dorsey and Danny Kaye, and every major newsmagazine recounted Bulkeley's adventures. By August, he was seated across from Franklin Roosevelt in the Oval Office and was soon collecting a spectrum of medals from the Navy Cross to the Medal of Honor.

Commander John Bulkeley would soon engage in other adventures against Japan's Axis partner, Germany, including participation in the screening force for D-Day and the invasion of southern France; however, the PT skipper may have exerted his most important impact on American history a few weeks later when he accepted an invitation for lunch with the former American ambassador to Britain, Joseph Kennedy.

The lunch invitation stretched into a seven-hour meeting that ended well after dinner was served, and the center point of the conversation was substantially about a match between the now hugely glamorous PT boat service and the ambassador's second son, John Fitzgerald Kennedy. Jack

Kennedy was a midshipman at Northeastern University in the naval officer training program, and Bulkeley opined that the personalized nature of the small crews and small craft could gain public relations value for a person who was both brave and intelligent.

A few weeks later, Bulkeley spoke to John Kennedy's cohort at Northeastern and shocked the young officer candidates by declaring, "Those of you who want to come back after the war and raise families need not apply. PT boat skippers are not coming back!" Two colorful, verbal, and confident young Irishmen now shared a connection, and as Bulkeley prepared for new adventures and fame in the European Theater, Lieutenant Kennedy's own legendary adventure was about to begin.

On April 25, 1943, John Kennedy assumed command of the soon to be legendary craft, PT-109. His sense of humor, personal attention to the needs of his small crew, and overall presence immediately attracted attention, even if one of his new crewmembers insisted, "I don't know if I want to go out with this guy. He looks fifteen!" The actual firepower Kennedy commanded was little changed from John Bulkeley's craft a year earlier, but unlike the "Mosquito Boats" serving in the Philippines, Kennedy's squadron was not surrounded or under siege. The American and Imperial forces were very nearly evenly matched, with both sides devising plans for new offensives. Patrols were initially centered around harassing Japanese efforts to resupply their bases in the Solomon Islands and search and rescue missions to assist either downed aircrew or survivors of sunken ships. Much of the action was at night, as PT boats conducted nocturnal patrols, and Japanese floatplanes attempted to spot the telltale phosphorescent waves that the boats produced. The PT boats suffered from two potentially deadly defects. First, their torpedoes were just as unreliable as those in their submarine counterparts, which meant that the boats launched dozens of torpedoes to gain even minor hits on enemy shipping. Second, the guns aboard the mosquito boats were virtually useless in any vessel-to-vessel confrontation; an encounter with an enemy destroyer was often a deadly meeting, as the destroyer was only slightly slower than the PT boat but carried guns that could rip through a mosquito boat in seconds. The fighting potential of the PT squadrons was also reduced by the vague guidelines concerning exactly where a squadron commander should exercise his command. Some squadron commanders accompanied squadrons out on a mission; others relied on often erratic radio commentary between their onshore headquarters' officers and the boats. Some commanders insisted on absolute radio silence between boats; others allowed such interactions. These often-erratic command procedures were beginning to have a major impact at the end of July 1943, when John F. Kennedy and his fellow PT boat skippers were assigned a major role in thwarting a Japanese plan to reinforce their garrisons on the Solomon island of Kolombangara in the key water passage of Vella Gulf.

On August 1, 1943, Lieutenant Kennedy was hard at work on PT-109, attempting to implement a suggestion from Adm. William Halsey that PT boats should be equipped with experimental high-caliber guns that might prove more effective in destroying enemy barges ferrying Imperial troops in the highly contested island battles. Kennedy had located a derelict Army antitank gun near the dockyard and lashed the weapon to the section of the boat that normally held the vessel's single life raft. The upgrade in firepower was based on reports that the enemy would attempt to provide a new round of reinforcements deployed down the channel that separated Kolombangara and Vella Lavella islands.

American cryptologists had intercepted Japanese plans for a major run down the channel called the "Slot," and one of the largest PT boat operations of the war was now about to be initiated. Japanese air units had been given orders to challenge any American interference with the massive reinforcement operation, and Imperial planes attacked the PT boat base just as Kennedy was casting off. Two other boats were turned into a hail of flying splinters, but the remaining boat commanders returned to dock for a final briefing of their nocturnal mission.

The surviving boats were distributed into four vessel divisions with orders to patrol an area known as Blackett Strait through which the Japanese transports would pass with their destroyer escorts. As fifteen PT boats formed into four assault groups along a six-mile stretch of water, there may have been some private confusion among boat commanders as to exactly who was the hunter and who was the hunted. The PT boats had more speed and armament than the enemy transport vessels, but Imperial destroyers escorting those ships could blow the Americans out of the water with their far superior heavy guns. The only positive note in this situation was that the PT boats were actually a final line of defense that started farther up the strait with American destroyers.

The disparity of American versus Imperial firepower was enhanced by the fact that at this point in the war, only one in every four PT boats was equipped with radar. The other boats would become blind if the vessels drew too far apart from one another.

In a series of negative consequences that might rival the *Titanic* experience for sheer bad luck, the nocturnal hunters gradually lost contact with each other, and at 2:15 a.m., PT-109 began a series of actions that would lead to a similar fate. The object looming far above the small craft was not an iceberg but still towered over the tiny boat. It was the Japanese destroyer *Amagiri*, which, without losing a knot of forward speed, essentially sliced the American boat in two.

As the stern and bow of PT-109 split into separate pieces, the rear of the boat and two crewmembers simply disappeared; nine others were propelled into the sea, and Kennedy and a single crewman remained onboard. Unlike the *Titanic*, the PT-109's watertight compartment did function properly, and the young man who would two decades later manage crises in Berlin and Cuba without resorting to another world war coolly issued orders that resulted in eventual rescue. Kennedy led the swimmers to a nearby island, swimming while towing the most badly injured crewman, connected by a belt between the skipper's teeth, and then swam an even greater distance when it was discovered that their refuge had neither food nor water, and dispatched a rescue request through friendly natives of another island. In short order, John F. Kennedy had morphed from war vessel commander to lifeguard to castaway to emissary with no sense of panic or hopelessness. Somewhere in that series of events a legend began to emerge that had found its origins in Comm. John Bulkeley's David versus Goliath attacks in the dark days after Pearl Harbor and its climax in the rebuilt model of PT-109 that accompanied the inauguration parade of a new president early in 1961.

CHAPTER 11

Yanks

WHEN THE CELEBRATED WAR CORRESPONDENT ERNIE PYLE SOUGHT A respite from the carnage of the battle for Sicily, he decided to recuperate in Britain, rather than making the three-thousand-mile journey back to the United States. Many aspects of the British lifestyle agreed with the worldly, chain-smoking "superstar" reporter with a vast American reading audience. Pyle wrote, "I had left London for Africa one dark and rainy night and many times since then. I had never thought to see England again." Yet, Pyle made it back to Britain once again, and "There it was, fresh and green and beautiful; and although I was still far from home and family, it was a wonderful thing to be returning, for I had loved London ever since first seeing it in the Blitz." Pyle admitted that Britain had become his new "overseas home," and the island nation, still in a state of semi-siege after Hitler's conquest of the Continent, seemed a special place for the tidal wave of Americans who had come to England to begin the first steps toward the liberation of the rest of Europe.

One of the first realizations that had captured the imagination of thousands of young American service personnel was that a crowded island still under aerial attack and desperately short of almost any item beyond the most basic foodstuffs refused to exhibit the slightest hint of panic or fear, and in fact, had begun a virtual nationwide countdown toward the date when their armed forces would return to the mainland of Europe. American aid and years of learning how to make do had at least slightly eased the really meager existence of the days of the German Blitz. Now there was more food, more people on the streets, more shopping, more Sunday strolls in the park, and the inhabitants continued to be kind and polite, not only to each other but to the tidal wave of newly arrived Americans who were called "Yanks," even if they grew up in Mississippi or Alabama.

Every month in 1943 saw a new wave of Americans arriving by ship and plane, and despite a long list of differences, these "invaders" had come not to conquer but to help Britain win the war and then return home as soon as possible, with at least some of them going home with a new British bride who would face the challenge of adapting to an equally strange environment on the other side of the Atlantic.

These peaceful invaders spoke English, played sports that had their inception in some equivalent British game, and were generally polite, well mannered, and were paid substantially more than their British counterparts. In essence, the path home led through Britain, as even in 1943, it was clear to most servicemen that an Allied invasion of the Continent would most likely occur sometime in 1944. While bomber crews and their fighter escort pilots were now often flying deep into the Third Reich, these airmen represented only a small fraction of the massive American presence in Britain, and given the twenty-five-mission limit to their tour, these aircrews would be on their way back home as later-arriving squadrons would cover the cross-Channel invasion. The young British servicemen wore much less stylish uniforms and had less opportunity to rise above their current social class. By 1943, despite these disparities the vast majority of the population, especially its younger members, were delighted that the Americans would both deter Hitler from invading the island, and in the relatively near future, team up with British forces to drive deep into the Third Reich.

The proof that there was little anti-Yank sentiment was evident in virtually every city that had one or more American bases nearby. For example, the Washington Club in London featured a huge map of the United States on which American service personnel pinned names and hometowns that new arrivals to Britain could check to catch up on news and information from home. This center was only one of sixty-four similar clubs that operated in Britain in 1943 partially paid by a $25 million fundraising campaign in both America and Britain. The club was staffed by a mostly female contingent of both American and British volunteers who would chat with lonely servicemen, offer huge amounts of American food, and direct visitors to a wide variety of American newspapers and magazines for the latest news from home.

A *Life* magazine correspondent noted, "Almost every club has a weekly dance where American soldiers and British girls (many in uniform) smoke, drink coffee, cuddle a lot and later get together for movies, outings and concerts." The center on Curzon Street in London offered rooms for fifty cents a night and could feed twenty-five hundred Americans three times a day and sleep 750. American-style doughnuts were available for one cent each, and hundreds were delivered every hour.

Another form of hospitality emerged from more informal sources in Britain. For example, Andrew Carnegie's granddaughter opened her sumptuous Edinburgh mansion to American soldiers and sailors, while Mrs. Theodore Roosevelt, daughter-in-law of the first American president named Roosevelt, entertained officers and enlisted men several nights a week at her London mansion, always reminding visitors that she had three of her own sons in the service.

The American service personnel who arrived in Britain in 1943 were the first troops to receive a new pamphlet that had just begun to be issued by the US War Department. The pocket-sized thirty-one-page booklet, which the staff of the London *Times* compared to the works of Washington Irving, Ralph Waldo Emerson, and Nathaniel Hawthorne, all of whom had attempted to interpret Britain to an American audience, was designed as a snapshot of wartime Britain. The British Ministry of Information had already charged the Strand Film Company to provide a documentary film that showed newly arrived Americans how to cope with everyday situations in pubs, public transport, and stores, and, in turn, presented a picture of the British people as a nation stoically coping with the problems caused by rationing and German bombing. While the Strand film reminded service personnel from the Deep South that, unlike their states, British public transport, theaters, and restaurants were all integrated, the American booklet simply reminded the Yanks that, "For the time being, you will be Britain's guest."

The mission of the newly arrived American service personnel was clearly defined in this book. "You are going to Great Britain as part of our Allied offensive to meet Hitler and beat him on his own ground. Hitler knows that they are both powerful countries, tough and resourceful. He knows that they, with the other United Nations, mean his crashing defeat in the end. So it is only common sense to understand that the first major duty he has given his propaganda chiefs is to separate Britain and America and spread distrust between them. If he can do this, his chance of winning might return."

This attempt to bond the British and American nations through the thousands of service personnel that were now disembarking in the United Kingdom was not an unreasonable project, as in 1943, much more than in the twenty-first century, American history textbooks still tended to portray the British government and monarch of the Revolutionary period as tyrannical and ill-disposed toward the colonies, while the subsequent War of 1812 was chronicled around the violent seizure of former British sailors now serving on American vessels and the subsequent destruction of the While House and Capitol by rapacious British soldiers.

In turn, the substantial number of American personnel of Irish Catholic descent were often exposed to the excesses of the Black and Tan constabulary against Catholics during the Easter Rebellion of 1916, and the virtual civil war in Ireland during the 1920s.

A key element in the ability of British society to temporarily absorb hundred of thousands of Americans in a relatively small nation was the special relationship that was developing by 1943 between the Yanks and the young people of Britain.

American servicemen taught British children how to chew gum, swing a baseball bat, and make extra money by wending their way through the long lines in fish and chips takeaway restaurants and delivering the meals to servicemen unable to leave their bases.

The Yanks threw huge Christmas parties for local children, distributing toys, candy, and snacks typically unavailable to young Britons, often presented by a sometimes strange composite of Father Christmas and Santa Claus.

On another social level, the posting of British service personnel on a global battle front from India to Italy created a significant gender imbalance between the young British males who were either exempted from the service or posted on British soil, and their female counterparts who substantially outnumbered them. While some social critics, academics, and young uniformed men still stationed in Britain sometimes uttered the refrain that the "Yanks were overpaid, oversexed, and over here," the majority of young women in Britain were delighted to develop relationships with the expanding flood of Yanks now posted in their country.

The difference between the American and British school systems also added a substantial edge for the Yanks. By 1943, the vast majority of American elementary schools and high schools were coeducational, while separate schools for British boys and girls were still largely the norm. The American servicemen exuded a level of informality with females that many British girls found different and exciting, compared to their previous experiences. American servicemen genuinely missed the company of their female friends back in the United States but often made the best of the situation by transferring that attention to typically flattered British girls, a relationship that initiated a tidal wave of "war brides" eventually landing on the other side of the Atlantic.

While the Yanks used their relatively generous wages and relatively limited free time to form new relationships, frequent pubs, and explore a still somewhat exotic British countryside, they also began to gain an appreciation of how close the enemy really was. A two-hour trip south from London to Dover would essentially place the American servicemen at the very edge of what was considered the "Allied territory." A visit to the medieval splendor of Dover Castle might also include gazing through high-powered binoculars that revealed the coast of France only twenty miles away. In early 1943, many servicemen pondered the reality that a coastal city such as Dover was the absolute edge of that "free world," and the French coast only a short distance away was the northern tip of a European continent that was essentially ruled by Adolf Hitler and his minions. At this point in time, the Continent consisted exclusively of either small neutral nations living in fear that Germany would find a reason to invade and occupy their country on a whim, and Fascist nations that were all effectively satellites of the Third Reich. While Allied bombs could hit Berlin, the reach of Allied ground forces ended at the south coast of Britain, and these young Americans could not go home until that nearby continent was released from tyranny. While American magazines and newspapers carried columns lauding the possible beneficial effects of an Allied invasion of the "soft underbelly" of the continent through Italy, few of the Americans in Britain in 1943 believed that operation alone could sweep into the heart of the Third Reich. The Yanks could dance to swing bands, interact with the locals in pubs, and even engage in relationships that could run anywhere from short-term affairs to marriage, but ultimately, that spectral coast twenty miles distant lay waiting to challenge the bravery of young Americans hailing from New York to California.

While American service personnel peered through optic devices staring at Nazi-occupied Europe on the other side of the English Channel, their president's wife left the White House to begin a five-week, twenty-five-thousand-mile tour of the Pacific Theater on behalf of the American Red Cross. Although Eleanor Roosevelt visited seventeen island outposts, nearly half of her sojourn was spent in Australia, where she walked through miles of hospital wards, talked to hundreds of American and Australian wounded soldiers and sailors, and inspected dozens of Red Cross hostels and clubs. A reporter who accompanied her noted that no stop on her journey received a greater harvest of gratitude and good will than her sojourn "down under." In Sydney and Melbourne, crowds massed early to view and cheer this high-profile visitor from America. Orators and editors competed with one another to find adequate expressions of affection and esteem. In an open letter to the American people, one journalist insisted, "We can only thank you for sending her here."

The Roosevelt visit was seen as tangible proof that the United States would make the front line of defense against Japan far beyond the shore of California, and the menace of a Japanese invasion of the Australian continent would be met with far more force than the Australian military could muster on its own. One reporter estimated that the First Lady walked more than three miles up and down the corridors of hospital wards. She shook hands with Australian army nurses evacuated from Crete and Greece, one of whom was also the only survivor of a Japanese torpedo attack on a clearly marked "hospital ship."

A few weeks after the First Lady arrived, the American cruiser *Montpelier* steered into Sydney harbor after long action in the Pacific naval war. One very young member of the crew, James J. Fahey, a truck driver from Waltham, Massachusetts, noted the arrival in a diary that would eventually be published in book form by Houghton-Mifflin on the advice of the premier chronicler of the Pacific war, Adm. Samuel Morison. On October 19, 1943, seaman Fahey and his shipmates disembarked in Sydney Harbor with that seaman $250 richer for winning the ship's "anchor pool" for predicting the exact moment the ship docked in harbor. Now, relatively flush with cash, the young man dove into the social whirl in which eligible young Australian women greatly outnumbered the young adult males who were available on the island continent. The young seaman encountered multiple offers from the young women to tour the island and drifted into a Hyde Park amusement center noting, "The first thing that catches your eye are all the beautiful girls. The place is full of them there [*sic*] are supposed to be five girls for every man, but I think there are even more than that." Noting in comparison with young ladies he had met in Massachusetts, "The girls in the States could really learn something from the girls here. I never saw such friendly people. They trust you as if you are related and invite you to their homes to meet their families. Even the normally very strict Sunday blue laws are bent to accommodate the Americans, as two movie theaters are open on Sunday exclusively for American personnel and their girlfriends."

Even the Australian Treasury Department added a tangible welcome to the Americans, as the government made American money legal tender and sweetened the deal with special exchange rates for American troops. Australian newspapers used very scarce newsprint to print Major League Baseball box scores and hometown news, and even carried suggested American recipes for Australian housewives inviting Yanks into their homes. As an ultimate tribute, at movie theaters and concerts, Australians stood as "The Star-Spangled Banner" was played.

Eleanor Roosevelt and James Fahey arrived in Australia from very different backgrounds, but each of them noted the unique bridge that Australia formed between the two most powerful English-speaking nations, the United States and Great Britain. While the Americans had wrested independence from the English in a long and bloody war, the Australians had created a "new Britain" down under, with a clear eye to the need for British protection as a European island in a very Asian Pacific.

Australia had only become a relatively self-governing nation twelve years earlier, when the British Parliament passed the Statute of Westminster in 1931. This legislation preserved the monarchy as the titular head of each of the dominions and encouraged rather than forced those nations to enter a war in which the mother country was involved, but essentially left the day-to-day governance of Canada, New Zealand, South Africa, Australia, and other members of the Commonwealth to their own elected parliaments and leaders. Officially, Australia was an "autonomous country within the British Empire, equal in status, united by a common allegiance to the Crown, and freely associated as members of the British Commonwealth of Nations." Yet rather than rushing significant air, ground, and sea forces to defend Australia from Japanese invasion after Pearl Harbor, the outbreak of the Pacific war found the cream of the Australian army battling the Axis in the deserts of North Africa, with only minimal forces left to defend against a Nipponese invasion of Australia's enormous coastline.

Now the Yanks had arrived in large numbers as a kind of substitute for the expected British defense presence, and the Australians found themselves drawing even closer to a United States that could and did pour their own forces into the extremely vulnerable nation. Australian war minister Francis Forde defined the new relationships as, "What we are, you were. What you are, we will be someday. We feel that our fate and that of America are indissolubly linked. We know that our destinies go hand in hand and that we rise and fall together."

Now Diggers and Yanks, despite occasional barroom brawls over female attention or the superiority of cricket and soccer versus football and baseball, sensed that their mutual British ally was so entangled in the defense of it own homeland and an eventual return to the Continent that these two English-speaking nations with a physical presence in the Pacific region would have to defeat Japan on their own.

Winston Churchill gave belated and grudging permission for at least part of the Australian army serving with Bernard Montgomery in North Africa to return home for the defense of their own homeland, but also made it clear that the prime task of the British army in the war against Japan was to prevent Imperial Japanese forces from invading the Crown of the Empire, India, from Japanese bases in occupied Burma. The Allies were attempting to push the Japanese back from a south New Guinea coast not very far from northern Australia (and New Zealand), and while Monty might still be toasted in Australian pubs, it was American commanders from Gen. Douglas MacArthur to Adm. Charles Lockwood who were seen as the main hopes for throwing the Japanese wave back to Nippon.

One of the most personalized accounts of the Yank presence in 1943 Australia emerged from the first-person account of a young Marine from New Jersey, Robert Leckie. While much of Leckie's account of war in the Pacific centers on the unrelenting danger, deprivation, and brutality of a war to the death with Japanese counterparts, an extensive interlude in *Helmet for My Pillow* focuses on the American impact on the Australian home front.

After only partially recovering from the malnourishment and fevers of the Battle for Guadalcanal, Leckie, along with his Marine companions, was housed in the Melbourne Cricket Grounds, sleeping on double-deck bunks stretching up the steps in the tiered sports palace. After receiving six month's pay in a lump sum, Leckie and many other Marines slipped through an ineffective military police quarantine and found themselves instant war heroes upon initial meeting of Australian civilians in town. Street vendors sold civilians pennants with the welcoming message, "Good on you, Yank. You saved Australia." Noting that adulation was "like a strong drink," he soon formed an insistence that, "I took it for a triumph and soon regarded every smile as a salute and every Melbourne girl as the fair reward of the sunburned deliverer."

Endless rounds of drinks, meat pies, and somewhat exotic ice cream led to off-key singing of "Waltzing Matilda" with local men and a complicated social life with women who, much like their counterparts in Britain, included more than a few young ladies who wished to settle in the United States as war brides.

American books, pamphlets, and magazine articles that compared British and American lifestyles now turned their attention to Australia

The arrival of American soldiers and weapons in Australia proved to the Aussies that the Japanese threat of invasion had now passed. This photo shows Australian and New Zealand army crews ready for review in front of American tanks.
LIBRARY OF CONGRESS

with figures indicating that Australians drink fourteen cups of tea to every one cup quaffed by Yanks, while the Americans captured the coffee sweepstakes at an even more robust twenty-six to one. Australians consumed twice the butter, twice the beef, and twelve times more mutton than the Yanks, who compensated with twice the ice cream and triple the pork products.

By 1943, the Americans pouring into Australia had begun to establish a special relationship with a people who now routinely uttered the forceful slogan, "Fight, work or perish." The American War and Navy departments that had developed the booklet, *Instructions for American Servicemen in Britain,* quickly added a companion equivalent, *Instructions for American Servicemen in Australia.* The booklet insisted that, "You won't have any trouble finding out that everyone in Australia is in the war all the way down the line. There aren't many cars on the streets, taxis are hard to get; streetlights have been turned off to save power and the Prime Minister recently announced that all non-essential industries will be turned off for the duration. Clothes and food have been severely rationed, and wages, prices and profits have been frozen for the duration. So life for the Australians isn't as free and easy as it was, but they're out to win the war and to hell with the comforts."

Thousands of miles from one another, living, training, and in many cases fighting the Axis powers from bases in Britain and Australia, the Yanks were helping to form an alliance; the Axis powers would soon rue the day that alliance between the English-speaking nations was formed. German, Italian, and Japanese leaders and many of their fighting men never really trusted one another, and their alliance in some ways replicated the temporary bonds formed in the 1920s by American gangsters. American service personnel in Britain and Australia quickly moved beyond tepid beer, tough mutton, and slightly exotic accents to join in a crusade against an alliance of gangsters that put Al Capone and Bugs Moran to shame. The British and Australians were not always perfect hosts, and the Americans were equally liable to be very flawed guests, but by 1943, the new Anglophone group was becoming a force to be reckoned with. Soon these young Americans with their British and Australian allies would be pushing into the heart of two stolen empires and would number the days of the Axis plague.

CHAPTER 12

The Battle for Salerno

THE ALLIED CAPTURE OF SICILY NOW GAVE THE ALLIES A PERMANENT base in Europe at a loss of five thousand personnel, compared to four thousand casualties inflicted on the Wehrmacht. The most heavily publicized rationale for the outcome was that the Allies had also captured the majority of the one hundred forty thousand Italian soldiers who had garrisoned Sicily on the day of the invasion. Axis and Allied commanders generally agreed that Operation Husky was merely a stepping-stone to the mainland of Fascist Italy, but the most heavily discussed question was where the actual invasion of the mainland would occur. The enjoyment of virtually total control of the sea provided Allied planners with a wide variety of follow-up campaigns, with the understanding that Axis commanders could not defend every foot of the coastline with in-depth defensive positions.

Adolf Hitler, in one of his rare attempts to ensure the loyalty of his senior commanders, ultimately agreed with his senior officers and authorized massively defended fallback positions along the bank of the Po River where the defenders would have easy access to reinforcing units currently posted in Germany. However, one of the Führer's favorite leaders, Field Marshal Albert Kesserling, convinced Hitler that the Axis forces could bleed the Allied invaders nearly to death if each of the deep, raging rivers and towering, often unclimbable mountain ranges were contested long enough to convince the Allied attackers into thinking that the war was unwinnable.

As the competing battle plans for the Axis defense of the Italian mainland were debated in the dusk to dawn "Führer Meetings," punctuated by

Hitler's seemingly endless supply of reminiscences about his activities in World War I, a reality check came storming from the east. Hitler and his closest advisors had concocted a daring counteroffensive against an increasingly powerful Red Army. Operation Citadel was planned as an attack on a huge Soviet assault force in the vicinity of Kursk, with more than a sprinkling of unwarranted optimism that a major victory on those plains would at least temporarily force the Russians to regroup in a time-demanding process that would allow a concentration of German forces that might achieve enough Axis victories to entice some portion of the Allied high command to propose a compromise settlement.

As Axis leaders debated the tangible benefits of successful advance into or retreat from Italy, Josef Stalin was cajoling his British and American counterparts to significantly distract the Führer as Soviet forces massed to push the invaders completely out of the Soviet motherland as the first step on the long road to Berlin.

While the Allied commanders alternately cajoled, flattered, and supported their counterparts, among a number of distinct units from a nearly double-digit roster of various nationalities, the senior German commander in Italy was somehow able to maintain a joint Italian/German force on a reasonable level of combat readiness. Kesserling, an Air Force officer, could be considered an unusual choice for a battlefield dominated by ground forces, but his energy was legendary and his generally positive view of the Italian allies complemented his popularity among rank and file German units.

Kesserling was one of the Italian population's most ardent advocates in the Gothic halls of the Nazi inner circle, yet would order the execution of Italian men, women, and children without a hint of remorse if they seemed to favor the Allied cause in even minor acts of defiance. These atrocities would earn him a seat among the accused war criminals at the postwar Nuremberg Trials, where he was sentenced to life imprisonment, though released a few months later on grounds of ill health that did not result in his death for another eight years.

Kesserling hated to fly but learned to pilot a plane near his fiftieth birthday, partially to justify the Führer's generous personal "allowance" of over seventy thousand marks a year and rapid promotion to command of an entire aerial army during the Battle of Britain in 1940. Now the heady days of British evacuation were long gone, and the field marshal would be forced to confront the British Eighth Army moving up from the south and an impending Anglo-American landing near Salerno in a massive amphibious assault designed to trap the Germans between two forces.

Kesserling had at his disposal a potentially awe-inspiring but actually deeply flawed Salerno garrison. The 16th Panzer Division was encamped on the sandy plain just beyond Salerno. The unit had a proud history, but was virtually annihilated during the collapse at Stalingrad and had to be reformed from a nucleus of personnel either evacuated from the city before the final battle or men recuperating from earlier wounds in hospitals back in the Reich and now back on duty training on the powerful new Panzer vehicles.

The 3rd Panzer Division had arrived in Italy in early June, and the unit was currently stationed near Rome with pending orders to move down to Naples at the signal of an Allied invasion of Italy. These elite troops had gained the professional admiration of the British units they had encountered in North Africa but had been practically annihilated in combat and fielded an increasing number of personnel who had not seen their first battle.

The third major German unit in the vicinity of Salerno was the 15th Panzergrenadier Division, which had more ghosts than living soldiers, as it had been virtually annihilated in North Africa. The division was caught in the middle of the Anglo-American landings in Sicily and was now essentially a "rookie" outfit with impressive battle flags gained by dead or maimed previous members who were no longer on the divisional rolls.

These once almost unbeatable and still formidable units occupied a sometimes confusing middle ground between past and future. Three years earlier, these men or their predecessors had gained revenge for the humiliating surrender to Britain and France in 1918 by becoming occupation troops in France. Less than eighteen months in the future, surviving soldiers would be backtracking to the gates of the Third Reich in an emotional tug of war between defending their hometowns against an Allied advance or attempting to surrender to the Anglo-Americans before being forced to experience sometimes merciless reprisals meted out by Soviet invaders. Yet in the summer of 1943, the front lines were still far from the heart of the Third Reich; letters from home still arrived on a regular basis; and Hitler promised the imminent entrance to the battlefield of jet fighters, guided missiles, and King Tiger tanks that could quite possibly squash the diminutive Allied Shermans into metal blocks headed to the junk pile.

On the other hand, the Allied invaders of mainland Europe had undergone a somewhat reverse process where the sun now started to climb above the darkness that had covered sites of defeat from Dunkirk to Kasserine Pass. Earlier films viewed by these Allied invaders featured a continuing theme of an Alamo-like desire to simply take as many enemies with you to the grave as possible. Films such as *Wake Island* depicted the elimination of the entire four-hundred-man Wake Island garrison by enemy invaders with their only consolation that the doomed defenders took many enemy soldiers with them before they themselves perished. *Bataan* featured a similar Alamo-like last stand in which Robert Taylor, portraying the sole survivor of an ambushed American patrol force, emptied numerous clips of pistol and tommy-gun fire against the surrounding hordes of Japanese soldiers before his inevitable death. *Purple Heart* centered on the sham "trial," yet very real execution, of the "terrorist" bomber crews that had the audacity to bomb Tokyo. By 1943, it was the Americans who were involved in the surrender of mass formations of Italian and German troops and even a few Nipponese warriors who had been wounded too seriously to commit ritual suicide.

American soldiers and their British counterparts were now about to enter an occupied European continent dominated by endless food shortages and absence of fuel for winter, and arbitrary arrests to a forced labor camp or a final destiny in front of a firing squad were becoming numbingly commonplace events, as the "Fascist Brotherhood" of the totalitarian states was giving way to maximizing personal survival in a grim world where the retreating Axis forces were often following a "scorched earth" policy.

The American leader who would, at that moment, embody this sense of liberation in a crusade against pure evil was almost as complex as the complexities of the American, British, and Soviet alliance itself. Gen. Mark W. Clark, who preferred to be called "Wayne" (his middle name) rather than "Mark," was a tall, angular officer who had at one point been the youngest cadet at West Point. After graduation, he had entered into one of the most mutually satisfactory marriages that might be imagined. While serving as an assistant to the assistant secretary of war, Clark met a young, slightly older divorced woman on a blind date, which resulted in a wedding between the six-foot-two general and the five-foot-one former Indiana college student that marked the first step in a climb toward power, responsibility, and controversy. "Rennie" Clark adored the future general, who seemed to laugh and smile only with her. Unlike many of the key decision makers in the senior American military hierarchy, Mark Clark remained faithful to his wife. While Mrs. Clark saw a husband who "no matter how busy with his work of soldiering, always found some unexpected little way to let me know that he was thinking of me," her husband was also perceived by his superiors to be one of the emerging stars of the Army.

On the eve of "Avalanche," the Allied invasion of Salerno, Clark was, at forty-seven, one of the youngest lieutenant generals in the history of American warfare, yet rarely demonstrated his communication skills beyond his wife, children, and his mentor, Gen. George C. Marshall. Clark was one of the most virulently anti-British officers in the American services. He was also arrogant enough to insist that reporters could only photograph him from his "better" left side and employed an inside staff of over fifty servicemen all instructed to ensure that his name appeared on every single page of any official reports or press releases.

Once Generals Montgomery, Eisenhower, and Patton left the Mediterranean Theater to assume key roles in the Normandy invasion, Mark Clark began a campaign within a campaign to liberate Rome before the first Allied soldier set foot on the Normandy beaches. The first step in this long march to Rome began with an attempt to secure the invasion beaches fronting Salerno.

The German defenders of Salerno had excellent morale, superior tanks, and were deployed on ground that offered ravines, orchards, ditches, and stone buildings from which the defenders could pour down fire on the Anglo-American invaders. Yet the Allies possessed one trump card that the Axis forces could not begin to match—a powerful fleet sitting just off shore with weapons that could destroy virtually any German strongpoint. The master mariner who orchestrated this maritime firestorm was Vice-Admiral Kent Hewitt, who was using Avalanche as a dress rehearsal for the even more complex Normandy invasion the next year.

The Allied assault on Salerno began in the predawn moments of June 9, 1943, just under one year from the Allied attempt to gain solid footing at the other side of the continent with Operation Overlord. Much as elite Allied airborne forces would land behind enemy lines to spread confusion and terror among the German defenders at Normandy, a force of American Rangers, under already well-known Col. William Darby, landed at the small fishing village of Maiori, while their British counterpart commando units poured into the town of Vietri, five miles to the east. While the commandos slammed into a significant Axis defense position, the Rangers had discovered a hole in the German line and pushed quickly to seize the highest structure in the area, the Capodoro lighthouse, while some advance units captured Darby's primary objective, the Chiunzi Pass, which offered road access to Salerno from the rear.

Ironically, as Darby's Rangers spread out across the Italian shoreline, they were no longer enemy invaders, as King Victor Emmanuel had just signed a capitulation document in which his kingdom formally switched sides. The Axis garrison in Italy had been reduced by two million men at the stroke of a pen, and now Allies became sworn enemies to Field Marshal Kesserling, long the most fervent supporter of Italy in Hitler's court. As Allied forces waded ashore along a majestic beachfront, "Smiling Albert" underwent a startling transformation from Italophile to Italophobe.

While Albert Kesserling had, in effect, switched identities from superhero to supervillain in a metamorphosis worthy of contemporary American comic book characters, the American soldiers pushing inland were in many respects transforming the identities and reputations of their parent divisions. The 36th Division had been formed around National Guard units in Texas and Oklahoma during World War I and had maintained much of its frontier identity into 1943. The unit insignia was an arrowhead superimposed on the letter T, with the arrow representing Arizona and the T, the Texans. The unit had no shortage of nicknames, as it was called the Panther Division, The Texas Army, Arrowheads, and T-Patchers. The National Guard division was activated in federal service in late 1940, literally in the shadow of the Alamo and stationed at Fort Jim Bowie before being transferred east to practice amphibious landing with mock assaults on bathing areas of Martha's Vineyard, Massachusetts.

Depending on individual viewpoints among the T-Patchers, the division had either been rewarded or punished for its invasion of Massachusetts, as Mark Clark selected the unit for Avalanche over the more experienced 34th Division. Even the very much Yankee born and bred division commander, Gen. Fred Walker, quickly adapted to his new environment by always carrying a Lone Star flag in his knapsack and tolerated the activities of his men when they forced every customer in any bar on either side of the Atlantic Ocean to stand and remove their hats as they bellowed the words to "The Eyes of Texas."

The Wild West atmosphere of Ernest Dawley's VI Corps Salerno assault force was carried in the T-Patchers' sister division, the Thunderbirds of the 45th Infantry Division. Dawley's second unit was formed around volunteers from Colorado, Arizona, New Mexico, and Oklahoma, with an unusually diverse roster of Native Americans, Latinos, Anglo cowboys, and "city slickers" from the relatively small number of population centers in the region. Ironically, the Thunderbirds shoulder patch was a red square with a yellow swastika in the middle, which began as a tribute to the Native American flavor of the unit but was switched on the eve of the war to a less controversial Thunderbird.

The Thunderbirds would go into combat under the command of Gen. Troy Middleton, a popular, intelligent officer on a short track to lieutenant general, who had demonstrated considerable courage outside the line of fire when he refused to ban journalist/cartoonist William Mauldin when George Patton demanded that he be fired for publishing cartoons depicting the difficult conditions under which the Thunderbirds were living and fighting. Middleton had escaped Patton's wrath but now had a dangerous assignment to cover over ten miles of beachfront that would become a bull's-eye for German artillery in the hills along the beach.

The long-term impact of Middleton's near career-ending faceoff with Patton was a reserved place from Dwight Eisenhower for command of

American VIII Corps in the Normandy battle of the Cotentin Peninsula, and subsequent Operation Cobra at the peak of the Overlord fighting. Yet on this balmy September morning, Overlord was both nine months and the length of a continent away, and the Allied advance forces would soon be dead or in prisoner of war camps unless the Allied main forces could establish a beachhead. Ironically, even though the vast majority of Americans scheduled to hit the beaches of Salerno came from someplace other than the Northeast and Midwest of the United States, their British counterparts in the invasion force continued to call virtually anyone with an American accent a "Yank." Yet beyond this minor irritant, the British units were assigned landing beaches that were in some respects even more daunting targets than those the Yanks were facing.

The British assault force in Avalanche centered around two combat divisions. The 46th Division was recruited primarily from Hampshire, the East Midlands, and Northwest England and was officially designated the North Midland Division. The core elements of this division had been evacuated from Dunkirk beaches three years earlier, and even if these men were reentering the continent at a huge distance from where they left it, there was an excitement gathering among the troops that Avalanche would at least provide a measure of revenge for being "Dunkirked."

The Midlanders' companion invasion force, the British 56th Division, was a far different unit, in that it was composed of men enlisted from wide recruiting sweeps through Britain and could not point to any particular "home base" for its diverse membership. This relatively impersonal unit was provided with some compensation, as it had been reinforced by the much higher profile 201 Guards Brigade which had experienced very active service in the desert war and which included a large number of comrades who had been stationed at Tobruk when Rommel had captured most of its garrison.

The target city of Salerno was hardly one of the most populous cities of Europe, but its seventy thousand residents placed it on a rough equivalency of Albany, New York, or Harrisburg, Pennsylvania, with the added prestige of housing one of the most famous and oldest universities in existence, an institution that rivaled Oxford and Cambridge for sheer academic brand recognition. The city of Naples, which loomed twenty miles farther up the coast, was clearly more important in the area of commerce, but Salerno offered far more cultural appeal. with its ancient learning center rivaled for attention by the Greek-era town of Paestum, which served as a constant reminder of Salerno's fame in the Greco-Roman world of the ancients.

As the Americans and their British allies began to push inland from the sea, Field Marshal Kesserling decided to take an enormous strategic gamble by largely ignoring the threat of Bernard Montgomery's slow march northward from the southern tip of Italy, while throwing the German 10th Army into a massive offensive to force the newly landed enemy invasion force near the Salerno beachhead back into the sea in a massive Teutonic one-two punch.

German intelligence had scored a major coup in correctly anticipating the landing areas of the Allied add-on forces, and now troops were cutting down trees and bushes to provide a clear field of fire, while their comrades dragged heavy guns right down to the beachfront to blast landing craft into splinters before their passengers could sprint to dry land. Machine guns were employed in specific zones that would provide interlocking fire, with some guns actually deployed right on the edge of the water in fifty-yard intervals. Another fifty yards behind the light machine guns, the heavier artillery was wheeled into place to provide another strongpoint in front of the mortar positions that could lob shells into the invaders' landing craft while they were at their most vulnerable position. Invaders who successfully navigated through this curtain of steel would suddenly find themselves targeted by the deadly 88mm guns that provided a crescendo to this symphony of death.

Much like the experiences of Allied soldiers the following spring when they would clamber ashore on the beaches of Normandy, a similar cast of characters now entered a terrifying middle world between the sea and the world beyond the coastal beaches. The American landing beaches ran along two miles of coastline that flanked the edges of the ancient ruins of Paestum. The man ultimately responsible for the success of this landing was Maj. Gen. Ernest Dawley, who now, briefly, took center stage in the first American invasion of German-dominated mainland Europe.

Ernest Dawley entered the Avalanche operation as a middle-aged general who looked a bit older than he really was. Most of his career revolved around assignments in artillery units and staff positions that culminated in 1918 with assignment as the chief of staff of artillery units of the Second United States Army. Dawley was a close friend of Lt. Gen. Lesley McNair, who was nominally the highest-ranking administrative officer as commander of Army ground forces in the United States and helped Dawley to secure command of the VI Corps, which was ticketed for service in the burgeoning Mediterranean Theater of operations.

Fifth Army commander Mark Clark and Ernest Dawley were never able to sustain close bonds, especially with the always looming reality that Clark was ten years younger than his subordinate. Now, in Dawley's first significant battle, his corps waded into a hail of steel that might very well end with a disaster on the level of Pickett's Charge at Gettysburg. Ironically, the main reason that the Paestum landing didn't replicate George Pickett's iconic fiasco was the intervention of artillery. The invaders had pushed inland just far enough to bring artillery batteries onto the beachfront, and soon, shells were tearing into the German assault units. Then the massive firepower of the Allied naval forces joined the action and tore another swath through the lines of field gray opponents. Lastly, the Allied air forces entered the contest just as the German high command received word that General Montgomery's slow-moving crawl northward had morphed into a full-scale charge. The Americans had their backs to the sea but were never forced into the water, and their foothold on the mainland would gradually expand. The chief career casualty during the battle for the beaches was General Dawley, who was replaced by Mark Clark with Gen. John Lucas, over the strong dissent of many of the commanders in the field, notably James Gavin, the new rising star of the paratroop forces.

Dawley experienced the indignity of being a failed commander sent home in semi-disgrace. He lost two stars with a demotion to colonel, was shifted to command the tank destroyer training school, later received one star back for his absolute discretion on the matter, and lived long enough to see the even more draconian career derailment of Watergate. Mark Clark, the youngest-looking senior officer in the room, turned over VI Corps to John Lucas, a general who looked even older than Dawley. The new corps commander would get his unwanted ticket home the next year at Anzio, but for the moment, the Allies still held a portion of the European mainland.

Now that the Allied forces were ashore, the next challenge was to push inland beyond the beachfront and eventually link American and British invasion areas. One of the earliest thrusts inland from the sea was centered around Col. William O. Darby's versatile Ranger units, as these elite troops pushed through resort towns like Linori and Amalfi, marched through a long line of lemon tree orchards, and made camp at the far end of Chiunzi Pass over five miles from the edge of the beach. Darby and Mark Clark kept in constant communication as the Rangers plunged ever deeper into the enemy defenses while the invaluable naval vessels provided vital fire support.

Darby climbed to the top floor of an abandoned building, which offered a sweeping vista of the region, and promptly called massive naval barrages on key targets, all coded to the identities of Snow White's seven dwarves. The San Francisco Hotel now became the fire control center for an offensive surge off the beaches that resulted in the capture of Vietri, a tiny port town squeezed between Darby's position and the actual city of Salerno. The Allies had now secured a viable, if tiny, port on the Italian coast, but the invasion force had been spread dangerously thin in order to accomplish this goal, and the American position now included a dangerous two-mile gap between the Sele and Calore Rivers that German commanders quickly utilized as a target in a planned counterattack. As Darby radioed firing directions from a front window of the hotel, the still fragile foothold on the Salerno area beaches was solidified by the arrival of British units that rivaled the American Rangers in daredevil operations.

Darby's new neighbors on the flank of the Allied line were an elite British force centered around the Royal Marines of number 41 Commando and the number 2 Army Commando which, in concert with the Rangers, provided a secure base from which to launch a thrust farther inland. Ironically, while these new positions were viewed as the launching pad for an Allied offensive toward the city of Salerno, four powerful German *Kampfgruppen* were already moving into position to push the Allies back toward the sea. Gen. Traugott Herr looked down from the high ground above the seashore and marveled at the opportunity presented by an Allied battle line filled with gaping holes that seemed to welcome a massive armored counterattack.

On Monday morning, September 13, General Herr ordered his armored units to swing around the rear of the still fragile Allied line and capture the river bridges that linked the invaders with their vital naval support forces. While startled British forces pulled back to defend a sanatorium, pushing onto what would soon be called "Hospital Hill," the Americans sprinted to the temporary safety of a complex of buildings called Fiocche Farm. The main American defensive position was formed around a huge complex constructed to process large amounts of tobacco.

The battle for the "tobacco factory" became a magnet for Allied and Axis forces who changed ownership of the building several times each. While American soldiers clung to a shell-damaged warehouse on the western edge of the large, circular complex, Panzergrenadiers captured the eastern side of the building. "Thunderbirds" and Panzergrenadiers blasted at each other across a wide central yard, but the Germans gradually worked their way around the curved corridors of the warehouse and pushed the Americans out of the entire complex.

After the sun set on "Black Monday," General Walker promptly fired all three of his regimental commanders, while even more senior officers realized that their own days of command were numbered. American theater commander, Dwight Eisenhower, made an emergency visit to the battle site, while a surprisingly jovial Adolf Hitler exclaimed of Allied future plans, "No more invasions for them! They are much too cowardly."

Yet only hours after the Führer's bold prediction, massive Allied reinforcements began landing on the still Allied-held beaches and threw back poorly coordinated Axis attacks. On September 18, American patrols discovered that the Germans had abandoned the bloody halls of the Tobacco Factory, and upon further inspection, the shocking truth settled in that the Germans had essentially declared victory and then retreated northward toward the far more important city of Naples, only a short distance up the coast. The whole German line simply swung northwards to span across the Italian peninsula to the east of Naples with a backup position on the Volturno River, north of Naples, if and when the Allies penetrated into that city. The Allied forces had suffered nearly thirteen thousand casualties to capture a relatively small city, while inflicting perhaps one-fourth as many casualties on their enemy. Yet the Allies were now on Italian soil to stay, and even if they crawled up the boot, they were always advancing with the Germans always in retreat.

CHAPTER 13

A Square Mile of Hell

The Battle for Tarawa

WHILE AMERICAN AND OTHER ALLIED UNITS CLAMBERED OVER THE rocky hills and icy streams that stood between their armies and the liberation of Rome, another contingent of troops stared out from the decks of transport ships at the vast Pacific Ocean that contained a tiny coral atoll that would soon assume the iconic status of Bunker Hill, Antietam, Cold Harbor, and the Argonne Forest as a site of sanguinary exchange between US personnel and their enemy. The tiny island atoll known as Tarawa represented the extreme edge of the Japanese Empire, the very outer limits of their stolen territories. Tarawa Atoll was an island group among several islands identified collectively as the Gilberts, a string of tiny specks that had until recently been an outpost of the British Empire.

In one of a number of one-sided victories in the immediate aftermath of Pearl Harbor, an Imperial invasion force scooped up the Gilberts, as a tiny British constabulary unit was captured, and Japanese engineers particularly focused on Betio Island and Makin Island as the location for significant garrisons and defense installations. Now, nearly two years later, the American high command had chosen the Gilberts as the location for the first intrusion into the Imperial Empire, with the Army tasked with the capture of Makin Island and the Marine Corps designated as the assault force on Betio. While the two Army battalions designated to assault Makin would face a mixed bag force of only a bit more than one-tenth of their own strength, the Second Marine Division tasked with the Betio operation would be confronted by a powerful garrison of five thousand Imperial Special Landing Force personnel who were basically the counterpart of American Marines.

The 7th Sasebo Special Navy Landing Force and the 3rd Special Base Defense Force formed the main components of Rear Adm. Keiji Shibazaki's garrison, which was, in turn, supported by a platoon of eight tanks, four huge long-range naval guns, and a dozen field pieces. That garrison could also greet any American assault force with dozens of heavy and light machine guns deployed along almost any conceivable enemy landing point. While this formidable garrison was theoretically committed to defend Betio Island to the last man, most of the garrison, from Admiral Shibazaki down to the lowliest private, fully expected the still impressive Imperial surface fleet to storm to the rescue and gain revenge for Midway and Guadalcanal.

The island entrusted to the care of these elite Nipponese fighting men was just under a square mile of coral shaped like a triangle with its bottom third facing the entrance to a coral-floored lagoon that fronted the Tarawa Atoll portion of the Gilbert Islands. The entire atoll featured a dozen villages scattered on about twenty islands that stretched over thirty miles at the longest point and held a mission station, a national government administration building, and piers stretching from the beachfront into the shallow waters beyond. While large numbers of palm trees dotted the island, Betio was in no sense a "jungle island," comparable to the green hell that was much of Guadalcanal and New Guinea as American and Imperial forces battled for supremacy in those locations.

Operation Galvanic was expected to emerge as the first really important Marine-dominated amphibious landing on a beach fully protected by Japanese defenders. All of the elements for the initiation of the first of a series of American amphibious assaults against a heavily defended Japanese stronghold island were fully coming together for the first time. Adm. Chester Nimitz, the officer responsible for the massive American naval effort in the Pacific Theater, was one of the primary proponents of the theory of an "island hopping" strategy that would leave several large Japanese garrisons withering on the vine, as they were simply bypassed rather than attacked. However, other islands could not be "hopped over," and Tarawa was one of them. Wresting a heavily defended island from the Japanese would emerge as a professional specialty for Gen. Holland McTyeire Smith, the profanity-loving, intense, short-tempered Marine now better known as "Howlin' Mad" Smith to friends and adversaries alike. While photographs depicted a superficially mild-mannered, bespectacled middle-aged man who could be the hometown doctor or high school principal, he barely concealed and often exhibited a ferocious temper that would lead to debates about his fitness to command on the part of congressmen the following year. At the moment, "Howlin' Mad" Smith was focused on ensuring that as commander of V Marine Amphibious Corps, his main subordinates including Maj. Gen. Julian Smith, commander of 2nd Marine Division, and Col. David Shoup, divisional operations officer, were on board for the looming assault on Betio Island.

Julian Smith had learned combat techniques in the jungles of Central America during the frequent "banana wars" of the 1920s and utilized his photographic memory to make the right decisions at the right moment. His chief planner and detail person, Colonel Shoup, was an extremely young-looking intelligence and managerial genius, addicted to chomping on unlit cigars and developing iconoclastic ideas that would eventually propel him into the highest levels of power as commandant of the Marine Corps under Presidents Eisenhower and Kennedy. Shoup was determined to utilize all of his intelligence and every possible innovative idea, even those emanating from young enlisted Marines, to avoid a World War II version of Civil War bloodbaths, such as Fredericksburg and Cold Harbor.

The plans for victory in the Pacific war germinated in the halls of Washington, centered around an initial penetration of the Japanese Empire in the Marshall Islands, the capture of which would provide a springboard for the recapture of Guam and the invasion of Saipan and Tinian. However, these targeted locations were all under the protective umbrella of the huge Imperial naval and air fortress of Truk that stood like a dagger that could be thrust into any planned American offensive. Adm. Raymond Spruance, one of the major architects of the victory at Midway, was less than enthusiastic about launching the first American naval offensive in the looming shadow of the Truk fortress and pressed for an alternative target—the Gilbert Islands.

Operation Galvanic was designed as a joint Army-Marine invasion of the Gilberts chain that lay within a reasonable distance of American support bases and was thought to be far less heavily defended than Truk. This assumption was partially correct, as Betio Island contained a Japanese airfield that was not yet fully operational and was devoid of protective aircraft, but that positive point was largely negated by the reality of a large ground garrison of over five thousand men that had enjoyed ample time to turn virtually every foot of the island into a potential death trap for American invaders.

Unlike Operation Overlord, which was put into operation after long and meticulous planning, Galvanic had the appearance of a rushed operation in which too many variables were simply put on a back burner. Fortunately, unlike the American intervention on Guadalcanal which was thrown together even more rapidly, Galvanic was at least not a "shoestring" offensive lacking essential ingredients for an expected victory. Unlike a year earlier, when the Marines on Guadalcanal had watched in shock as their support fleet retreated from the battle zone to safer waters, a powerful fleet was now on call for support of the landing on Tarawa, and the vessels would be in action for the entire length of the operation.

However, this significant advantage was at least partially nullified by the alarming lack of intelligence about the ability of the Betio garrison to throw the invaders back into the sea and the significant physical barriers that would face the assault troops as they attempted to make landfall. Even more challenging was one of the facts that Galvanic planners *did* know about their target. The water around Betio was a complex aquatic environment susceptible to periodic "dodging tides" that would draw the sea so far away from the beaches that the invasion troops might have to push toward the beaches from water only three feet deep, shallow enough to rip the bottom out of standard "Higgins Boat" landing craft. Luckily for the landing units, unlike the invasion of Normandy just over six months later, the Marines had supplemented their Higgins boats with a new landing craft called an Amphtrac (or Amtrac) that was more of an amphibious landing tractor than a traditional landing craft. However, there was still a limited supply of these vessels.

The 2nd Marine Division that was tasked with the Betio operation had been involved in the later stages of the grueling battle on Guadalcanal and had then been pulled back to New Zealand to rest, recuperate, and train for future operations. After the green hell of Guadalcanal, the Marines alternated recreational activities and training exercises against the backdrop of a West European/North American climate and a huge welcome extended by New Zealanders, who feared an imminent Japanese invasion of an island in which most of the physically fit young men were either fighting in the European Theater or trudging through the jungles of New Guinea to halt Nipponese offensives.

Maj. Gen. Justin Smith commanded an oversized division centered around five regiments—the 2nd, 6th, and 8th Marine Infantry Regiments, the 10th Marine artillery regiment, and an 18th Marine regiment that was a mixture of combat engineers, pioneers, and construction workers. In a Pacific Theater that seemed to have an unending supply of both Army and Marine generals named Smith, Justin Smith answered to Maj. Gen. Holland "Howlin' Mad" Smith and Rear Adm. Richmond Kelly Turner, the short-tempered, ill-humored naval officer usually identified simply as "Terrible Turner." These two leaders' less than warm personalities were tempered somewhat by the fact that Holland Smith was a personally brave commander who acknowledged the heroism of his troops, while Turner often behaved courteously toward junior officers and enlisted personnel who were less likely to get in his way than their superior officers. "Howlin' Mad" Smith also proved popular with his men when they learned that he had expended significant personal capital to ensure that the invaders would be carrying the new M-1 Garand semi-automatic rifles in place of the much-slower-firing World War I era Springfield bolt-action weapons that had been used in many previous battles..

The five thousand Imperial troops tasked with literally holding Betio Island to the last man would now be outgunned in small-unit combat, as they were armed with slower-firing, five-shot bolt-action rifles and moderately cumbersome hand grenades, but they had an ample supply of machine guns, and reasonably good cover from which to fire at intruders. They retained at least some hope in the prospect that if they could simply kill enough invaders, the Marines, who seemed to value individual lives more than their Imperial counterparts, might simply back off and try to slice into the inner Empire from somewhere else.

Contrary to the innuendoes by reporters and some Hollywood films of the era, the Marines who were about to land on Betio Island and the soldiers preparing to invade Makin Island generally had great respect for one another with most of their ire reserved for personnel regardless of branch who had been thought to have actively plotted to serve a rear echelon posting. The link between the two services was about to be forged even closer in the near future as, to the utter shock of both active and inactive Marines, this would be the last invasion composed entirely of leatherneck volunteers. The rapidly growing need for combat personnel had finally forced the Marine Corps to concede to the necessity of enrolling draftees designated to the Corps regardless of their personal desire for choice of service. This would be the last time that an entirely volunteer Marine invasion force would storm onto an enemy beach. After Tarawa, a Marine Corps that traditionally secured a large portion of its recruits from smaller communities and warmer weather parts of the nation would contain a much larger proportion of leathernecks from more populous cities and major Northeast and midwestern cities. The "Old Breed" was not exactly dying, but it was morphing into an organization quite different from the world of the pre–Pearl Harbor Corps.

Regardless of this demographic transition, the men of the Marine assault force were tasked with a very difficult mission of landing on an enemy-held island with virtually no advantage of surprise. The recent battles to recapture the Aleutians had been fought on less than ideal terrain with frigid instead of torrid weather conditions taking a significant toll on the invasion force. The Imperial garrison had essentially fought to the last man, and the same mindset was expected to confront the Marines on Betio Island. The Marines expected to confront much more immediate enemy fire than in the Aleutians as the defenders had very little space in which they could retreat, but the positive aspect of this topography was that American tanks and other armored vehicles could be thrown much more rapidly into the battle with much less risk of being rendered immobile as on Attu, where snow, ice, and rugged terrain significantly reduced the effectiveness of American armored support.

Now, in the predawn hours of Saturday, November 20, 1943, the invaders made final preparations for the assault, while enjoying a last moment of satisfaction from the pre-Thanksgiving dinner they had just enjoyed. According to the participants, their pre-invasion breakfast showed a significant decline in culinary satisfaction as "The next morning, before leaving the ship, the officers were served their standard 'steak and eggs' while 'grunts' had beans and ketchup." After this less than sumptuous final meal, the heavily laden assault troops clambered toward their embarkation positions, still largely expecting the air and naval bombardments to annihilate most of the garrison. Yet as one participant, Bernard Lee Riggs, noted in his memoir of the battle, "If anyone had known what the next four days had in store for us, I'm sure that we would have embraced one another, written some long last letters home with signatures of 'goodbye,' and each would have made peace with his maker." Even though Riggs was still confident of a relatively rapid victory on that predawn morning, he admitted, "I did not have any faith in the intelligence given us before we were dropped in those small assault crafts."

Now the choreography of a classic Pacific war amphibious assault began to lurch into motion with its strange combination of repetition of previous operations and unexpected surprises. The battleships and cruisers spat orange flames from their barrels, and a whistling sound followed and ended with a thump and multicolored explosion on the island. The Imperial defenders returned the greeting with their huge British eight-inch guns that they had transported to Betio after the mammoth pieces had proved no value when the Japanese army captured Singapore from the land side instead of from the sea. *Colorado* and *Maryland* had completed their first task, and now allowed other vessels to get in closer to fire at their assigned targets. Smaller surviving Japanese guns opened fire on two American minesweepers until destroyers *Dashiell* and *Ringgold* entered the Betio lagoon and covered the minesweeping operation with their five-inch guns.

The Higgins boats then chugged at a stately pace through the almost achingly beautiful turquoise lagoon to deposit their passengers at prearranged landing sites. These craft, developed in New Orleans designing centers, would become one of the most iconic elements of D-Day

The Marine battle for the control of Tarawa was a harbinger of the difficulty of conquering the vast Japanese Empire. Here, Marines manage a light-hearted moment as their landing barge approaches the Japanese-held island.
LIBRARY OF CONGRESS

in Normandy just over six months later. Under the protective cover of Dauntless and Helldiver bombers, the boats chugged toward a pair of piers that stretched out into the water. There would be no festive mood on Betio on this day as the American invaders nudged closer to the protruding structures. Well-concealed Japanese automatic weapons opened up a ferocious barrage as damaged American landing craft left their passengers half swimming, half walking in neck-deep water as the Imperial defenders engaged in a ghoulish version of a boardwalk arcade shooting game.

Now as the Marines scrambled out of their now largely useless assault craft and headed toward shore, virtually every weapon that the defenders could fire opened in a grand crescendo of flying death. The first dozens of what would eventually be thousands of casualties began to stain the azure water with a red hue. One survivor of the assault insisted that, "This was the largest 'shooting gallery' that the US Navy could provide. This left every Marine exposed as 'wingless ducks' might be in a pond or small lake, drifting toward the shore. These men were friends, brothers, husbands and good Marines who could have been here today writing this story instead of me."

At the peak moment of potential disaster, a series of events unfolded to turn the American landing on Betio Island from an aquatic Pickett's Charge to a still sanguinary but winnable battle. First, unlike the men in the Higgins boats, the occupants of the newly designed Amtracs, more often than not, were able to either clamber out of the vehicles on the beach or at least disembark in shallow water. These part sea craft, part wheeled vehicle devices were largely exclusive to the Pacific Theater and were seemingly largely ignored by the officers responsible for planning Overlord the following June. Unlike the Higgins craft, Amtracs could alternately float and crawl on aquatic or solid surfaces and deposit their twenty-four to thirty-six passengers closer to their enemy tormentors than the Higgins craft. Most of the men in the Amtracs landed on Betio unwounded and fully armed, and their good luck was enhanced when, almost an hour behind schedule, Hellcats, Helldivers, and other warplanes swooped from the blue skies above them and began to rip through the Japanese defense positions. Imperial Zeros rose to challenge the intruders, but craft with red suns on their wings were soon crashing into the sand or sea far more often than their opponents.

Adm. Keiji Shibazaki had correctly surmised that the American invasion would center on the north beaches of Betio and had concentrated his most powerful anti-invasion weapons toward that direction. Now the admiral began to sense that he had just acquired a second advantage in the battle that was essentially a self-inflicted wound in the American ranks. The Marine invaders reached the invasion beaches with the one or two canteens they had brought along from their transport ships, but an island located only eighty miles from the equator produced massive dehydration issues which required a far more ample supply of water than any individual could possibly carry. Yet in one of the worst oversights of the entire battle, the units responsible for delivering additional water to the combat units had managed to simply reuse oil drums that had previously stored fuel without bothering to clean out the inside of the containers. The result was that Marines who had so far managed to dodge enemy bullets doubled over in agony from their reactions to the tainted liquid.

High above this gruesome panorama of American assault troops either dropping to the ground with bullet wounds or doubled over after ingesting toxic water, aircrews took in a scene that looked like a diorama of a Civil War battlefield such as Antietam or Gettysburg. Instead of landmarks such as Devil's Den or the Burnside Bridge, the square mile of this contemporary hellish battlefield was rapidly producing its own points of maximum confrontation. One man-made object that was already entering the conversation of battle was the long pier that thrust out between Red Beach 2 and Red Beach 3 on American invasion maps. A second focal point a few hundred yards down the beach was a wharf that also extended into the azure lagoon. On an island with very few distinctive man-made objects, these two structures would be contested as if each was a priceless exhibit of architecture. Marines from California viewed these objects as some bizarre knock-off of the famous piers that provided everything from ice cream to arcade games along the West Coast, while their counterparts from the East Coast saw them as replicas of fishing piers that jutted out from seaside boardwalks such as Atlantic City and Virginia Beach.

News correspondent and author Robert Sherrod spent the night following the invasion attempting to make out the few landmarks visible in the darkness while noting, "I did not see a single Marine fire his rifle during the night. Such a firing might have given away our position. Whatever else I decided, these Marines were not trigger happy!" As the second morning of battle dawned, only about two out of three Marines who had landed the previous day were still both alive and capable of combat action. As fighting resumed, the invaders were shocked to learn that much of the most deadly enemy fire was coming from a seemingly abandoned freighter sitting in the lagoon. Imperial troops had made their way out to the vessel during the night and now nearly succeeded in drawing the Americans into a crossfire from both the sea and the interior of Betio. The deadly crossfire dropped scores of American Marines, eventually adding two hundred more names to the frighteningly long death list that was surging upward by the hour.

Col. David Shoup, the youthful-looking Second Division operations officer, was now thrust into the unexpected position of implementing the plan he had developed in the quiet of an office. The future Medal of Honor recipient and commandant of the Marine Corps was now tasked with turning a bloody stalemate into an American victory. The emergence of a seemingly old-fashioned weapon was about to change the course of the Battle of Tarawa. The century-or-more-old shotgun was neither banned for Marine use nor mandated as a necessary weapon. However, many of the more experienced Marines insisted it was more likely to hear an enemy than to see him, and the scattered shots of multiple metal pellets seemed to be particularly useful in this lush battlefield. This new tactic seemed particularly valuable in countering the numerous Japanese defenders who had climbed trees or hidden in bushes as they peppered away at the Americans who seemed to be more frequently fighting on open ground. As one veteran Marine insisted, "It's something like hunting turkeys; sometimes you have to flush them out." Now, as some of the invaders let loose with their shotguns against enemies hiding in the foliage, other Americans were throwing demolition charges down vents and shafts which would often force the defenders to emerge out into the open where they often faced the deadly fire of multiple flamethrowers.

As this deadly game of hide and seek was acted out in the interior parts of Betio on the second day of battle, just as darkness was about to fall, Marines anywhere in sight of the main pier cheered as they watched jeeps towing 37mm and 75mm self-propelled guns in preparation for a massive attack that would eliminate one of the most dangerous threats to American advances. Soon the massive firepower snuffed out a key Imperial position, and medical staff supervised the transfer of wounded Marines to the sea end of the pier, as stretchers were positioned to facilitate extraction of the casualties by naval craft for their journey out to hospital ships. By nightfall of the second day of the battle, the remaining Japanese defenders had been forced back to the eastern end of the island and were so often without living officers to command them that they were reduced to forming small attack groups or fighting as individuals to at least ensure that the invaders would be forced to pay a significant price in blood for control of Betio Island.

Then, as the third day of Galvanic dawned, Howitzers, battleships, destroyers, and carrier planes all combined into a riot of explosive violence that one Marine insisted, "Shook the island like an eight point Richter Scale earthquake," as the fire turned the darkness into a brightly lit island. Now, it became the hour of the banzai, as swarming Imperial troops attempted to smash through the American flanks to inflict at least some critical loss on the enemy invaders. Almost by instinct, surviving Japanese defenders drifted toward their most easily defended positions in preparation for an extensive last stand.

On the morning of November 23, 1943, the climax on Betio Island developed in a manner predictable for a battle in which one of the armies had no concept of an honorable surrender. At one Japanese-held blockhouse, the garrison charged toward an American Sherman tank that knocked down several dozen attackers with a single round. Along a one-mile stretch of beachfront, the Marines wiped out 475 defenders at a cost of nine of their own men killed. Tanks roared through the prehistoric-looking battlefield like predatory raptors, picking off an accelerating number of doomed defenders. Perhaps five dozen Koreans forced to labor on the Imperial defense were happy to end their service for their Nipponese master, but among the thousands of defenders, the number of prisoners taken did not climb into double figures, with a single, noncommissioned officer representing the highest-ranking live captive.

Yet the cost for this island victory was a stark preview of what would occur as the American naval offensive pushed ever closer to the Japanese home islands. A total of 1,026 Americans would never leave Betio Island, as they were interred there. Col. David Shoup would be awarded the Medal of Honor for his actions on Betio and would emerge as a colorful, controversial senior officer during the trying days of the Vietnam War, while 3,401 other Marines would receive the Purple Heart, which averaged out to about one American casualty a minute during the engagement. Those Marines who were still capable of eating were rewarded by the Navy with a second Thanksgiving dinner, as the men slowly lost sight of Tarawa Atoll, fading in the distance. The Gilbert Islands were now entering the rearview mirror of American amphibious invasion planners with the Marshall Islands the next designated target on the long road to Japan. Now, from the vast reaches of the Pacific and Atlantic Oceans and the Mediterranean Sea, the last month of 1943 was approaching with 1944 looming on the horizon, and from the Imperial Palace in Tokyo to the Führer's mountain retreat, men with little intent of peace and goodwill to other men would begin to wonder how, when, and where an aroused alliance of nations would attempt to change the nature of war in the last weeks of 1943 and the opening weeks of 1944.

CHAPTER 14

The Devil's Playground

Naples to the Volturno

THE BATTLE FOR SALERNO WAS THE FIRST MAJOR ENGAGEMENT ON THE mainland of Europe since the German Blitzkrieg of May and June 1940. In that confrontation, the British had fought with one eye on the beach behind them, focused increasingly on the Channel and the safe haven of Britain twenty miles across the water, and the French had clearly come to the conclusion that life in a German-dominated Europe was still better than burial in the middle of an increasingly unwinnable battle. In 1943, the British returned to the Continent with a new ally far more powerful than the French and, with their allies, largely controlling the sea and for much of the time, the airspace above the battlefield. Now it was the Germans who were marching in long lines toward prisoner of war camps or leaving the battlefield to the Allies in hopes of better fighting odds on another day. After Salerno, Naples was the next logical target for an Allied advance, another major milestone on the long road to Rome and a seeming death knell for Benito Mussolini's two-decade-long exercise in that odd combination of pageantry, showmanship, and brutality known as Fascism. Gen. Mark Clark outwardly cheered the capture of Salerno, yet privately admitted that the battle had been a "near disaster," in which his counterpart, Field Marshal Albert Kesserling, had proved himself to be "one of the ablest officers in the Hitler Armies, well-qualified as a commander and an administrator," though Clark was privately relieved that his nemesis had been transferred back to Germany, noting that, "I was glad to see him go."

The cost of capturing Salerno was not cheap. The British X Corps had lost four thousand men, including 531 killed in action, while the

American contingent had suffered sixteen hundred casualties with 225 fatalities. Yet, the Anglo-Americans now occupied a moderately important Italian city and had already begun to advance to the even more celebrated precincts of Naples, thirty miles farther up the coast.

Nearly two decades after World War II, *Life* magazine initiated a series of features on the Centennial anniversary of the American Civil War with a photo essay of a Civil War era costume ball at The Citadel college in Charleston, South Carolina. The event highlighted the commemoration of the Union surrender of Fort Sumter, and most of the cadets wore Confederate officers' uniforms, as their dance partners adopted nineteenth-century female ball gowns. The central couple in the feature was Gen. Mark Clark and his wife looking every bit as comfortable in a Civil War atmosphere as they did at the peak of World War II. However, on that particular evening Clark's main purpose was simply to obtain positive publicity for his relatively small college; two decades earlier, wearing more drab but practical gear, the general, in command of descendants both Yankees and Rebels, with offspring of British Redcoats mixed in, prepared to advance on a city of over three-quarters of a million people that was about to become the epicenter of another civil war between the Fascist and anti-Fascist elements of one of the most important port cities of Europe. Clark would live long enough to become the oldest surviving four-star general of World War II, but in 1943, he was about to witness a real-life civil war erupt before his eyes.

On September 16, 1943, Mark Clark and Dwight Eisenhower conferred on the next logical step in the Allied offensive, the liberation of Naples. Clark insisted to his superior officer, "We are in good shape now. We are here to stay." Yet it was clear that the Germans were still setting the pace of the campaign as they found ample time in their evacuation activities in Naples to settle scores with a broad list of "traitors," which often meant Neapolitans who were simply at the wrong place at the wrong time.

The German garrison of Naples had enjoyed relatively amicable relations with the Neapolitan population when the two nations were still considered equally valuable allies. The stunning beauty of a sun-drenched city sitting at the base of an ever-present Mount Vesuvius smoking in the near distance encouraged the German soldiers to distribute candy to children, invite their older sisters to go driving, and issue salutes to senior citizens. Then, to the genuine shock of many men serving in the military of the Third Reich, Italy simply switched sides and left a Pact of Steel that was assumed would last for decades. Most Neapolitans probably wished that the Germans would simply leave, and they were prepared to greet the newly arriving Allies in a transition that had been acted out numerous times in the long history of the city. However, in attics, basements, and closets all around the city, some Neapolitans pulled out smooth bore muskets, antique swords, surplus Italian army rifles, and even stolen German guns and prepared to send the occupiers out of the city just ahead of a hail of gunfire. American news photographers snapped photos of these mostly young guerrilla fighters, many of them nine and ten years old, defiantly brandishing weapons with cigarettes dangling from their mouths. In some respects, these young warriors seemed to be precursors of the guerrilla fighters that battled the Soviet occupation of the American heartland in the 1980s film *Red Dawn*—simultaneously without fear yet knowing deep down that they were hopelessly outgunned and doomed. In the film, virtually all the male teenage guerrillas are killed in action before the enemy is driven out at some unspecified date in the future. In the real world of Naples in 1943, the death toll swept far beyond the actual insurrectionists, but for the survivors, relief was only days or even hours away. American political and military analysts insisted that they could detect real anguish in the voice of Adolf Hitler as he gave a speech which accused the Italian government of treachery, an action which in turn prompted the Germans to occupy the northern half of Italy and treat that region as enemy territory. American analysts insisted that the defection of Italy from the Axis was "paying off" in a big way for the Allies, which demonstrated the superiority of having invaded Sicily and mainland Italy instead of the Sardinian and southern France invasion that had also been considered. Military analysts now asserted that the threat of a rapidly expanding campaign in the Mediterranean had compelled Italy to throw in the sponge sooner rather than later. Yet in the moon crater landscape of the city of Naples, the results seemed far less beneficial to the Neapolitan population.

The thirty-mile trek from newly captured Salerno to German-occupied Naples would be an odyssey through a seemingly endless series of mountains and hills occupied by German riflemen and mortar and machine-gun squads topped off with heavily concealed batteries of 88mm cannons that either tore apart advancing American platoons or sent men scurrying toward roadsides festooned with cleverly concealed German mines. The soaring casualty lists of personnel injured or killed by seemingly ubiquitous mines actually secured a minor public relations victory for Mark Clark when he overrode British medical officers' insistence that nurses and female Red Cross personnel should not be deployed in the advance. The American general welcomed the arrival of these distaff members of the Allied forces, and these angels in olive drab sent morale soaring, even if their contributions would soar as the casualty lists skyrocketed.

The shuffling of such Mediterranean luminaries as Bernard Montgomery, Dwight Eisenhower, and George Patton to the rapidly expanding planned invasion of northwest Europe in 1944 pushed Mark Clark even higher on the list of influential Allied commanders in Italy, and he realized that he had roughly a year to dominate center stage before Operation Overlord would threaten to push the Mediterranean conflict to a secondary status. The liberation of Rome before the first Allied soldiers set foot on the beaches of northern France became an almost obsessive goal for the still largely talented officers who had drawn the "other" invasion of Europe, rather than the iconic operation far to the north.

Mark Clark would now be either blessed or cursed with the command of this "other" major battle for Europe, and at least for the time being, the general was prominently featured in American news media. To Clark's credit, in a conflict in which a number of American commanders would seek the companionship of females not their wives in a wide variety of relationships, the normally humorless Clark adored his wife and displayed a sense of humor and compassion that would have shocked the men in his command who called him Marcus Aurelius Clarkus, due to his display of grandiose splendor. Maurine "Rennie" Clark and her husband were a middle-aged couple that essentially rebelled against the complacency and diminishing affection displayed by their age group in the 1940s and even brought iconic figures such as Gen. George Marshall and President Roosevelt into their live version of a romantic comedy film. When Clark was scheduled to return to Washington to report on his progress in the Mediterranean, Marshall hid Rennie on the back seat floor of a staff car to surprise her husband when he arrived at a stateside

Gen. Mark Clark emerged as the face of the American campaign to capture Italy.
LIBRARY OF CONGRESS

air base and then posted a guard of military police around their apartment so that the couple would not be interrupted as they enjoyed a brief second honeymoon. The commander-in-chief then changed his schedule to accommodate Clark so that he would not be rushed unduly to the capital and White House to issue his report.

Yet, in the early autumn of 1943, the very deadly business of adding Naples to the list of captured Axis cities was a grim reality which took the entire focus of Mark Clark, the general, not the husband and doting father.

While Naples shimmered in the distance as Allied forces drove north from Salerno, it began to occupy its own special chamber of hell. When Clark arrived at Place Garibaldi in the city center, the general felt uneasy that he still saw no Italians. "I was becoming conscious of the eyes that peeked out at us from the closed shutters of every house and every building. It was an eerie sensation." The general had a right to feel that eerie sensation, as the largest city yet captured by the Allies was undergoing a trial by fire in which Allied and Axis soldiers rarely even shot at one another. Naples no longer belonged to the Axis, but more than a few Neapolitans would never participate in the victory celebrations.

A military analyst for an American weekly magazine noted the importance of the Allied capture of Naples as, "Its capture is something equal to an Axis capture of Hollywood, Miami Beach and Brooklyn, the iconic centers of American life beyond mere centers of finance and politics."

Much like the horrific experiences of citizens of occupied Holland almost exactly a year later, the residents of Naples could see the Allies marching northward from Salerno and assumed that the German occupiers would merely fall back to better defensive positions. Dutch citizens watching the Germans prepare to retreat from Arnhem and vicinity in 1944 largely stayed out of the way of the Germans, and when the Allied offensive ran out of steam suffered more from a massive shortage of food than over German acts of retribution. The Neapolitans were determined to do much of the Allies' job for them by chasing the Nazis out of their joyful metropolis before the first Allied soldiers arrived. But joy soon turned to stark terror as violence careened upward on both sides.

While citizens of Naples, especially those belonging to Leftist organizations such as the Party for Italian Liberation, grabbed carefully concealed weapons and determined to free their city, American Ranger battalions pushed from the town of Maiori six miles into a mountain range dominated by Chiunzi Pass, not far south of a smoking Mount Vesuvius. As reinforcements from paratroop and infantry battalions arrived on the scene, the German defenders dropped artillery shells on the Allied positions from guns carefully hidden in a little village at the foot of the looming mountain range. While Allied commanders cobbled together a major assault force, the advance party of Americans set up positions around a thick-walled Italian farmhouse on the floor of the pass and named it Fort Schuster in honor of an officer who had set up a first-aid station on the premises.

The German defenders lacked the numbers to push the Americans and newly arriving British units back out of Chiunzi Pass, but the Allies, even with massive tank support, could not concentrate enough firepower to break through the pass. While the battle of Chiunzi Pass seesawed back and forth, the commanders of the German garrison in Naples made plans to accomplish an orderly evacuation of Naples once it became apparent that the city could no longer offer military value. More than a few German officers and men seethed in anger at the "treachery" of Italian allies abandoning the Axis cause, and the opportunity for massive violence skyrocketed as Italian partisan groups decided to "escort" the invaders out of the city with gunfire. "Payback" now replaced "correctness" in the German evacuation as recent Axis allies were now deemed to be mortal enemies. German soldiers began to admit that they had never really trusted their Italian comrades, and Field Marshal Kesserling's order to conscript young Italians into labor battalions provoked open rebellion.

Newly energized Neapolitans hurled roof tiles at German truck convoys and grabbed any weapon that might somehow kill a German. Schoolchildren now morphed into snipers and posed in menacing stances for anyone with a camera. An iconic photo in an American news magazine depicted a trio of Neapolitan "liberators" with two young teenagers cradling rifles and flanking a nine-year-old comrade puffing a cigarette and standing barefoot while holding a submachine gun. College professors led students in street fighting while twenty young boys from a local school died in a single firefight with the now hated German occupiers.

German demolition units responded to desultory sniper fire by blowing up the Naples sewage disposal plant, destroying the city's main power generator, torching the public library, and concealing time bombs to blow up at staggered times after the Germans evacuated the city. The leading government officials were kidnapped and held as hostages, and citizens were used as human shields in each retrograde movement out of the city. German troops stormed into maximum-security prisons, freed what appeared to be the most dangerous prisoners, gave them arms, and encouraged them to get "revenge" on their more law-abiding fellow citizens.

Gen. Mark Clark entered a newly liberated city that in many respects seemed to rival the destruction caused by the burning of Atlanta in Margaret Mitchell's iconic *Gone With the Wind* film, at the time still hugely popular for American theater patrons. Clark, in a very modern way, echoed the style of famous Roman generals entering cities by flying into Naples in a Piper Cub spotter plane and landing on one of the main plazas in the city. He further enhanced his reputation among the Neapolitan population on the following Sunday by attending a Thanksgiving mass in the Naples Cathedral followed by a letter to his wife, "giving" her the city as her birthday present. However, the Germans quickly informed Clark that they were still capable of killing Neapolitans, even after the German evacuation. One by one, preset time bombs exploded all over the city. Seventy people were killed or wounded when the main Naples post office turned into a fiery volcano. An explosion in the downtown shopping district created a deadly scythe along the city center, killing almost two dozen of the Rangers who had battled for Chiunzi Pass so recently. To his credit, the often imperious Clark rolled up his sleeves and worked as hard as a common private rescuing survivors. Starving residents acted out in an almost cartoonish style as they ate the fish in the Naples aquarium, roasted stray cats, and sold family heirlooms to Allied soldiers to purchase black market food. Mark Clark interspersed his letters with both the joy of victory and the loneliness of his increasingly high rank as his old friends, now in lesser ranks than Clark, no longer felt comfortable dropping by his headquarters to play cards. He sought a consolation prize from his wife: the dispatch of the family dog to Italy as the court of "Marcus Clarkus" now added a cocker spaniel to its ranks.

The capture of Naples meant that the Allies now controlled most of the southern third of Italy with little apprehension that the Germans had enough power to push them back into the sea. However, much of the rationale for the invasion of Italy was the opportunity to capture one of the three most important Axis capital cities. The Germans might be in retreat mode, but they were not yet on the run, and a glance at the map of Italy revealed a daunting list of mountain ranges and rivers looming between the Allied forces and the Eternal City. The next major barrier was the Volturno River, and a thrust toward the Italian capital seemed ludicrous until that wide, cold river was occupied on both banks by the Allies.

As the searing heat of an Italian summer gradually gave way to a preview of the wet, cold disagreeable winter that hovered over sunny Italy for several months each year, a massive force of over one hundred thousand American and British soldiers began to deploy for the jump across the first of many rivers that stood as barriers to a victory parade in Rome. Mark Clark's overall plan of action was to deploy the British 10 Corps under Gen. Sir R. I. McCready in an advance along the fertile coastal plain of western Italy with the British right flank extending fifteen to twenty miles in from the sea. American VI Corps drew the more physically difficult assignment of covering the British right flank in the process of groping its way through mountainous terrain studded with relatively wide rivers sure to be contested by German defenders. While much of this difficult advance would be undertaken by units that received relatively minimal publicity for their efforts, the already high-profile troops of Darby's Rangers would be paired off in this particular adventure with another newsworthy unit, the 100th Infantry Battalion composed of Japanese-Americans about to enter their first major battle.

This unit, fighting under the slogan, "Go for Broke," was one of the most carefully monitored forces in the entire American Army. It was a composite of Nisei residents of Hawaii territory and other Japanese Americans from the American mainland, each of whom had experienced a very different version of World War II up to that point.

The contingent from the mainland had been almost exclusively recruited from the detention camps established inland from the West Coast after the roundup of Japanese residents in the wake of Pearl Harbor.

As the need for American combat troops escalated enormously in 1942, young Nisei men in the detention camps were given a questionnaire that asked, "Are you willing to serve in the Armed Forces of the United States on combat duty wherever ordered?" Internees who answered in the affirmative now began to be assigned to the 442nd Regimental Combat Team, which was expected to serve in the Mediterranean Theater.

The other major component of the first Japanese-American combat unit was volunteers from the large Japanese-American community in Hawaii. These men had largely avoided incarceration due to the enormous numbers of men of Japanese ancestry in the future fiftieth state. In fact, a substantial portion of the prewar ROTC enrollment at the University of Hawaii was made up of the islands' Japanese population, and a number of them would become officers in the new unit, although senior command positions were reserved for white officers. The mixed message on racial identity continued in training exercises in southern US military training camps where the "Go for Broke" men were designated as "honorary whites" in segregated transportation and dining facilities, yet endured the stares of civilians still fixated on the racial ancestry of the enemy that had attacked Pearl Harbor. Now the men of Go for Broke attempted to advance against an enemy for which racial identity was an overriding concern but was a close ally of the ancestral homeland of that elite American unit.

On October 12, 1943, the Nisei troops formed part of the assault units of the 34th Infantry Division tasked with making a successful crossing of the Volturno River and pushing the enemy just a bit closer to the defenses of Rome. General Clark admitted in the post-battle report that the troops had "covered a distance of almost twenty miles in twenty-four hours despite extreme difficulty of the mountain road and a German defensive position that was about as good as could be imagined for the defense of a river, even after the 45th Division had taken the high hills that protected the right flank."

The Germans held the high ground, enjoyed perfect observation of every American move, and were energized with a generous supply of artillery batteries that they knew how to employ. The German high command now designated the Volturno position as the Gustav Line and settled in to see where the Americans would attempt to cross the river. The Nisei volunteers were now joined by a battalion of Darby's Rangers, and in the gloom of a short, late autumn afternoon, American forces attempted to push one step closer to the Eternal City. The crumbling ruins of ancient castles provided hints of earlier battles between almost forgotten adversaries. Yet unlike most of those earlier battles, the German defenders were not fighting directly to protect their homes and families. Wehrmacht engineers were already constructing a fallback position farther north which would eventually become famous as the Winter Line and develop its own tales of triumph and frustration.

The contest to hold and secure the Volturno River played out against an eerie backdrop of both murky weather and murky senses of identity. The men of the 100th Battalion were fighting for an American republic that was currently imprisoning some of their kinsmen as political traitors. On the other hand, a Ranger unit was deployed across a ravine from a German unit commanded by a sergeant who was a hotel management major at Michigan State University and was drafted into the Wehrmacht when he had returned for Christmas vacation. The adversaries enjoyed friendly banter during a series of informal truces when horrendous weather trumped military priorities.

During the first week of November, operating largely at night, the Rangers, the Nisei soldiers, and much of the rest of Mark Clark's Fifth Army crossed the Volturno under cover of darkness, against severe German defensive fire. A twelve-day battle roared day and night as high ground and Italian villages exchanged hands regularly. The capture of each piece of high ground on the far side of the Volturno River simply led to another formidable German position on the next visible high ground. Colonel Darby sent reports to higher commands stressing the enormous difficulties in advancing on such rough terrain. "The mountains are miserable, and we heartily desire movement and new action. The enemy brought up heavier artillery, shelling the Rangers continually. Clouds that cover the peaks are used by both sides for moving in patrols for attacks." Darby hinted that the battle was devolving into a World War I–like stalemate as invaluable experience and training of the Rangers was being shot to pieces in this type of combat.

Yet the high number of American casualties was not entirely in vain. A major British push across another part of the Volturno River forced the defenders to thin the ranks of defenders facing the Americans, and by Thanksgiving of 1943, the battle had shifted northward to a series of fortifications the Germans called the Winter Line, a term that would be etched in blood and frustration as the year 1944 began.

As the new year loomed in the near future, high profile units such as the "Go for Broke" 100th Battalion and Darby's Rangers would be joined by another highly publicized band of "special" forces, the joint Canadian-American special unit known officially as the Special Service Force, but more popularly called by the public "The Devil's Brigade," which like Darby's Rangers and the "Go for Broke" men would be chronicled in a major film a quarter of a century later. One by one, the pieces of the chessboard were fitting in place for the march on Rome that would begin to accelerate in the new year.

CHAPTER 15

December 1943

THE UNITED STATES AND ITS ALLIES ENTERED THE FINAL MONTH OF 1943 enjoying a strategic position that was enormously improved compared to December of 1942. During the past year, the European war had taken a drastic turn as the Wehrmacht collision with the Red Army had wiped dozens of German divisions from the table of battle on a long front that included Leningrad, Stalingrad, and Kursk. By December 1943, the German army was engaged in a fighting retreat that would eventually shift the field of battle from the streets of Stalingrad to the alleys of Berlin. On the Western Front, Paris, Rome, and Berlin were still Axis-controlled capitals, but Italy had been knocked out of the war. Axis forces had been ejected from North Africa, Sicily, and nearly half of Italy, and the imposing high ground of Kasserine Pass that marked the center point of action the previous winter had now migrated all the way to the equally imposing barrier of Monte Cassino Abbey in central Italy. While German defenders peered down from the high ground of Monte Cassino as they waited for the eventual Allied assault, their counterparts far to the north now began peering across the English Channel and North Sea, knowing that somewhere along this long stretch of landing beaches Allied troops would make their first foothold in northern Europe backed by near total control of the air and sea that defined the perimeter of the looming battle.

During the same twelve months since December 1942, in the Pacific Theater the Imperial army and fleet had been expelled from the Aleutian Islands, a large part of eastern New Guinea, Guadalcanal, and the Gilbert Islands. The Rising Sun still flew over Guam Island in the Marianas and all of the islands in the American protectorate of the Philippines, and the high command in Tokyo assumed that it was only a matter of time until major land, sea, and air battles would be fought in these two island chains. The garrison on Betio Island would not be the last Imperial force that would fight almost literally to the last man in the coming year.

The American Army and the British and Commonwealth allies would enter 1944 with a numerical superiority far below the traditional equation that assumed the need for a three-to-one superiority in attackers over defenders to provide a reasonable chance for success. In December 1943, it seemed probable that American ground forces during the next year would top out at eighty-eight infantry divisions and perhaps thirty British, Canadian, and Australian divisions which, in aggregate, came nowhere near the ideal margin. This looming shortfall was expected to be compensated by possibly drafting seventeen-year-olds who had already graduated from high school and men over thirty-five; transfer of African-American units from support roles to combat status; and shifting potential Army Air Corps personnel over to infantry or other combat arms designations. Younger servicemen and older soldiers would become much more noticeable in the units that would fight the decisive battles of 1944.

The officers who were planning the campaigns of 1944 had now received a significant opportunity to study the alacrity of American armored and air combat units to match or possibly surpass those of their Axis enemies. The American combatants in the Mediterranean/European Theater were now encountering the impact of German initiation of the use of the soon to be dreaded Panzer V and VI models but seemed to be at relative parity with the increasingly numerous Panzer IV models that in some cases could still outpower the far more numerous Shermans. Now, these two new German "super tanks," the Panther and Tiger, were beginning to emerge, and American armor experts were closely watching their impact on the battlefield. One expectation for the coming year was that the sheer number of Shermans could beat the Panzers on the battlefield, but this concept was not always proven workable, as in the shockingly one-sided battle soon after D-Day when a single Panzer VI Tiger tank annihilated much of a British armored battalion near the invasion beaches. During 1944, even the British army began to use more Shermans than their home-designed Cromwells, Churchills, and Matildas.

The Sherman M-4s were numerous, faster than most German tanks, and could fire without stopping, which at least partially compensated for their tendency to catch fire easily and display weaker penetrating power than the powerful 88mm German tank cannons.

Late 1943 and early 1944 would see the rapid intensification of the air war over the Reich, with the growing infusion of the P-51 Mustang fighter escort to deter the deadly incursions of the ME-109 and FW-190 interceptors. American B-17 Flying Fortresses and B-24 Liberators would continue to drop like flies in the early days of 1944, with as many as sixty bombers (and six hundred crewmembers) spiraling to their destruction in a single raid. During the coming year, the Luftwaffe would also begin to deploy its futuristic-looking ME-262 jet fighter that would invoke fear of even more massive Allied losses if enough were made available, despite Hitler's insistence that they should be utilized as bombers, rather than interceptors.

The last month of 1943 and the first month of 1944 would produce a similar evaluation of Japanese versus American technology as plans were devised for future invasion of the Marshalls, the Marianas, and the Philippines. American plans largely dismissed the threat of Japanese armored forces in these island slugging matches, as the Imperial Chi-Ha tanks were small, undersized, and underarmed and could barely match the firepower of American light Stuart tanks, let alone the Shermans. During the upcoming battle of Saipan, the utilization of an entire regiment of Imperial tanks proved useless to the defenders, as the unit was nearly annihilated in a single eerie night battle.

On the other hand, the Japanese Type 0 "Zeke" fighter was still a major threat at the end of 1943 and early 1944. The odds would begin to swing more in the favor of the American air forces when the still dangerous, but increasingly underarmed P-40 Warhawk was tasked with ground attack missions as the Army Air Force introduced the deadly trio of the twin-engine P-38 Lightning, the bottle-shaped and hugely durable P-47 Thunderbolt, and the streamlined P-51 Mustang to the Pacific air war. While these Army Air Force planes were turning the tide in battles between the Zeros and the American ground-based planes, the tide continued to turn against the Japanese naval air force even more significantly when the US Navy introduced the Hellcat, a plane designed specifically to shoot down Zeros. The one-sided destruction of American aircraft at Pearl Harbor would be avenged finally during a single summer day in 1944 in Leyte Gulf when the Hellcats and their companions would destroy more Japanese planes than the Americans lost at Pearl Harbor, while maintaining a twenty-to-one kill ratio in the aerial duels over the American invasion fleet. In concurrent aerial duels between Army Air Force fighter pilots and their Nipponese adversaries, the one-sided scores racked up by Zero pilots when they initially encountered obsolescent Army Air Force aircraft, such as the P-36 Mohawk and even the more obsolete P-256 Peashooter, were a thing of the past. Now the skies were filled with P-51 Mustangs, "the Cadillac of the Air," which were sending more than a few of the 1942 Japanese aces to their graves, while the spectacularly advanced B-29 Super Fortress was nearing combat status and would eventually turn Japanese cities into funeral pyres.

On January 1, 1944, as one hundred thirty million Americans celebrated a New Year's Day that optimists expected to be the last year of the war, a variety of Americans who were currently abroad and at least one pair of British children who were experiencing an extended stay in the United States all commented on the feelings of being far from home over a holiday period. Richard and Vanise Harninden were British children aged fourteen and eleven who had been evacuated from Britain to Long Island, New York, earlier in the war and had morphed into truly transatlantic youngsters. A *Time/Life* correspondent coupled a feature on the attitudes of American GIs stationed in Britain with this pair of children who now included a boy who was the star pitcher of his high school baseball team and a preteen girl who insisted that she would love to marry a cowboy. The correspondent noted that "spending their formative years in the United States has really made them children of two countries. Using a readily interchangeable mix of British and American accents, they are quite at home in the mannerisms of normal American teenagers. Vanise would be hardly recognizable to her parents as she has gained eleven inches and forty pounds since arriving and is now an active Girl Scout while Richard admits a keen interest in football, motorcycles and cowboys."

Three thousand miles across the Atlantic Ocean, award-winning correspondent Ernie Pyle spent New Year's Day 1944 hunkered down on an Italian battlefield wondering how "sunny Italy seemed to offer little more than chilly rainfall and a bleak gunmetal sky." Pyle was camped only eighty miles from Rome, but there was a powerful German army barring almost any significant movement northward. The correspondent admitted to his home front readers that "the steadily forward advancement" they were reading about in their newspapers and magazines was actually proceeding "at the speed of an earthworm" while the scenery he was observing was "from an earthworm's eye view." There was little glamour or optimism in an environment that featured "a cast of tired, dirty soldiers who more ingest than eat tasteless lukewarm food followed by anti-malaria pills and who might vote to go home immediately even if peace is less than an enemy surrender." Pyle insisted that "rather than a lust for battle and triumph, most soldiers would even trade eventual defeat of the Axis for a guarantee of female companionship back home." He further claimed that the GIs "stranded between a present stalemate and a murky future, the soldiers want the gentling effect of femininity and are so impatient with the strange culture of the country that they now inhabit, they insist that if they get home alive, they never want to see a foreign country again."

While Pyle would at least temporarily escape the hill fighting in Italy as he returned home to New Mexico, one of the commanders of the men he was interviewing was about to lead an assault that put any thoughts about his own family and home far back in his consciousness. Gen. Fred Walker commanded the 36th Infantry Division that was tasked with breaking the stalemate in Italy by crossing the Rapido River and opening a path for a drive toward Rome. The fact that he was coordinating an assault that had elements of some of the bloodiest setbacks in the Civil War was not lost on Walker and his men.

Now, early in the New Year of 1944, Walker's Texans were carrying cumbersome assault boats up to the southern shoreline of the wide, icy Rapido River that featured a powerful combat force of German defenders on the far side who were waiting patiently to open fire Walker wrote in his diary that, "I do not know of a single case in military history where an attempt to cross an unfordable river that is incorporated in the enemy's main line of resistance has succeeded." Walker's protests fell on deaf ears in relatively distant, well-lit, and warm headquarters' offices, and the fully alerted German defense forces opened a murderous fire as soon as the first boats left the southern shore of the river. At a cost of only sixty men killed and a modest toll of wounded, the defenders on the north bank of the Rapido inflicted over twenty-one hundred casualties on the assault force before Walker called a halt to the carnage. The only glimmer of a positive note to the whole affair was that the commander of the German defense force offered the attackers an extended truce after the shooting ended. In a scene reminiscent of Civil War truces along the Rappahannock River in 1862 and 1863 and the Christmas truce on the Western Front in 1914, the adversaries shared photographs of families, exchanged souvenirs, and wished each other good fortune to survive the war before the grim business of combat was eventually resumed.

On the other side of the world in January 1944, a different kind of truce was unfolding in the main public park in Honolulu, Hawaii. This time, the truce was among Americans in different uniforms, as the traditional Army-Navy rivalry was set aside for a day for a unique event called the "Great Texas Barbeque." The event was the idea of Adm. Chester Nimitz, the blond, youthful-looking mariner who had progressed from growing up in the Texas home of a widowed mother to the cusp of appearances on the covers of virtually every national magazine during the coming year. On a gorgeous tropical morning, Nimitz walked into the main entrance of the municipal park, arm in arm with Gen. Robert Richardson, senior Army commander in the Central Pacific. As they strolled through the park, they were joined by an ever growing cascade of men in Army and Navy uniforms who were either themselves Texans or given the minimal identity checks in force, had become Texan for the day. The two senior commanders became Pied Pipers for the day as a tidal wave of revelers swapped stories and observations on their day off from Army-Navy rivalry.

Nimitz and Richardson had spent the last few weeks reviewing the accounts of the Gilberts invasion as they prepared for the next combined Army-Navy engagement, Operation Flintlock, which would be an invasion of the Marshall Islands as the final run up to the long awaited reconquest of Guam and the other Marianas islands in June. Unlike the abysmal planning that had turned the Rapido operation into a one-sided defeat, the genial yet highly focused Nimitz and the often underrated Richardson, who occupied an uncomfortable back seat behind Douglas MacArthur in the Pacific, expedited the distribution of an extensive critique of exactly what had turned the Tarawa operation into a bloodbath. Adm. Richmond Kelly Turner had completed a sometimes scathing report titled "Lessons Learned at Tarawa," which would essentially emerge as the game plan for future Pacific amphibious operations. Operation Flintlock would benefit from vastly expanded reconnaissance, greater integration of submarines for scouting missions, and a tripling of the bombardment capabilities of the invasion force.

Adm. Raymond Spruance, the acclaimed hero of the "miracle at Midway" the previous year, was now back in the command chain for the assault on the Marshalls. Spruance shared Nimitz's passion for daily brisk walks, solicitous attitude toward his officers and seamen, and love for wideranging conversations free of the influence of variations in rank. Spruance made it clear to Army and Marine assault commanders that, unlike the debacle on Guadalcanal when the American battle fleet fled the scene and left the ground forces on their own, that the warships involved in the Marshalls invasion would always be nearby for any needed support.

A colorful quartet of American senior officers would comprise the team that would be the most directly involved individuals in the Flintlock operation. Adm. Richard Connelly was already displaying the hell for leather attitude that would result in the almost legendary status of "Close In Connelly" in both the Pacific and European Theaters during the coming year. The equally colorful and newsworthy Gen. Holland "Howlin' Mad" Smith would reprise his duties that he performed in the Tarawa operation, while at least temporarily toning down the worst of his tantrums until emerging in even more publicly demonstrated fury in the invasion of the Marianas during the upcoming summer.

Smith would face the same challenge at the Marshalls operation as he would in the Marianas—a mixed command of Army and Marine assault divisions. The Army commander was Gen. Charles Corlett, who would face his own challenge, serving in both the Pacific and Atlantic invasions with a command of the 7th Infantry Division for Flintlock, which in turn would operate in tandem with the 4th Marine Division under the steady hand of Gen. Harry Schmidt.

The first month of 1944 in the Pacific war would be one of final organization for the February invasion of the Marshall Islands, while the main action in the Pacific Theater would be centered around Douglas MacArthur and his quest to return to the Japanese-occupied Philippines as quickly as possible.

General MacArthur, backed by the strong support of admirals William Halsey and Thomas Kinkaid, was convinced that a massive American and Australian offensive along the northern coast of New Guinea, supported by amphibious invasions of offshore islands, would eventually place his massive, colorfully designated "Alamo Force" at the very northwest tip of the island with the southernmost islands of the Philippine chain at least figuratively looming on the distant horizon. During 1943, MacArthur's American and Australian forces had soared from 351,000 personnel to 697,000 men formed around thirteen combat divisions and numerous supplementary units, supported by thirty-two air groups, augmented by an additional four hundred thousand air and naval personnel available for duty.

On January 2, 1944, the fighting tip of this massive military spear, seven thousand men of the 32nd Infantry Division, staged a massive leapfrog over Imperial forces in northern New Guinea and occupied the town of Saidor in a quantum leap toward the ultimate target of Leyte Island in the Philippines.

While the men of the "Alamo Force" pushed their way through the green hell of New Guinea, Maj. Greg "Pappy" Boyington, an alumnus of the famed Flying Tigers who dueled with the Japanese air force in pre–Pearl Harbor China, led his now almost legendary squadron of Marine aviators, VMF 214, on a particularly high-profile mission. Major Boyington had put together a squadron of highly individualistic pilots seen as misfits by their original unit commanders and quickly designated them the "Black Sheep Squadron" to the delight of an ever-growing group of reporters and publicity personnel.

Boyington was so attuned to the advantages of publicity for his "bad boy" unit that the exploits of his squadron were chronicled three decades later in the hit television program, *Baa Baa Black Sheep*, which starred actor Robert Conrad of *Wild, Wild West* fame as Pappy, with the real Boyington as a technical advisor. However, on a bright December morning in 1943, the Black Sheep took to the air, accompanied by Navy Hellcats, Royal New Zealand Air Force Kitty Hawks, and a few other assorted aircraft on a mission to compromise the threat of the enormous Japanese air presence on Rabaul. The plan was for the slower Kitty Hawks to serve as bait for Japanese planes taking off to defend their Rabaul airfields, at which point the more powerful American Navy and Marine aircraft would dive down in ambush. Twenty Kitty Hawks proved to be an inviting target for dozens of Zeros until the much faster Hellcats and Corsairs seemed to appear from nowhere, and the Imperial attackers now became the prey. At one point, a Zero flew so close to a Kitty Hawk that the two aircraft became essentially fused with one another, forcing both pilots to bail out almost simultaneously. Ironically, one of the most highly chronicled missions of the Black Sheep would largely end Boyington's run of luck, as a few days later he was shot down by a Japanese ace who had grown up as a baseball star in his native Hawaii before choosing the Imperial side in the war. Boyington would spend the coming year, 1944, as a brutally treated guest of the Japanese Empire.

Adm. William Halsey would spend the early days of 1944 in far more comfort, as the colorful sea dog dropped anchor by the American mainland, highlighted by his appearance as guest of honor at the New Year's Day East-West all-star football game in San Francisco, give a national radio address on the NBC network, and fly into Washington for meetings with Navy commander Ernest King and enjoy a Senate luncheon in Halsey's honor.

Halsey used each public speaking opportunity to voice his agreement with Douglas MacArthur that the liberation of the Philippines was a far more worthwhile enterprise than an invasion of Rabaul, as an offensive from the Marshalls to the Marianas and beyond would mostly likely entice the entire Japanese fleet to emerge into the open sea for a confrontation that the Americans had an excellent chance of winning. The decisive American victories at the Philippine Sea and Leyte Gulf in 1944 would soon demonstrate the wisdom of Halsey's plans.

While the senior officers in the Pacific Theater spent the last days of 1943 and the opening days of 1944 preparing to fight the iconic battles that would shake the Pacific in the coming year, a small team of British engineers and related personnel was moving quietly along a French beach in German-occupied territory. As Wehrmacht soldiers in nearby villas and taverns celebrated the onset of 1944, the intruders were taking samples to determine if the beach they were landing on could support the weight of tanks and other heavy vehicles. The beach had acquired a new name back in Allied headquarters in Britain; it was designated Omaha and would become the epicenter of a massive battle five months in the future. The fact that the Anglo-American allies could actually decide when and where they would return to the European mainland in the coming year was testimony to the sacrifice and success of members of an ever more powerful alliance that during 1943 had turned a year filled with peril and more than a few near or real defeats at the hands of the Axis into the proving ground for what Gen. Dwight Eisenhower would call a Crusade. During the coming year the Allies would push the German and Japanese aggressors far back toward their own homelands and ensure that 1944 would be the last full year of World War II. Each day of 1943 had indeed been a day of peril, but those 365 days in total would be remembered as a year of remarkable victory for the increasingly vast assemblage of nations determined to snuff out the global contamination that was the Axis.

Conclusion

WHILE PESSIMISTIC AMERICANS WHO EXPERIENCED AMERICA AT WAR in 1943 seemed reconciled to the slogan, "The Golden Gate in '48," and more optimistic citizens rallied around the cry of "end the war in '44," there seemed to be no catchphrases that covered an end to the conflict in 1943. Even the most optimistic citizens were unable to produce a scenario in which Italy, Germany, and Japan would all surrender before the end of 1943, and this intuition proved entirely correct as the year entered its final few weeks.

Most residents of the Allied nations during the Great War were caught by surprise when the Kaiser abdicated, and the German military leaders sued for peace in November 1918, even as the Allied press was featuring stories on the projected 1919 offensive. The best that could be said about 1943 was that by the end of the year, the chances of an Axis victory were far less possible than twelve months earlier; one of the three major Axis powers had surrendered; and a tangible plan now seemed to be set in motion to push the Japanese back to their home islands and the Germans back into their own homeland in some calculable if not necessarily imminent future. In some respects, the summer of 1943 in the war against Germany was comparable to the summer of 1863 in the Union prosecution of the war against the Confederacy. During that summer eight decades earlier, Union forces repelled Robert E. Lee's most powerful thrust into the North; captured the key Tennessee city of Chattanooga; and split the Confederacy in two with the surrender of Vicksburg and took control of most of the Mississippi River. Yet at the end of that summer of Federal triumph, the Confederacy still had enough power to carry the secessionist nation for nineteen or twenty more months of existence. As the war in central Italy began to congeal into a slow-motion advance in early autumn of 1943, the Third Reich had about the same span of time remaining, with the Japanese Empire afforded an additional few months, due to the much more extensive distances in the Pacific war.

The Anglo-American allies and their Soviet partner had much to celebrate about the trend of the war in 1943. Stalingrad, Kursk, "Tunisgrad," Sicily, Salerno, Buna, Tarawa, and the Solomons had all sent Axis armies reeling or even to their annihilation, but several thousand Americans had been marched into the Colosseum in Rome as prisoners after Kasserine Pass, thousands more American and British bomber aircrew members were now residents of Luftwaffe prison camps as bombers dropped from the skies by the score all over Europe, and thousands of Marines were either in hospitals or cemeteries after the shooting ended on Tarawa. At the end of 1943, far more American homes displayed the gold star of the supreme sacrifice of one or more members of their family with victory parades still far in the future. Huge, if diminished, swaths of the planet were still displayed on maps with a swastika or rising sun superimposed on the territory with little hope that V-E or V-J Day would be occurring anytime in the next twelve months.

The year 1943 had seen the Axis powers largely pushed out of the Solomon Islands, the Aleutians, the Gilbert Islands, much of eastern New Guinea, all of North Africa, Sicily, and southern Italy, and much of the airspace over each of these battlefields. Yet vast swaths of a stolen Axis empire were still very much under the boot of the occupiers at the end of 1943. The promised July 4, 1946, date of full independence for the Philippines held little imminent impact for the Filipino people, as Imperial soldiers and sadistic "thought police" ravaged the islands' bounty, raping, taking hostages, and making a mockery of the "independence" they had granted the islands after the surrender of Bataan and Corregidor. The band of twenty thousand American soldiers, sailors, and Marines that had emerged with raised hands at Bataan and Corregidor were a shrinking population, as a combination of cruelty and neglect was rapidly thinning their ranks as smuggled matchbook covers with Douglas MacArthur's "I shall return" promise heralded a still apparently distant event that, if the Japanese mistreatment continued, might leave no prisoners to release.

As Filipinos adapted, collaborated, hid out, or died during their unwanted membership in the Greater East Asia Co. Prosperity Sphere, the residents of France, the Low Countries, eastern Europe, and Scandinavia collected incomplete shreds of information from illegal radio broadcasts or banned papers and pamphlets that reminded them that they were not forgotten by the Allies. Resistance groups formed, sometimes were infiltrated, sometimes annihilated, and sometimes were successful at putting a dent into the body of the now sprawling Reich. Ever larger fleets of Allied bombers flew overhead and sometimes caused massive destruction and death to the people who cheered their arrival in an era well before the targeting accuracy of "smart" bombs and laser guidance systems. Yet, even if the Allied air force could not liberate territory, they were seen as harbingers of the future land invasion that might just occur before the next twelve months ended. For those held hostage to Hitler's dreams, the Allied bombing attacks and land victories at the southern edge of the continent in 1943 were seen as portents of still more substantial hope for the coming year. The "Yanks" who included large numbers of men whose ancestors fought for the Confederacy eight decades before and the "Brits," who included non-English subjects from Scotland to Canada, would soon be stirring from massive camps from Glasgow to Salerno to catch Hitler's armies in the western side of a pincer as a massive and now victorious Soviet army plunged toward the Reich from the east. Meanwhile, American soldiers and sailors, Marines and pilots, Australians and New Zealanders, were going through similar rehearsals to push the Imperial invaders much of the way back to their home islands during 1944.

When nations go to war against one another, more often than not in history, each side tends to form a rough timetable to produce a victory for itself. In 1775, King George III and his key ministers were certain that "one strong blow" would bring the rebellious colonists to their senses, while four decades later, the usually level-headed Thomas Jefferson asserted in 1812 that the American conquest of Canada would be "a mere matter of marching" into the desired northern addition to the Republic. A hot-headed southern politician in 1861 offered to "wipe up with his handkerchief" all the blood spilled over the looming secession of the Southern states. Somehow, none of these perceived rapid victories ever managed to meet their timetables, so American military planners of World War II learned caution about predictions from these earlier missed calls. Thus, the American war effort in 1943 remained free of catchy "end the war" slogans, at least for that year. This was a prudent decision, as almost every day of 1943 was played out against a backdrop of a crisis some place, somewhere over the vast expanse of war from the White House to the War Office to Pearl Harbor to Army Air Force offices in London. Yet, in their composite, the myriad crises, from the location of potential German submarine attacks on merchant ships to the revision of battle plans on a bloodstained beach at Tarawa, produced a generally positive direction to the war between January and December of 1943. American forces that were fighting to hold Kasserine Pass and Henderson Field early in the year were preparing for the invasions of Guam, the Philippines, and France by the end of the year. By the end of 1943, American victory was not assumed, but it was certainly in the air in the not too distant future.

A Note on Sources

As in my previous book on the American war experience in 1944, I have remained convinced that any attempt to gain a proper understanding of how Americans actually experienced that war is incomplete without exploring the literature written by the participants of the events of 1943. One of my first activities in conducting research on *Days of Peril* was to immerse myself in the newspapers and magazines that Americans read anywhere from the safety of the home front to the foxholes on the tip of the battlefield. I consulted a wide variety of publications including *Life, Time, Fortune,* the *Saturday Evening Post, Look, Newsweek,* and *U.S. News and World Report,* along with a sampling of daily newspapers from across the nation. While none of these publications carried anything near exclusive focus on the battles then being fought, the vast majority of advertisements actually featured some tie-in to the war, from female aircraft production workers lauding a particular cigarette as a "pick me up" on the aircraft production line to a gaunt, ragged prisoner of the Japanese begging home front Americans to carefully consider impulsive purchases as he is confronted by a bayonet-wielding Japanese guard advancing menacingly on the other side of the barbed wire cage.

Extensive perusal of contemporary periodicals provided an excellent counterpart to the autobiographical and biographical works centered on the significant leaders during 1943. Among the most valuable autobiographical works on the war in 1943 were Dwight Eisenhower's *Crusade in Europe,* George Patton's *War As I Knew It,* Mark Clark's *Calculated Risk,* and Winston Churchill's *Closing the Ring.* These works are invaluable in understanding the broad-based strategy and decision-making in 1943 and are supplemented by later biographical works enjoying a less biased view of the commanders' actions and decisions. Notably valuable in this category are Eric Larrabee's *Commander in Chief: Franklin Delano Roosevelt, His Lieutenants, and Their War*, William Manchester's *American Caesar: Douglas MacArthur*, Walter Borneman's *MacArthur at War*, Thomas Hughes's *Admiral Bill Halsey*, and Adolf Galland's *The First and The Last*.

While works by or about the individuals who made the command decisions during 1943 are invaluable, I also focused a significant amount of my research on enlisted personnel and junior officers who were at the front of the firing line and then produced some form of memoir of their experiences. Two of the most famous of these memoirs were Robert Leckie's chronicle of Marine combat in the Pacific, *Helmet for My Pillow*, which formed a major component of the HBO series *The Pacific*, and Greg "Pappy" Boyington's chronicle of Marine air combat in *Baa Baa Black Sheep*. James Fahey's chronicle of combat from the perspective of a teenager stationed on a cruiser, *Pacific War Diary*, received less media attention but was one of the most valuable sources utilized concerning the Tarawa bloodbath.

An invaluable middle space between works by professional historians and memoirs designed for family or other minimal circulation was provided by the accounts of the brave war correspondents who reported the battles of 1943 at some considerable risk to themselves. Two of the most famous of this brave corps were Robert Sherrod and Ernie Pyle, who between them covered most of the major battles of the year. Sherrod, who doubled as a correspondent for *Life* and *Time* magazines, produced the first book-length account of Tarawa only weeks after the battle, and *Tarawa: The Story of a Battle* became an instant success. The ever popular Ernie Pyle chronicled the battle in Tunisia in *Here Is Your War* and the Sicilian campaign in *Brave Men*, both of which are important sources from a writer who would not survive his transfer to the Pacific Theater.

While Sherrod and Pyle provided "on the ground" accounts to American home front readers, British ministry of information accounts of US combat activities in both North African and the Pacific provided another fascinating primary source on America at war in 1943. *Tunisia: Armies at War* and *Ocean Front: The Story of the War in the Pacific* were mass-circulation, heavily illustrated campaign histories sold at a modest one shilling each that provided glowing accounts of Allied amity and unity during the 1943 multi-theater campaigns. These works paired well with the American War and Navy Departments *Instructions for American Servicemen in Britain* and *Instructions for American Servicemen in Australia* in official American and British attempts to cement a still relatively new alliance.

This wide variety of primary sources was enhanced by a significant contribution from secondary sources that spanned several decades in publication. The Battle of the Aleutians is bookended by two excellent works in *The Thousand Mile War: World War II in Alaska and the Aleutians* (1969) by Brian Garfield and Mark Obmascik's *The Storm on Our Shores* (2019). A similar time span bridges the disaster at Kasserine Pass with Martin Blumenson's *Kasserine Pass: Rommel's Bloody Climactic Battle for Tunisia* (1966) and Rick Atkinson's *An Army at Dawn: The War in North Africa 1942-1943* (2002). The Battles from Buna to the Bismarck Sea extend from an account of the evacuation of the Imperial Garrison from the Solomons in Irving Werstein's *Guadalcanal* (1966) to the slugfest at Buna in John Prados's *Islands of Destiny* (2012). The expulsion of the Axis armies from North Africa are discussed in Geoffrey Perret's *There's a War to Be Won* (1991) and Carlo D'Este's *Patton: A Genius for War* (1995).

The multi-ocean submarine campaign received an Atlantic Ocean perspective in Jonathan Dimbleby's *The Battle of the Atlantic* (2015), while the American submarine in the Pacific received primary attention in Edward Monroe-Jones and Michael Green's *The Silent Service in World War II* (2012).

The air war over the Reich is discussed in two excellent books on the bombing of Hamburg: Martin Middlebrook's *The Battle of Hamburg* (1980) and A. C. Grayling's *Among the Dead Cities* (2006). James Dugan and Carroll Stewart provided the most comprehensive treatment of Ploesti in *Ploesti: The Great Air-Ground Battle of 1 August 1943* (1962).

The most comprehensive treatment of the Battle of Sicily is *Bitter Victory* by Carlo D'Este (1988), while Rick Atkinson provides an excellent wider chronicle from Sicily to the advance up the Italian Peninsula in *Day of Battle* (2007).

When compared to the massive Pacific naval battles in 1944, naval operations were considerably more limited in 1943. However, two volumes of Adm. Samuel Eliot Morison's magisterial multi-volume *History of United States Naval Operations in World War II* provided excellent accounts of operations from the Aleutians to Tarawa in *Volume VII, Aleutians, Gilberts and Marshalls* (1951) and *Volume VI, Breaking the Bismarcks Barrier* (1951). On a much more limited strategic scale, yet with enormous political ramifications for the 1960s, John F. Kennedy's command of PT-109 and other effects of those operations are the primary topics in Richard Tregaskis's *John F. Kennedy and PT 109* (1962) and William Doyle's *PT 109: An American Epic of War, Survival and the Destiny of John F. Kennedy* (2015). The adventures of Darby's Rangers and the Nisei members of the 100th Infantry Battalion and 442nd Regimental Combatants in the Battle for the Volturno River are chronicled in H. Paul Jeffers's *Onward We Charge* (2007) and Chester Tanaka's *Go for Broke* (1982).

Acknowledgments

Although I am privileged to have the opportunity to write books such as this one, I have never given up my membership in the fellowship of men, women, boys, and girls who are avid readers. I always hope that readers will enjoy each book as much as I enjoy writing them. A unique bond is always created between an author and the reading audience that has taken the time to read the book.

My always exciting and rewarding role as an author is complemented by my other roles as a teacher and a parent. I have enjoyed the great good luck of spending my entire near half-century teaching career at Villanova University, gradually morphing from a twenty-something, new recipient of a doctorate to one of the most senior members of the entire faculty. The Reverend Peter Donahue, OSA, was one of my first students and has somehow managed to combine his priestly duties and passionate love for the theater with an astounding role as president of a university, in which he has made every member of the Villanova family, from housekeeping staff to students, parents, and faculty alike, feel that they are acknowledged, remembered, and all equally important. I would also like to acknowledge the crucial support of Dr. Adele Lindenmeyr, the dean of the College of Arts and Sciences and a fellow historian, and Dr. Christopher Schmidt, chair of the Department of Education and Counseling for their academic support for this project, and Anne Feldman who has combined the vital roles of both typing the final manuscript and serving as a unique sounding board as this project has come to fruition. In turn, this book could never have been written without the support and encouragement of Niels Aaboe, who has always used his calm, friendly manner to encourage ideas to become books.

My activities in researching and writing this book have always been accomplished against a backdrop of the magical role of parenting my children, Matthew, Gregory, and Stephen, and my grandson Liam, all of whom continue to look forward to a life of excitement and adventure, thanks in no small measure to the young people from America, Britain, Canada, Australia, and the other Allied nations who sacrificed their comfort, their physical well-being, and in many cases, their lives so that future generations could have the opportunity to dream of an always better future.

Index